Southern
Africa
by Rail

CW00951963

The Bradt Story

In 1974, my former husband George Bradt and I spent three days sitting on a river barge in Bolivia writing our first guide for like-minded travellers: *Backpacking along Ancient Ways in Peru and Bolivia*. The 'little yellow book', as it became known, is now in its sixth edition and continues to sell to travellers throughout the world.

Since 1980, with the establishment of Bradt Publications, I have continued to publish guides for the discerning traveller, covering more than 100 countries and all six continents; in 1997 we won the *Sunday Times* Small Publisher of the Year Award. *Southern Africa by Rail* is the 148th Bradt title or new edition to be published.

The company continues to develop new titles and new series, but in the forefront of my mind there remains our original ethos – responsible travel with an emphasis on the culture and natural history of the region. I hope that you will get the most out of your trip, and perhaps have the opportunity to give something in return.

Travel guides are by their nature continuously evolving. If you experience anything which you would like to share with us, or if you have any amendments to make to this guide, please write; all your letters are read and passed on to the author. Most importantly, do remember to travel with an open mind and to respect the customs of your hosts – it will add immeasurably to your enjoyment.

Happy travelling!

Hilary Bradt

41 Nortoft Road, Chalfont St Peter, Bucks SL9 0LA, England
Tel/fax: 01494 873478 Email: bradtpublications@compuserve.com

Southern
Africa
by Rail

Paul Ash

Bradt Publications, UK
The Globe Pequot Press Inc, USA

First published in 1998 by Bradt Publications,
41 Nortoft Road, Chalfont St Peter, Bucks SL9 0LA, England
Published in the USA by The Globe Pequot Press Inc,
6 Business Park Road, PO Box 833, Old Saybrook, Connecticut 06475-0833

The author and publishers have made every effort to ensure the accuracy of the
information in this book at the time of going to press. However, the publishers
cannot accept any responsibility for any loss, injury or inconvenience resulting
from the use of information contained in this guide.

British Library Cataloguing in Publication Data
A catalogue record for this book is available from the British Library
ISBN 1 898323 72 0

Library of Congress Cataloging-in-Publication Data
Ash, Paul
    Southern Africa by Rail / by Paul Ash.
        p.   cm.
    ISBN 1-898323-72-0 (alk. paper)
    1. Africa, Southern—Guidebooks. 2. Railroad travel--Africa,
    Southern--Guidebooks. I. Title
    DT1017.A84 1998
    916.804'65--dc21   98-28278
                                                                              CIP

Maps
Steve Munns; *except sketch maps in Chapter 17,* Donald Sommerville

Photographs
Front cover: Rovos Rail, South Africa (Ariadne Van Zandbergen)
In text: Paul Ash (PA); Ariadne Van Zandbergen (AZ)

Typeset from the author's disc by Donald Sommerville
Printed and bound in Spain by Grafo SA, Bilbao

Contents

Introduction/Author

INTRODUCTION

I am crazy about trains – watching them, hearing them pass at night, and riding on them. There is, really, no other way to travel, drifting as you are in the palm of a giant, rocking hand, lulled during the day by a slow-changing landscape, soothed at night by a steady rhythm and distant rumble. However, happy train travel requires a shift in priorities. Time often has little meaning in Africa and trains seem especially prone to the fatalism of 'It will go when it is ready'. It was a delight to take to the rails and discover Africa again. However, unlike in Europe or countries like India, Africa's passenger trains are an endangered species. Underfunded by governments and battling against often unfair competition as well as disinterest from some national rail operators who think railways should be for freight trains only, passenger train services in Southern Africa have been cut to the bone. Just two things ensure their survival: continued demand from Africans who rely on trains to carry them across huge distances, and travel and tourism, which have begun booming in the region. The growth in luxury and special train services has been dramatic in the last few years and these – more expensive – trains have a devoted following.

With travellers pouring into Southern Africa, it should be time for an ordinary, everyday passenger train revival. Some national railway operators have woken up to this and are trying to provide a service for travellers. Ride these trains, and then tell the people in charge how excellent it is to go by train. Enthusiasm from passengers will help save a heritage and the world's best way of getting around.

AUTHOR

Paul Ash is a journalist with a passion for railways. His family sold steam locomotives in Southern Africa for decades, instilling a love of rail travel which has inspired him to journey by train across India and throughout Southern Africa. His particular favourites are Zimbabwe, Namibia and Mozambique and, of course, his home country of South Africa. Paul is currently features editor of South Africa's Out There magazine

Acknowledgements

It would have been impossible to write this book without the consistent help and patience of many people. I would like to offer my thanks to Eric Conradie at the Transnet Museum Library and Walter Rusch at the TransNamib Museum for sharing their enthusiasm and knowledge of Southern Africa's railway history; Bheka Manana, Mattie Geldenhuys, Hanlie Kotze at Mainline Passenger Services; Mr Gombera at NRZ headquarters and Mr Simonda of Zambia Railways; Leander Borg at Rovos Rail; Geoff Cooke at Rail Safaris; Geoff Clark for the book; Terry Hutson of the RSSA for answering endless questions; Jane Wilson-Howarth. Thanks also to Ophrus Mmagobo for his outstanding cooking which got me through many long nights and Tom Sauer and the other train crews and enginemen everywhere who were quick with advice, beer and stories. Best of all, thanks to Fiona Summers who joined me on the rails, married me, and then took on all the bitty work – this is for you.

LIST OF MAPS

Riding African Trains

ENJOYING AFRICAN TRAINS

Trains are the Ugly Sisters in Africa's transport scene. Bushveld law dictates the survival of the quickest so passenger trains are an endangered species. This is nothing new – services are constantly threatened with closure and yet southern Africa's train network, while more threadbare in this era of 'downsizing', somehow continues to survive.

Trains are about the best way of getting around Africa, whether you want to meet the smiling face of Africa as run by private operators and aimed unashamedly at flush travellers from countries with proud, strong currencies, or whether you want to travel the African way on the standard national passenger trains, some of which barely function, at least when compared to trains in super-slick Switzerland, say.

Tanzanians may warn you, for example, that the trip between Dar es Salaam and Kapiri Mposhi, 1,600km away in Zambia, can take up to two weeks instead of the advertised two days. I was sceptical of this claim until being compelled to spend 38 hours at the unenchanting siding of Mlimba in rural Tanzania because an earlier derailment had blocked the single track line. There was no food and very little beer and not much to do except wait. It was an educational time.

Many African train services continue, against the odds in a part of the world which aid agencies seem to believe should be dominated by trucks, to provide regular and vital transport to thousands of people every day. Not a single country in the region can compete with Indian Railways' boast of 10 million passengers a day, nor is there a train to compete with the exquisite timing of the three-hour blur between London and Liverpool. No, African train travel is an altogether unique animal. Think slow, be patient, and watch the vast landscapes slide by at somnambulent pace. Do it this way and the stress of first world living will slide away faster than it takes a trackside hawker of ripe bananas to unload his wares at a fair price for both of you.

The main point of using Africa's trains is that they put you among the people, in the country. My numerous journeys on South Africa's *Trans-Karoo*, which ambles daily between Johannesburg and Cape Town, have introduced me to South Africa. There is something about long-distance train travel which makes people open up and talk. I learned more about the country this way than in 12 years of school.

The slow pace of the trains is the finest preparation for more general travelling in the region. Arriving by train in a new country gives you time to acclimatise, vastly better than a shattering arrival at some tropical airport.

That's not to say there will never be stresses. Travel by African train can be an immensely frustrating, or liberating, experience, depending a little on luck, but also on how you adapt to it. There are a few tricks you can benefit from, quirks which reflect the frustrations of life here, as well as Africa's sometimes staggeringly different view of the world.

The first thing to remember is that unlike India or Europe, or even the USA, the trains do not go everywhere you might want, nor do all the countries in the region have cross-border services. A bit of research and forward planning is vital to avoid truly disturbing moments like arriving in a hot South African desert town to find you have missed the weekly train to Namibia by one day. Study the timetables like a trainspotter and check the fine print.

There are going to be gaps, often huge ones, in the area covered by rail, but there is always a solution. It is likely that if you are planning a rail-based trip in Africa, you are also going to be doing a fair amount of flying, bus, and boat travel, or even hitching if you are going really off-track. In many places the services are sparse – maybe once a week – so if you are travelling by train to catch the plane home, allow a few extra days in your planning.

Combining train travel with cycling is probably the best way of seeing Africa – the bike gives you the transport you need in towns, as well as providing a way of filling some of the gaps not covered by the rail system.

TRAIN SURVIVAL

An American aid worker once told me that the truck was Africa's natural transport solution, able to cope with the difficulties of getting around on a continent which, in many places, has nothing in the way of infrastructure at all. But while trucks and buses do rule, trains are still mass transport for the people. The reason is often a simple matter of baggage allowances. People going to market, or moving home, can put all their stuff on the train. One can do a lot with the standard 50-kg (110-pound) baggage allowance. Cost is the other reason – train travel is absurdly cheap, especially by European and north American standards. One reason for this is that many of Africa's passenger trains are regarded as strategic assets, and are accordingly subsidised by governments.

This all means that the trains are usually jammed full of people and their belongings. At times, it will feel like the whole continent is on the move with you. With so many people on board, reservations can sometimes become a meaningless concept, but a few survival hints may help.

Tickets

If you can, buy your ticket several days in advance. Get to the station early on the day of travel and board as soon as you can. Make friends with the conductor or train manager (if there is one) as quickly as possible. Seat possession is nine-tenths of the law here. If there is a problem, be relaxed and friendly; there may well be a way to sort it out.

Food and drink

Most of the long-distance trains provide some kind of food, often in a full service, sit-down dining car. The quality varies, often from train to train. On my first Tazara train ride, the food on the first leg was appalling but the improvement was staggering when the crews changed half-way. Meals, especially on any train north of the Limpopo River, are based around maize meal porridge (*sadza*) with chicken, meat and sometimes fish. Africa is very meat oriented and being a vegetarian can be hugely frustrating; your vegetarian option will often be the *sadza* and vegetables with a fried egg dropped on top.

Take comfort food with you on long-distance trains. If the train is delayed, you will at least have a stash to keep you going when the train food runs out. Other passengers will often also share their food with you and an offer in return is greatly appreciated.

Most trains have clean drinking water in each coach, although on long journeys this may not be replenished. If you are nervous of local water, take your own. All the dining and catering cars sell beer and soft drinks of some kind.

Warning There have been incidents of passengers being deliberately poisoned by thieves. Use your judgement when accepting food or drink from a stranger. Most of the time, the offer is genuine, and safe, but if you have any doubts, plead a stomach upset and refuse.

Security

Trains are fantastic hunting grounds for thieves. The huge number of people, the bags everywhere, and the long journeys, provide plenty of opportunity for criminals. Your stuff will be fine while you are in your compartment. If you leave, ask someone to look after it for you, or have the conductor lock the door while you are away. Close the windows, too: an open window and slow-moving (or stopped) train is a golden opportunity for the quick-witted
. You can chain your bag to the overhead baggage rack if you really do not trust your travelling companions.

Keep windows and doors locked at night. There is often a latch on the inside which prevents even the conductor from opening the door more than a centimetre or two. Most sleeper coaches have metal or wooden louvred shutters which you can close at night instead of the window, but which still allow some fresh air in. It is often a trade-off, however, between wanting to sleep as cool as possible and worrying about your kit.

If you do have a problem, tell the conductor immediately. In addition Zimbabwean trains are often accompanied by a travelling contingent of police which is a welcome deterrent.

Patience

There may be a timetable but in many places this is just a rough outline of what was once expected. Trains move slowly – the track is mostly 3ft 6in (107cm) gauge (narrow compared to main lines in Europe and the USA) and

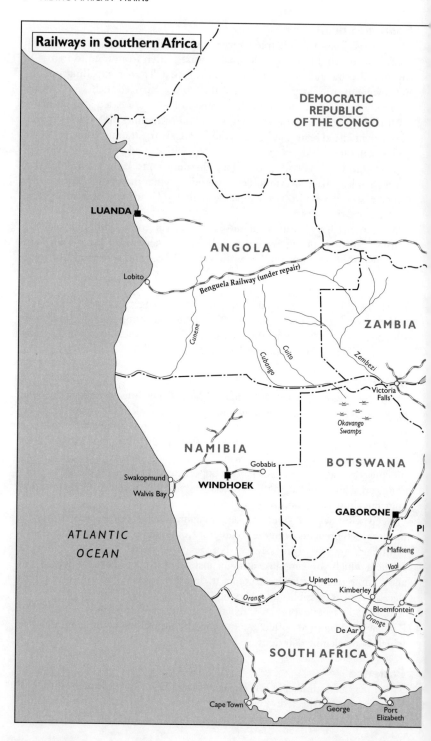

Railways in Southern Africa

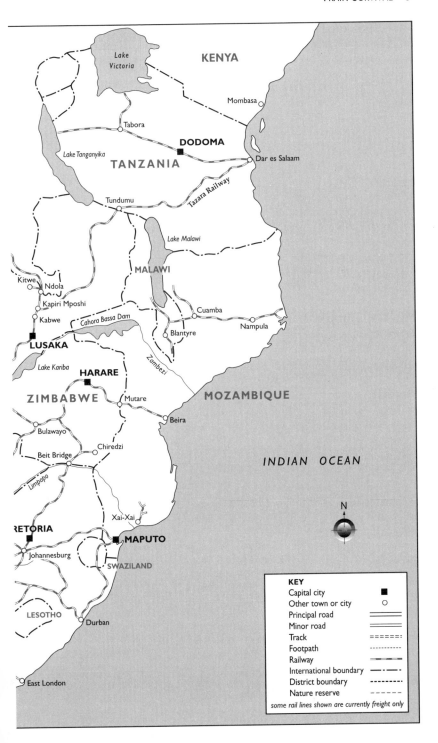

often in poor condition. Locomotives sometimes break down. A lot of the time the train will be delayed for hour after hour, and no-one will be able to tell you why. A fatalistic attitude helps at times like this. Africa will wait patiently – mimic it and you might find the stress fades away.

Litter

The amount of rubbish to be seen along the line of the railway is often staggering. All of it has been dumped from moving trains and, unfortunately, it is likely to remain there – there is not a lot of money for refuse collection in the African bush. The problem is a cultural versus a packaging one. Before packaging, Africa knew only organic waste, stuff that could be discarded reasonably readily, since it would eventually disappear on its own once it hit the ground. The old attitude is ingrained even though the packaging is now polystyrene, tin cans, plastic bags and cardboard. I saw one passenger fill the plastic refuse bag (provided for later disposal on all South African and Zimbabwean trains), tie a knot in the top and dump it gently from the speeding train. Use the bags correctly, please, and tell your governments that plastic is evil.

Meeting people

Trains offer a real opportunity for cross-cultural exchange. A lot of people will ask you all sorts of questions, some of them deeply personal. Don't be offended. You will meet Africa this way and the stories will be amazing.

Health

Malaria is rampant in many parts of southern Africa (see *Healthy Travelling*, pages 10–11) and mosquitoes do travel on trains. Standard rules apply for not being bitten – long sleeves, repellent and a mossie net if you can find somewhere to hang it. Fellow travellers may laugh at the net but you will get the last laugh when you visit them in hospital.

The toilets on many trains are basically holes in the floor of the coach which become more of a health hazard as the journey progresses. First class will be a lot cleaner than third so head that side if you can. Take your own toilet paper and guard it carefully.

Bicycles

Probably one of the best ways of seeing Africa would be on a combined bike/train tour. The freedom of having your bike to pedal away from the station of your choice is priceless. Africa really is bike country, especially in the remote rural areas where public transport is patchy. It is a brilliant way of exploring those parts of the country that trains don't reach.

Bike travel is slow and gives both you, and the people you will be running into, time to adjust to each other. As always, you should find out as much as you can about the area you intend cycling in beforehand. This will prevent you from cycling into embarrassing situations like civil wars.

Bikes are easily transported by train although in most cases they will be going in the guard's van. In most countries, other than South Africa where bikes travel free, you may have to pay the equivalent of the lowest priced ticket for the journey. However, fares are low in this part of the world, no matter what kind of miserable, dried soya-mince budget you are on.

Bike-wise, the best machine for the job is a sturdy, preferably broken-in mountain bike with whose quirks you are familiar – nothing like taking a brand-new bike out of the box at Dar es Salaam airport and discovering that you have no idea how to use it, or worse, how to put it together.

Remember that specialist spares are likely to be very scarce, so you should bring a reasonable selection of those you might need with you. On the other hand, with many parts of Africa reliant on bikes as a means of transport, even the smallest *shambas* will have a crew of resident bike experts who will doubtless be able to fashion some sort of rudimentary, but eminently workable, bush repair. And if you cannot yet fix your own punctures, take a course.

Flying with a bike
Sadly, the airlines no longer let you take your bike for free and it is now part of the baggage allowance. To transport it, take the wheels off, turn the pedals inward and bind the whole lot up in cardboard packing. Some people prefer to leave the bike unpacked in the hope that baggage handlers will treat it with care when they see what it is... or you might prefer to put another layer of cardboard on while you are about it.

Healthy Travelling

Dr Jane Wilson-Howarth
with thanks to Dr Vaughan Southgate
of the Natural History Museum, London

MAJOR HAZARDS

People new to exotic travel often worry about the range of dreadful tropical diseases waiting to attack the instant they arrive at their destination, but it is accidents which are most likely to carry you off. Road accidents are very common in many parts of Africa so be aware and do what you can to reduce risks. Try to travel during daylight hours and refuse to be driven by a drunk. Listen to local advice about areas where violent crime is rife.

PREPARATIONS

Preparations to ensure a healthy trip to Africa require checks on your immunisation status. It is wise to be up-to-date on tetanus (ten-yearly), polio (ten-yearly), diphtheria (ten-yearly), and for many parts of Africa immunisations against yellow fever, meningococcus, rabies, and hepatitis A are also needed. If your trip is a short, once-in-a-lifetime visit you could have hepatitis A immunoglobulin, which is short-lived but cheap; it gives some protection for a couple of months and costs around £5. However, most travellers are best to have hepatitis A immunisation with Havrix which costs about £40 per inoculation but protects for ten years. Typhoid immunisation is rather ineffective; it needs boosting every three years unless you are over the age of 35 and have had four or more courses; these travellers do not need further immunisations. Immunisation against cholera is no longer required anywhere. If you need most of these immunisations go – if you can – to a travel clinic a couple of months before departure.

Travel clinics
United Kingdom

MASTA, (Medical Advisory Service for Travellers Abroad), London School of Hygiene and Tropical Medicine, Keppel St, London WC1 7HT; tel: 0891 224100. This is a premium line number, charged at 50p per minute. Readers on the Internet may prefer to check the MASTA website: <http://dspace.dial.pipex.com/masta/index>.
British Airways Clinics: There are now 35 clinics throughout Britain and three in South Africa; tel: 01276 685040 (UK) for the address of your nearest one. Apart from providing inoculations and malaria prophylaxis, they sell a variety of health-related travel goods.

Other clinics include:

Berkeley Travel Clinic, 32 Berkeley St, London W1X 5FA; tel: 0171 629 6233.
Nomad Travel Pharmacy and Vaccination Centre, 3-4 Wellington Terrace,
Turnpike Lane, London N8 0PX; tel: 0181 889 7014.
Trailfinders Immunisation Clinic, 194 Kensington High St, London W8 7RG;
tel: 0171 938 3999.
Tropical Medicine Bureau This Irish-run organisation has a useful website
specific to tropical destinations: <http://www.tmb.le>.

USA

Centers for Disease Control This Atlanta-based organisation is the central source
of travel health information in North America, with a touch-tone phone line and fax
service. Travelers' Hot Line: 404 332 4559. Each summer it publishes the invaluable
Health Information for International Travel which is available from the Center for
Prevention Services, Division of Quarantine, Atlanta, GA 30333.
IAMAT, (International Association for Medical Assistance to Travellers),
736 Center St, Lewiston, NY 14092; tel: 716 754 4883. IAMAT is also represented at
Gotthardstrasse 17, 6300 Zug, Switzerland. IAMAT is a non-profit organisation which
provides health information and lists of English-speaking doctors abroad.

MALARIA

Malaria is a debilitating, potentially fatal, disease that no sensible traveller will
risk contracting. There is no vaccine against malaria, but there are other ways
to avoid it. Since most of Africa is very high risk for malaria, travellers must
give some thought to malaria protection. Seek current medical advice on the
best antimalarial medication to take. If mefloquine (Larium) is suggested, start
this two weeks before departure to check that it suits you. Stop it immediately
and seek medical advice if it seems to cause vivid and unpleasant dreams,
mood changes or other alterations in the way you feel. Anyone who is
pregnant, who has suffered fits in the past, who has been treated for depression
or psychiatric problems, or who has a close blood relative who is epileptic,
should avoid mefloquine. The usual alternative is chloroquine (Nivaquine)
two weekly and proguanil (Paludrine) two daily.

Travellers to remote parts would be wise to carry a course of treatment to
cure malaria in addition to taking preventative measures. Presently quinine
and Fansidar is the favoured regime, but it would be best to take up-to-date
advice on the current recommended treatment. The symptoms of malaria
include fever, aches and pains, headache, and lethargy and in a high risk
malarious area such a fever is very likely to be malaria. See a doctor if you
possibly can.

There is no malaria transmission at altitudes above 3,000m; at intermediate
altitudes (1,800m–3,000m/6,000ft–10,000ft) there is a low but finite risk.
Much of South Africa is free from the disease, although it is a risk in some
game and wildlife parks; Lesotho is also generally free from malaria; elsewhere
in Africa the risk to travellers is great. It is unwise to travel in malarious areas

while pregnant or when accompanied by children. The risk of malaria is considerable and such travellers are likely to succumb rapidly to the disease.

In addition to antimalarial medicines, it is important (and more comfortable) to avoid mosquito bites. Mosquitoes are most active between dusk and dawn. Pack a DEET-based insect repellent and a permethrin-impregnated bednet or carry a permethrin spray so that you can 'treat' bednets in hotels. With permethrin treatment, even very tatty nets give good protection and mosquitoes are also unable to bite through a treated net if you roll against it. Putting on long clothes at dusk means you can reduce the amount of repellent needed, but be aware that malaria mosquitoes often hunt at ankle level and will bite through socks, so apply repellent under socks, too, and on any exposed flesh. As well as protecting you from malaria, this will also help ward off elephantiasis and a range of nasty insect-borne viruses.

Travel clinics usually sell a range of nets, treatment kits and repellents, and malaria tablet memory cards, as well as providing their immunisation service.

COMMON MEDICAL PROBLEMS
Travellers' diarrhoea
At least half of those travelling to the tropics/developing world will suffer from a bout of travellers' diarrhoea during their trip, and the newer you are to exotic travel, the more likely you will be to suffer. The unpleasant truth is that travellers' diarrhoea comes from getting faeces in your mouth. This most often happens from whoever is cooking not washing their hands after a trip to the toilet but, even if the cook does not understand basic hygiene, you will be pretty safe if your food has been properly cooked and arrives piping hot. The maxim to remind you what you can safely eat is: Peel It, Boil It, Cook It – or Forget It. This means that fruit you have washed and peeled yourself (making sure your own hands are clean first) and hot foods should be safe, but raw foods, cold cooked foods and salads are risky. And foods kept lukewarm in hotel buffets are usually dangerous.

It is much rarer to get sick from drinking contaminated water, but it happens, so try to drink from safe sources. Water should have been brought to the boil (even at altitude it only needs to be brought to the boil), or passed through a good bacteriological filter or purified with iodine; chlorine tablets (eg: Puritabs) are less effective and taste nastier.

By taking precautions against travellers' diarrhoea you will also avoid typhoid, cholera, hepatitis, dysentery, worms, and other unpleasant problems. If, despite all precautions, you are struck down, see the box overleaf for the appropriate treatment.

Avoiding insect bites
In addition to the precautions against mosquito bites already described, there are other potential insect problems to avoid. During the day it is wise to wear long loose clothes if you are pushing through scrubby country; this will keep ticks off and also tsetse and day-biting mosquitoes which may spread dengue and yellow fevers. Tsetse flies hurt when they bite and are attracted to blue.

TREATING TRAVELLERS' DIARRHOEA

It is dehydration which makes you feel awful during a bout of diarrhoea, and the most important part of treatment is taking lots of clear fluids. Sachets of oral rehydration salts give the perfect biochemical mix you need to replace what is pouring out of your bottom, but they do not taste very nice. Any dilute mixture of sugar and salt in water will do you almost as much good, so if you like Coke or orange squash, drink that with a three-finger pinch of salt added to each glass. Otherwise make a solution of a four-finger scoop of sugar with a three-finger pinch of salt in a glass of safe/treated water. Or add 8 level teaspoons of sugar (18g) and 1 level teaspoon of salt (3g) to about one litre (roughly two pints, there is no need to be precise) of safe water. A squeeze of lemon or orange juice improves the taste and adds potassium which is also required. Drink two large glasses after every bowel action, and more if you are thirsty. If you are not eating you need to drink at least three litres a day, depending on the weather and temperature and your level of activity, plus whatever is pouring into the toilet. If you feel like eating, take a bland diet; heavy greasy foods will give you cramps.

If the diarrhoea is bad, or you are passing blood or slime, or you have a fever, you will probably need antibiotics in addition to fluid replacement. A three-day course of ciprofloxacin or norfloxacin or nalidixic acid is good for dysentery and bad diarrhoea.

Locals will advise on where they are a problem and where they transmit sleeping sickness.

Minute biting blackflies spread river blindness in some parts of Africa between 17°S and 19°N (from northern Zimbabwe to the Sahara). The risk of the disease occurs close to fast flowing rivers; flies breed there and the larvae live in rapids. The flies bite during the day but long trousers tucked into socks will help keep them off. Citronella-based repellents do not work against them.

Tumbu flies or putsi are a problem in areas of East, West and southern Africa where the climate is hot and humid. The adult fly lays her eggs on the soil or on drying laundry and when the eggs come in contact with human flesh (when you put on clothes or lie on a bed) they hatch and bury themselves under the skin. Here they form a crop of 'boils' each of which hatches a grub after about eight days, when the inflammation will settle down. In putsi areas dry your clothes and sheets within a screened house, or dry them in direct sunshine until they are crisp, or iron them.

Jiggers or sandfleas are another kind of flesh-feaster. They latch on if you walk bare-foot in contaminated places, and set up home under the skin of the foot, usually at the side of a toenail, where they cause a painful boil-like swelling. These need picking out by a local expert; if the distended flea bursts during eviction the wound should be dowsed in spirit, alcohol or paraffin (kerosene) otherwise more jiggers will infest you.

Skin infections

Any mosquito bite or small nick in the skin gives an opportunity for bacteria to foil the body's usually excellent defences. It will surprise many travellers how quickly skin infections start in warm humid climates and it is essential to clean and cover even the slightest wound. Creams are not as effective as a good drying antiseptic such as dilute iodine, potassium permanganate (a few crystals in half a cup of water) or crystal (or gentian) violet. One of these should be available in most towns. If the wound starts to throb, or becomes red, and the redness starts to spread or the wound oozes, antibiotics will probably be needed; a five-day course of flucloxacillin (250mg four times a day), or cloxacillin (500mg four times a day), or for those allergic to penicillin erythromycin (500mg twice a day), should help. See a doctor if it does not start to improve in 48 hours.

Fungal infections also get a hold easily in hot moist climates so wear 100% cotton socks and underwear and shower frequently. An itchy (often flaking) rash in the groin or between the toes is likely to be a fungal infection which will need treatment with an antifungal cream such as Canesten (clotrimazole) or if this is not available try Whitfield's ointment (compound benzoic acid ointment) or crystal violet (although this will turn you purple!).

Prickly heat

A fine pimply rash on the trunk is likely to be heat rash; cool showers, dabbing (not rubbing) dry and talc will help, and if it is bad you may need to check into an air-conditioned hotel room for a while. Slowing down to a relaxed schedule, wearing only loose baggy 100% cotton clothes, and sleeping naked under a fan can reduce the problem.

Protection from the sun

The incidence of skin cancer is rocketing as Caucasians are travelling more and spending more time exposing themselves to the sun. Keep out of the sun during the middle of the day and, if you must expose yourself, build up gradually from 20 minutes per day. Be especially careful of sun reflected off water and wear a T-shirt and lots of waterproof high SPF sun cream when snorkelling or swimming. Sun exposure ages the skin and makes people prematurely wrinkly; cover up with long loose clothes and wear a hat when you can.

Foot protection

If you wear old trainers, plimsolls or jellies on the beach you will avoid getting coral or urchin spines in the soles and you are less likely to get venomous fish spines in the feet. If you tread on a venomous fish soak the foot in hot (but not scalding) water until some time after the pain subsides; this may take 20–30 minutes submersion in all. Take the foot out of the water to top up otherwise you may also scald the injured foot. If the pain returns re-immerse the foot. Once the venom has been heat-inactivated, get a doctor to check and remove any bits of fish spine in the wound.

Safe sex

Travel is a time when we may enjoy sexual adventures, especially when alcohol reduces inhibitions. Remember the risks of sexually transmitted disease are high, whether you sleep with fellow travellers or locals. About 40% of HIV infections in British people are acquired abroad. Use condoms or femidoms. If you notice any problems get treatment promptly.

Animal attacks

If you are venturing into the bush remember that it is inhabited by some threatening wildlife. The most dangerous species are the big primates, wild buffalo, and hippos if you happen to frighten them and you are between them and the safety of their waterhole. Small monkeys who are used to being fed in parks may bite and can carry rabies; village dogs must also be assumed to be rabid. Any suspect bites should be scrubbed under running water for five minutes and then flooded with local spirit or dilute iodine. A post-bite rabies injection is needed even in immunised people, and those who are unimmunised need a course of injections. These should be given within a week if the bites are to the face, but if the bites are further from the brain the incubation period is longer and you probably have more time; make sure you get the injections even if you are a very long way from civilisation. The incubation period for rabies can be very long, so never say that it is too late to bother. Death from rabies is probably one of the worst ways to go.

Snakes rarely attack unless provoked and bites in travellers are unusual. You are less likely to get bitten if you wear stout shoes and long trousers when in the bush. Most snakes are harmless and even venomous species will only dispense venom in about half of their bites. If bitten, then, you are unlikely to have received venom; keeping this fact in mind may help you to stay calm. Most first aid techniques do more harm than good; cutting into the wound is harmful and tourniquets are dangerous; suction and electrical inactivation devices do not work; the only treatment is antivenom.

In case of a bite which you fear may have been from a venomous snake try to keep calm. It is likely that no venom has been dispensed. Stop movement of the bitten limb by applying a splint and keep the bitten limb below heart height to slow the spread of any venom. If you have a crepe bandage, bind up as much of the bitten limb as you can, but release the bandage every half hour. Evacuate the casualty to a hospital which has antivenom.

Never give aspirin; you may offer paracetamol which is safe. Never cut or suck the wound. Do not apply ice packs. Do not apply potassium permanganate.

If the offending snake can be captured without risk of someone else being bitten, take this to show the doctor, but beware that even a decapitated head is able to dispense venom in a reflex bite.

Bilharzia or schistosomiasis

Bilharzia or schistosomiasis is a common debilitating disease afflicting perhaps 200 million people worldwide. Those most affected are the rural poor of the tropics who repeatedly acquire more and more of these nasty little worm-lodgers. Infected travellers and expatriates generally suffer fewer problems because symptoms will encourage them to seek prompt treatment and they are also exposed to fewer parasites. However, it is still an unpleasant problem that is well worth avoiding.

When someone with bilharzia excretes into fresh water, bilharzia eggs hatch and swim off to find a suitable freshwater snail to infest. Once inside the snail, they develop, change and emerge as cercariae (torpedo-shaped worm or tadpole-like organisms). These are only just visible to the naked eye, but they can digest their way through human or animal skin. This is the stage that attacks people as they wade, bathe or even shower in infested water, and unfortunately in Africa many rivers, irrigation canals and lakes, including Lake Malawi, carry a risk of bilharzia. Two thirds of expatriates living in Malawi have evidence on blood testing of having encountered bilharzia and in 1995 75% of a group of people scuba-diving off Cape Clear in Lake Malawi for only about a week acquired the disease.

The pond snails which harbour bilharzia are a centimetre (0.4in) or more long; they like well-oxygenated, still or slowly moving fresh water, with plenty of vegetation (water-weed, reeds, etc.) for them to eat. The most risky shores will be close to places where infected people use water, where they wash clothes, etc. Winds disperse the cercariae, though, so they can be blown some distance, perhaps 200m (220yd), from where they entered the water. Scuba-diving off a boat into deep off-shore water, then, should be a low-risk activity, but showering in lake water or paddling along a reedy lake shore near a village carries a high risk of acquiring bilharzia.

Water which has been filtered or stored snail-free for two days, or which has been boiled or treated with Cresol or Dettol is also safe. Covering your skin with an oily insect repellent like DEET before swimming or paddling is also protective.

Cercariae live for up to 30 hours after they have been shed by snails, but the older they are, the less vigorous they are and the less capable they are of penetrating skin. Cercariae are shed in the greatest numbers between 11am and 3pm. If water to be used for bathing is pumped early in the morning, from deep in the lake (cercariae are sun-loving), or from a site far from where people excrete, there will be less risk of infestation. And afternoon swims will be a much higher risk than an early morning plunge. Since cercariae take perhaps 10 to 15 minutes to penetrate, a quick shower, or a splash across a river, followed by thorough drying with a towel should be safe. Even if you are in risky water longer it is worth vigorously towelling off after bathing for this will kill any cercariae which are still in the process of penetrating your skin.

Only a proportion of cercariae which successfully penetrate will survive and cause disease. Although absence of early symptoms does not necessarily mean there is no infection, infected people usually notice symptoms two or more weeks after penetration. Travellers and expatriates will probably experience a fever and often a wheezy cough; local residents do not usually have symptoms. There is now a very good blood test which, if done six weeks or more after likely exposure, will determine whether or not parasites are going to cause problems. The infection can then be treated. While treatment generally remains effective, there are treatment failures and re-treatment is often necessary. The reasons for treatment failures are not yet fully understood, but there now may be some drug resistance. Since bilharzia can be a nasty illness, avoidance is better than waiting to be cured and it is wise to avoid bathing in high risk areas.

Summary

If you are bathing, swimming, paddling or wading in fresh water which you think may carry a bilharzia risk, try to get out of the water within ten minutes. Dry off thoroughly with a towel. Avoid bathing or paddling on shores within 200m of villages or places where people use the water a great deal, especially reedy shores or where there is lots of water weed. Preferably cover yourself with DEET insect repellent before swimming. If your bathing water comes from a risky source try to ensure that the water is taken from the lake in the early morning and stored snail-free, otherwise it should be filtered or Dettol or Cresol added.

Bathing early in the morning is safer than bathing later in the day.

If you think that you have exposed yourself to bilharzia parasites, arrange a screening blood test (your doctor at home can do this) more than six weeks after your last possible contact with suspect water.

FURTHER READING

Self-prescribing has its hazards so if you are going anywhere very remote consider taking a health book. For adults there is *Bugs, Bites & Bowels: the Cadogan Guide to Healthy Travel* by Jane Wilson-Howarth, and if travelling with children look at *Your Child's Health Abroad: A Manual for Travelling Parents* by Jane Wilson-Howarth and Matthew Ellis, published by Bradt.

South Africa: Background Information

FACTS AND FIGURES
Size and location
The Republic of South Africa lies at the foot of the African continent and is bordered by Namibia to the north-west, Botswana and Zimbabwe to the north, Mozambique to the north-east, and surrounds, or almost surrounds, Swaziland and Lesotho. South Africa covers an area of 1,221,040 square kilometres (471,443 square miles), making it one of the largest countries in sub-Saharan Africa.

Capital
Pretoria is the capital of South Africa. The South African Parliament meets in Cape Town, but in 2000 this function will move to Pretoria which was previously the administrative capital only.

Population
The population of South Africa is roughly 45 million. Apart from the towns, the most densely populated areas are KwaZulu-Natal, the highveld, the Orange Free State, Eastern and Western Cape and along the coastline. There are 11 main linguistic groups of whom the Zulus are probably the most numerous.

Government
The ruling party is the African National Congress which won the country's first truly democratic elections in 1994 by a sizeable majority. The party failed to win the two-thirds majority it needed to govern alone, but it dominates the Unity government. Nelson Mandela was inaugurated as the country's first black president in May 1994; his nominated successor is long-time ally Thabo Mbeki. The next elections are to be held in 1999, in line with provisions laid down by the country's post-apartheid constitution.

Major towns
Johannesburg is by far the largest town in South Africa. Spreading over hundreds of square kilometres, it has all but expanded into Pretoria 50km (30 miles) to the north, and is home to approximately 6.5 million people – there hasn't been a census in a while and illegal immigrants flood in daily.

Cape Town and Durban are second and third in size respectively, followed in rough order by Pretoria, Bloemfontein, Port Elizabeth, Pietermaritzburg, Kimberley, East London, Nelspruit, Pietersburg and George.

Economy

South Africa has the continent's most developed economy, highly diversified with a modern infrastructure. The varied resource base includes substantial reserves of strategic minerals. With big business historically tying up much of the country's wealth and production, South Africa has long been a capitalist nation. Its per capita GNP is estimated at US$2,520. There is, however, a great imbalance in the distribution of wealth and one of the government's challenges is to even out the inequalities and find work for the seething mass of jobless people – unemployment is about 45%.

Languages

There are 11 official languages, all of which are supposed to enjoy equal attention. In practice English is the language of government. Afrikaans is widely spoken, especially on the Platteland (countryside). isiXhosa, isiZulu and seSotho are also commonly spoken and tend to predominate in urban areas. The remaining languages are isiNdebele, sa Lebowa, siSwati, Xitsonga, Setswana and Tshivenda, which are concentrated in their areas of influence.

Climate

South Africa enjoys a varied climate ranging from sub-tropical heat and humidity on the lowveld and east coast, through the temperate highveld to hot and very dry in the semi-desert west. The humid lowveld and east coast regions can be unpleasant in summer, while the Cape summers are very hot but dry.

Average summer temperatures range from 26°C (78°F)on the highveld, and upwards of 30°C (85°F) in the lowveld and Western Cape. Summer temperatures in the Karoo and the Kalahari desert are regularly up around 40°C (104°F).

Winters – from May to August – are generally mild and dry although the highveld and desert regions do get bitterly cold, with temperatures often falling below freezing. Snow and frost is common in the high country, and the high mountain ranges such as the Drakensberg will be blanketed in snow. The Western Cape is unique in that it has a Mediterranean climate – hot dry summers and mild, wet winters.

South Africans take their summer holidays between December and January and prices rise accordingly. Accommodation in national parks, seaside towns and resorts is heavily booked over this period.

Geography

South Africa falls into two distinct physical regions, a great plateau in the interior which occupies most of its area, and a narrow coastal strip which fringes the plateau on three sides. The two regions are divided by a continuous range of mountains which forms the Escarpment. The plateau ranges in altitude from 600m (2,000ft) in the Kalahari Basin in the west to over 3,400m (11,155ft) in the Maluti and Drakensberg mountains which form the eastern part of the Escarpment.

The country is mostly arid. Good and regular rainfall occurs only on part of the land. The west-flowing Orange River is the country's main watercourse, but there are a few other perennial rivers which run through the dry western parts. The eastern part of the country has the bulk of the country's perennial rivers including the mighty Tugela. The legendary Limpopo River demarcates the northern borders with Botswana and Zimbabwe, but it is a small river by world standards.

The country's coastline is 2,990km (1,860 miles) long, lapped by two oceans – the Indian to the east and the Atlantic to the west. Coastal vegetation ranges from sub-tropical, in northern KwaZulu-Natal on the east coast, to barren desert on the west coast. The west coast is thinly populated. The south and east coasts are the prime tourist destinations along with the many game parks.

HISTORY

The word turbulent comes up a lot in any review of South Africa's history. Little is known about South Africa's pre-history before Iron Age people moved down into the area from the north. There is evidence, gathered from archaeological sites in the east, of humanoid activity going back about three million years.

More recently, people called the Khoisan moved into the region around 40,000 years ago. The San, otherwise known as Bushmen, were hunter-gatherers while the Khoikhoi (called the Hottentots by the first Dutch settlers at the Cape) were nomadic pastoralists. The Khoikhoi settled in the Cape about 2,000 years ago while the Bushmen roamed at will across the country. The first pressure on the San came from Bantu-speaking tribes, who were slowly pushing down the eastern coastal belt, looking for new grazing lands for their sheep, cattle and goats.

By the 15th century, Bantu-speaking tribes had settled most of the eastern half of southern Africa, limiting themselves to areas where they could grow their crops and keep livestock. Growing populations meant that the search for new grazing lands continued. The late 18th century saw the beginnings of the mighty Zulu kingdom whose rapid expansion put further pressure on the Xhosa people, forcing them further south and towards the rivers in the Ciskei where they would run into the newly arrived British settlers.

Portuguese exploration and the arrival of the Dutch

The Portuguese are the first westerners on record at the Cape of Good Hope. For 45 years in the middle of the 15th century Portugal's King Henry the Navigator equipped and sent expeditions to discover the mysteries of the sea routes south from Europe along the African coasts. The mission was to find a sea route to the East and its spices. A few years later, in February 1488, Bartolomeu Dias de Novaes was the first European explorer definitely to

round the Cape, although his three-ship flotilla was driven so far south by a
strong south-easter, that the Cape was passed unseen. It fell to Vasco da Gama
to make the first landing in what is today South Africa, at St Helena Bay on
November 7 1497. His was the first white face the Hottentots who watched
the landings had ever seen.

The South African coast was, and is, a perilous one for sailors, and the
Hottentots made it clear the Portuguese were not welcome. Portugal largely
ignored South Africa as a result and no settlements were founded. Table Bay
was a place for refuge from storms and somewhere water might be found in
emergencies.

By the beginning of the 17th century, the Dutch were the rising trading
force in the region, having wrested the spice trade from the Portuguese. The
Dutch East India Company, the key player, needed a half-way station where
supplies of fresh water and food could be taken on board its ships. The Cape
of Good Hope was the logical place to do this and, in 1652, three Dutch ships
under the command of Jan van Riebeek arrived in Table Bay.

A fort was built, vegetable gardens planted and fresh water located. The
Cape was open for business and white dominance of the region had begun.

Before long, van Riebeek was finding it tough just to feed his own people,
let alone supply passing ships with fresh produce. He was under pressure from
the company to make the settlement profitable and in desperation got
authorisation to release company employees from their contracts, allowing
them to start farming and trading. The company bought crops from these free
burghers (citizens) at fixed prices and suddenly the settlement was no longer a
garrison but the nucleus of a colony. Slaves were imported from the East to
solve the labour shortage and the settlement grew rapidly. Farmers began
pushing into the Western and Southern Cape and, by the late 18th century,
were encountering the Xhosa people who were drifting southward in their
quest for fresh grazing lands.

Many of these sturdy pioneers, the *trekboers* (trek farmers), wanted
nothing to do with the mainstream of European development and had adapted
to the hardship of survival in Africa, competing with the native peoples who
were also roaming cattle farmers. Their descendants were the Afrikaners and
they differed from other African tribes in their individualism and Calvinist
faith. They believed they were an elect of God, and that the black tribes against
whom they clashed had no rights either against them or to the land which they
claimed as their own.

By 1779 clashes between the *trekboers* and the Xhosa had begun along the
natural border of the Great Fish River, sparking a series of wars which were to
continue for 100 years.

By the end of the 18th century, the Netherlands had slipped dramatically in
the international power rankings and the Cape Colony passed into British
hands during the Anglo–French Napoleonic wars of 1803–15. The British
valued the naval facilities at the Cape as a strategic asset, but the vast, dispersed
and somewhat unruly colony extending inland from the Cape was seen as little
more than a nuisance.

The 1820 Settlers
To strengthen the frontier area and dilute the Boer power base, Britain landed 4,000 settlers in the Eastern Cape in 1820. Many were veterans of the Napoleonic Wars who had returned home from fighting to no jobs and many relished the chance of a new start. (See also page 76.)

The Great Trek
The advent of British rule sparked new restlessness among the Boers who wanted nothing to do with the British, or any government control for that matter. A growing humanitarian attitude among the British toward subject peoples worried the Boers who still believed in their right to the land and, more significantly, their right to use native labour on their own terms. New legislation granting some rights to the natives along with a decision to return a huge tract of annexed land along the frontier to the Xhosa were the last straws for many of the Boers. By 1836 a few exploratory journeys had been undertaken and large parties were now organised to trek north across the Orange River and into the interior. The Great Trek – an event which lies very close to the heart of traditionally-minded Afrikaners – was under way.

These hardy people called themselves *Voortrekkers*, literally meaning 'those who journey forward'. Whole families travelled, along with all their possessions, in sturdy wagons pulled by teams of oxen. It was a migration of a culture and something which many Afrikaners claim as part of their soul, this urge to keep moving in search of new – and most important – uninhabited land for farming and grazing. The Great Trek was also to lead them straight into the rich country which had already been settled by African peoples who, over centuries, had been moving steadily down from further north.

Some Voortrekkers moved north towards the Limpopo River, clashing with the Matabele tribe and forcing them north, but the bulk of the parties headed for the rich grasslands of Natal which had been temporarily depopulated by the growing and aggressive Zulu nation. The promise of a peaceful occupation was shattered after trek leader Piet Retief was lured to the royal enclosure of Dingane, the Zulu king, and murdered along with a number of his followers. The result was a short, sharp campaign by a new Boer leader, Andries Pretorius, who used mounted *commandos* and superior European firepower to overthrow Dingane's rule. In 1839 the Boers declared Natal an independent republic.

This move was regarded with some displeasure in Britain. The British government felt that, just because the Boers had trekked beyond the boundaries of the Cape, that did not stop them from being British subjects. Troops were sent to the British settlement at Port Natal (now Durban) and Natal was formally annexed in 1845. So the trekkers packed up and began moving back over the Drakensberg into the highveld, preferring the peril of dragging their loaded wagons hand over hand up the steep slopes of the mountains to British rule.

The Boer republics

The Boers were soon well spread out across the highveld, living their fiercely independent lives. While central government was an anathema to them, constant pressure on them from the Bantu tribes meant some form of cooperation was necessary. The result was the formation of the two republics of the Transvaal (later known as the Zuid-Afrikaansche Republiek or South African Republic) and the Orange Free State, with each governed by a *Volksraad* (People's Council) and headed by state presidents who could invoke supreme authority in times of crisis.

Britain, seeing that there was little going on other than farming and cattle ranching, decided the republics were not a threat and formally recognised their independence in 1854. But the pressures from expanding Bantu tribes continued and the thinly populated republics were barely capable of maintaining their borders. By 1871, when diamonds were discovered north of the Orange River in Griqualand West (on the border of the Orange Free State), the British Cape Colony was self-governing, and colonial officials hoped that its model of government elected on a non-racial franchise could be applied throughout the region. Of course this would mean annexing the recalcitrant Boer Republics, and in 1877 Sir Bartle Frere tried to do just that with the South African Republic, sparking the First Anglo–Boer War.

The campaign ended with the astounding defeat of the British on a mountain called Majuba in northern Natal. The Boers encamped on top of the steep-sided hill must have been amazed to see the British troops marching in open order up the mountain, their red tunics standing out starkly against the green countryside. All the campaign achieved was to deepen the rift between Briton and Afrikaner.

Gold and war

The South African Republic was muddling along as a bankrupt farming nation when Australian prospector George Harrison and his friend George Walker stumbled across a particularly rich gold reef on a small mountain ridge called the Witwatersrand (Ridge of White Waters) in July 1886. It was not long before other strikes were made and the sheer size of the reef became apparent. The government declared nine farms to be public diggings the same year, and prospectors from all over the world began pouring into the Transvaal.

President Paul Kruger of the Transvaal was very aware of the power the gold strike gave his country. So, too, was mining magnate Cecil Rhodes, who had a vision of a British-influenced federation in southern Africa and an extension of the British Empire all the way north to Cairo. Rhodes had made a massive fortune in the Kimberley diamond fields, buying up the claims of small prospectors and gradually assuming almost complete control of the industry. Extending his business to the Transvaal gold fields was the next logical step.

Rhodes had already helped Britain get into the territory known today as Botswana, and in 1890 sent a colonising force of policemen and settlers to occupy the Shona territories north and east of Matabeleland, creating what was to become the state of Rhodesia. The idea was to encircle the Transvaal to force it to cooperate with the Cape Colony.

All this Kruger interpreted as a threat to the independence of the Republic and he took further steps to isolate the Transvaal from the clutches of Empire, partly by authorising the construction of a railway from the east coast port at Delagoa Bay in Portuguese East Africa (later Mozambique) to Pretoria. The railway would give Pretoria a route to the sea, allowing it to avoid having to use the railways from Cape Town, Port Elizabeth and Durban.

Internally, Kruger had a bigger problem. The gold was being mined by an extraordinary mix of *uitlanders* (foreigners) – most Boers had distanced themselves from the squalor and social evils of the mining camp of Johannesburg. As the miners grew richer, they demanded more say in government, but Kruger maintained that they would have to subscribe to Afrikaner ideals first.

Eager to manipulate the volatile situation, Rhodes began planning a military invasion of the republic, which would be launched apparently in support of an uprising by the *uitlanders* (Rhodes having organised the 'uprising' beforehand), and which would replace Kruger with a more pro-Cape government. There were plenty of divisions among the *uitlanders*, though, and a few days before the uprising was due to begin, it was clear that it would be an utter disaster. Rhodes sent repeated telegrams to force commander, Dr Leander Starr Jameson, waiting at Pitsani just over the border from the western Transvaal, telling him the raid had been delayed. Jameson ignored the telegrams, crossed the border with 500 mounted policemen and was swiftly beaten by a waiting Boer force at Krugersdorp, ruining Rhodes' political career as a minor side effect.

The (Second) Anglo–Boer War

Direction of British foreign policy in Africa passed to Joseph Chamberlain who believed the Boers had to be conquered and anglicised. Sir Alfred Milner, the British High Commissioner in South Africa, continued to press the *uitlanders* cause to the point that war broke out at the end of 1899.

The conflict, often known simply as the Boer War, lasted three years during which time it changed from a war of set-piece battles and sieges to a guerrilla conflict in its closing stages. When hostilities began, there were just 27,000 British troops in South Africa, compared to the 35,000 fielded by the two Boer republics. The Boer army was a people's army, made up largely of mounted *commandos* raised in every farming district and backed by small, but superbly trained, state artillery regiments in each republic. When war broke out, the Boer generals were urged to ride for the coast and capture the ports before the bulk of British reinforcements, then still at sea, could land. But on the ride to the coast, the towns of Ladysmith and Harrismith in Natal, and Mafeking (as it was spelled then) and Kimberley to the west, proved too tempting and, instead of bypassing them, the greater part of the Boer army was tied up laying siege to these towns.

The British landed reinforcements unopposed and, after a series of stunning setbacks, began to gain the upper hand through sheer weight of numbers, eventually taking formal possession of the two republics. The war continued, however, as the Boer *commandos* took to the bush and began raiding towns, blowing up supply trains and depots and attacking forts and garrisons in daring hit and run raids.

The *commandos* were sustained by their countrymen on the farms. To deny them this support, Lord Kitchener, who took command of the British forces in November 1900, took the war to the people, building a line of blockhouses to defend the railway to the Cape, and establishing concentration camps for Boer non-combatants, mainly women and children. Farms and houses were torched and the *commandos* lost their main source of food. The scorched-earth policy reduced the countryside to a wilderness and, along with the horrors of the concentration camps, created a bitter legacy which Afrikaners would be slow to forget.

Their support gone, it was only a matter of time before the *commandos* had to give in. In 1902 they surrendered. The peace terms set out in the Treaty of Vereeniging were generous and, bizarrely, opened the way for the survival of Afrikaner ideals which would eventually culminate in the rise to power of the National Party in 1948.

In 1908 and 1909, the union of the two former Boer republics and the two British colonies was debated by an all-white convention and a single country, the Union of South Africa, was created in 1910. The country's black majority were not consulted on this move and remained as subjugated and marginalised as ever.

The *Apartheid* years

When the National Party swept to power in 1948 on the back of fervent Afrikaner nationalism, it did not introduce *apartheid* – it was already there in the race laws enacted in the four decades since Union in 1910. What the National Party did, however, was to gather up all the restrictive and discriminatory legislation and refine it into a systematic body of law.

The key piece was the Group Areas Act of 1950 which applied total segregation in cities and towns. Where before there had been places where people of different races lived together, now the lines were clearly drawn. Black people did most of the moving out and away. Other laws governed freedom of movement, racially-based identity documents, classification according to colour and regulated workplaces. Inter-racial marriages were banned and, under the terms of the Immorality Act, sex across the colour line was forbidden. The Reservation of Separate Amenities Act was the law which gave the country all those 'Whites Only' signs on park benches, beaches and station toilets. The more sinister aspect was stiff security legislation and rule by fear.

The Liberation Movement

Long before the Afrikaners came to power, the black opposition was already a strong force. Fuelled by disappointment that black aspirations had been ignored in the run-up to Union, the South African Native National Congress – which became today's African National Congress – was formed in 1912 to campaign for black rights by peaceful means. It kept its non-racial, liberal stance right up into the 1950s, despite pressure from more radical elements to use force to achieve its demands.

In 1952 the 'Defiance Campaign' began – black people began ignoring 'Whites Only' signs and curfews and breaking other apartheid regulations. They offered no resistance if arrested, and pleaded guilty in court. The government strengthened the laws and imposed tougher penalties for breaking them.

The turning point came at Sharpeville on March 21 1960 when nervous policemen opened fire on people protesting the pass laws, killing 69 demonstrators. Riots were soon breaking out in townships all over the country. The government banned the ANC, and also a radical breakaway group, the Pan-Africanist Congress. The ANC launched its armed wing, *Umkhonto we Sizwe* (Spear of the Nation), shortly afterwards.

The Sharpeville shootings were condemned overseas and South Africa became steadily isolated as international opposition to its policies mounted. In 1976 school children in the sprawling township of Soweto hit the streets to protest about being taught in Afrikaans. The police response was brutal and riots followed across the country, continuing for eight months.

The government was unrepentant. P.W. Botha (prime minister 1978–89) implemented a new constitution in 1984 which gave Indian and so-called Coloured communities a political voice, while Blacks remained excluded, as they were deemed to be citizens of the numerous 'independent homelands' which the government had started creating all over the country.

The tri-cameral parliament was a disaster. The country was becoming steadily ungovernable as resistance continued. By the 1980s, South Africa, heavily involved in a war on the Angolan/South West African border, was also at the brink of a civil war. In 1985, the first of a series of Emergencies was declared, giving the government and security forces terrifying powers.

Hello, Democracy

In 1989 Botha's replacement, F.W. de Klerk, realised that change was overdue. In Parliament on February 2 1990, he announced the un-banning of the ANC and other political organisations and nine days later ANC president Nelson Mandela, jailed in 1963 under the Terrorism Act, was set free. The negotiations which followed were somewhat tense as whites sought to avoid being totally swamped, as they saw it, by black majority rule. De Klerk wanted a federal system of government, the ANC preferred to go to the polls and see who came out on top. In 1993 Mandela and de Klerk were jointly awarded the Nobel Peace Prize.

The first democratic elections, in April 1994, were held in complete peace. Most of the nation was caught up in the euphoria. The ANC won most of the votes but failed to get the two-thirds majority which would have allowed it to rule on its own.

The four years since the elections have not passed altogether smoothly. The new government inherited a number of disasters including a creaking health care system, a shortage of houses, and an education system which is still in disarray. The post-election glow soon faded as the crime rate spiralled and numerous corruption scandals broke. The government desperately needs to create jobs but this means more outside investment is needed, something which rampant crime has reduced to a trickle.

On the positive side, a new constitution, seen as a model for the world, has been drafted and established, and some progress has been made at reducing the housing shortage.

The country's next elections are scheduled for mid-1999. Four years ago, the ANC was a sure-fire winner. Now all bets are off as voter dissatisfaction at government's seeming ineptness keeps growing.

PRACTICAL INFORMATION
Tourist information and services

Every town has some kind of tourist authority and in the recent years, since international boycotts were lifted and tourists began arriving in the country in far greater numbers, most now offer genuine practical help instead of clamming up whenever questions are asked.

The overall body is the SA Tourism Board, generally known as Satour, which has offices in all the major centres. The head office is in Pretoria, tel: 012 347 0600, fax 012 45 4889.

International Satour offices

Australia	Sydney, tel: 2 9261 3424
Canada	Scarborough, Ontario, tel: 416 283 0563
France	Paris, tel: 1 456 10197
Germany	Frankfurt, tel: 69 92 91290
UK	London, tel: 0181 944 8080
USA	New York, tel: 212 730 2929
	Los Angeles, tel: 310 641 8444

When to visit

The mild climate means that almost any time of year is suitable. Winters on the highveld can be bitterly cold, but at least it is a dry cold, and what little snow there is generally falls only in the mountains and in the high country around Belfast in Mpumulanga and Barkly East in the Eastern Cape. Winter is the best time to visit the game parks, most of which are in the lowveld, as that region gets unpleasantly hot in summer. Winter days here are mild with cold, crisp nights, and there are fewer malarial mosquitoes around.

Durban and the sub-tropical east coast is also lovely and mild in winter, hot and humid in summer. Winters in the Western Cape region, however, are wet and miserable, with rain falling or winds blowing most days between May and September. El Niño may change everything, but right now, the best time to visit Cape Town is still between early February and mid-April – most of the

South African tourists will have gone back to Johannesburg after Christmas and the students and schoolkids are back in the classroom.

Public holidays
South Africa seems to have an inordinate number of public holidays and at one stage, big business was calling for government to scrap them as the economy is seriously affected by constant stopping and starting. Existing holidays are:

New Year's Day (January 1)
Good Friday and the Family Day the following Monday
Human Rights' Day (March 21)
Freedom Day (April 27)
Workers' Day (May 1)
Youth Day (June 16)
National Women's Day (August 9)
Heritage Day (September 24)
Day of Reconciliation (December 16)
Christmas Day and Boxing Day (December 25, 26)

There are also two others –

National Holiday (August 10)
Public Holiday (June 17)

Red tape
Visas
Citizens of British Commonwealth countries, the US, Canada, Australia and most EU countries do not need visas for holidays or business visits. Check with the South African embassy or high commission in your home country. Otherwise call the Department of Home Affairs in Pretoria, tel: 012 314 8911; or fax: 012 314 8516, or contact one of the international Satour offices listed above.

South African Embassies and High Commissions
Australia Rhodes Place, Yarralumla, Canberra, ACT 2600, tel: 06 273 2424, fax: 06 273 2669.
Canada 15 Sussex Drive, Ottawa K1M 1M8, tel: 613 744 0330, fax: 613 744 8287.
UK South Africa House, Trafalgar Square, London, tel: 0171 930 4488.
USA 3051 Massachusetts Av NW, Washington DC 20008, tel: 202 232 4400, fax: 202 265 1607.

Foreign embassies and consulates in South Africa
Australia 202 Orient St, Arcadia, Pretoria, tel: 012 342 3740.
Canada 1103 Arcadia St, Hatfield, Pretoria, tel: 012 422 3000.
New Zealand New Zealand citizens' affairs are handled by the British Consulate.
UK 19th Floor, Sanlam Centre, corner of Jeppe & Von Wielligh St, Johannesburg, tel: 011 337 8940; or Cape Town, tel: 021 253 670

USA 877 Pretorious St, Arcadia, Pretoria, tel: 012 342 1048;
or Johannesburg, tel: 011 331 1681; or Cape Town, tel: 021 21 4280.

Immigration and customs
Like everywhere else, you are only allowed to bring a minimal amount of booze (two litres of wine and one litre of spirits) and 400 cigarettes into the country. The allowance for gifts and other goods is a paltry R500 so make sure that laptop you are carrying looks used. As always, look smart and unrumpled and you are more likely to be left alone.

Drugs
A real no-no. Following the opening of its borders post-apartheid, South Africa has become a transit point for global cocaine and heroin cartels and the authorities are understandably eager to put a stop to this. There are stiff penalties for being caught with hard drugs. While local consumption of ecstasy and cocaine has also boomed in recent years, it is a good idea not to indulge.

Bribery
Stories of corruption are rampant. It probably is rife but unlikely to affect the average tourist. If the opportunity is presented, please decline politely, and stand up for your rights as a traveller.

Bureaucracy
Layered and treacly. Getting visa extensions and the like can be an immensely time-consuming and frustrating thing with queues lasting for days. If you need paperwork done in the major centres, try going to one of the smaller Home Affairs offices in a nearby municipality. Remember to take all your documentation with you – including photocopies of your passport and a stock of passport photographs. There is nothing like standing in a queue for a day only to be told by the recalcitrant behind the counter, when you get there, that you must come back tomorrow unless you have photographs with you.

GETTING TO SOUTH AFRICA
By air
South Africa is well-served by airlines – the London–Johannesburg flight is one of the world's most competitive routes and astonishingly low fares can be found. All the major European airlines and, of course, South African Airways fly into Johannesburg, with a number also serving Cape Town. London is the best place for bargain air tickets – try looking for adverts in the various travellers' magazines available free in racks outside many London tube stations. *TNT* is the best of these publications.

Fares from the UK to Johannesburg or Cape Town can start as low as £380 return, but these are often booked out long before anyone thinks to change the ad. Look to pay between £450 and £550 for a direct flight – some of the cheaper flights involve two legs, one to the Middle East or Eastern Europe followed by an onward flight to South Africa. The stopovers can be lengthy.

Asian and Australasian routes are also quite competitive with flights to/from Bangkok, Kuala Lumpur, Singapore, Hong Kong, Tokyo, Taipei, Sydney and Perth. A high season, one-way youth fare from Sydney via Perth to Johannesburg costs around A$1,580, excluding airport taxes. Student fares are slightly lower at A$1,450. Malaysian Airline System reportedly offers the best deals from Asia. Note, too, that Bangkok is probably the world's best place for cut-price air tickets after London.

Air links to North and South America are sparser and much more expensive. At the moment South African Airways has direct flights linking New York, Miami and Rio de Janeiro. A return (round-trip) flight from the US should cost US$1,300–US$1,600, while an open jaws fare going via another African capital such as Harare or Windhoek, could be as low as US$1,900 including taxes.

Overland

Border crossings are mostly simple, although onward transport options may be limited in some places. This is especially the case if you are coming by train from Namibia – the weekly service crosses the border and stops at Upington, usually late at night. There is as yet no onward train service and bus or minibus taxi is the only way out.

Border posts close at night; some are open later than others, but none are 24 hours. The areas around border posts, with their usual mix of shady frontier characters, are not the most salubrious places to hang around in, even during the day. Do not ever think of sleeping outside one. Rather get there early enough in the day to be able to get away on the other side, or spend some money on safe accommodation.

Cross-border trains are presently limited to the Johannesburg–Gabarone–Bulawayo route (to and from Botswana and Zimbabwe respectively), Windhoek–Upington (Namibia–South Africa), Durban–Maputo (Mozambique), via the kingdom of Swaziland, and a daily shuttle between Maputo and Komatipoort (South Africa).

Long-distance, cross-border bus services do run between most of the capital cities in the region. Some are good, others decidedly dodgy. Use them if you must, but check them out before getting on. If the bus or its crew or its passengers look suspect, find an alternative.

WHAT TO TAKE

Plan to travel as light as possible, whether you are going by train or not. Travelling with minimal gear really does make life much more pleasant, especially on those occasions (and they will happen) when you have to walk with all your kit. Independent travellers should take a backpack, preferably with an internal frame, as these are easier to stow in overhead luggage racks on trains and buses. Ensure that it is durable with strong zips and pockets. A smaller day pack is very useful in addition. Bring a tent if you plan on camping, and a lightweight sleeping bag for those cool winter nights when the train bedding runs out before the bedding steward reaches you.

Since the country is largely westernised, there are few of the sartorial problems that one finds in countries to the north. Shorts are completely acceptable, although in African culture it is only little boys who wear them and you may be giggled at. Women in trousers will not cause any riots nor will bikinis. However, a streak of conservatism runs deep in many people and certainly, outside of well-trodden regions, it is worth trying to look as spruce as possible.

Clothing should be kept to a minimum – you will be carrying it, after all. Cotton clothing is best in Africa, especially in summer. Lightweight cotton trousers are far more practical than jeans and could double as reasonably smart evening wear. Lightweight long-sleeved shirts and T-shirts are comfortable, and bring a sweater – it gets cold in the mountains, and winter nights in the bushveld and the highveld get bitterly cold. Bear in mind also that long sleeves and long trousers can protect against sunburn and insect bites.

Odds and ends

Almost everything you might need can be bought locally, and fairly cheaply, too. Things like insect repellent, toilet paper, tampons and so on are widely available, even in rural areas. Bring a spare pair of contact lenses and the fluids you need to go with them. Camping shops are widespread and there are a number of chains. Names to look for include Cape Union Mart, Cymot, ME Stores, Drifters and Outdoor Centre. Camping gear can also be hired, see page 34 below.

Electricity

Power is normally 220/230 volts AC at 50Hz. Plugs are either 5amp, 2 pin or 15amp with three rounded pins. Special adaptors will almost always be needed for equipment from overseas.

Hunting and fishing licences

Hunters will need a licence to shoot any game. The easiest way of going about this is to join an organised party which will take care of the details. Operators include African Connection (011 468 1526) or the SA Hunters' and Game Conservation Association (012 565 4856).

You will need a fishing licence if you want to fish in designated reserves such as Kosi Bay National Park. Most fishing equipment suppliers or one of the national angling associations, tel: 011 824 2140, should be able to arrange this for you. You can also try the SA Deep Sea Angling Association, tel: 021 96 4454, or call the Rock and Surf Angling Association, tel: 0423 5 1140.

MONEY

The South African rand, while still regarded as a hard currency in the region, is not the strongest unit around and those travelling on US dollars, UK pounds and Deutschmarks, among many others, will have a ball. The rand is divided into 100 cents. The rate of exchange in autumn 1998 was around £1.00 = R10 and US$1.00 = R6.10. However, unlike in some other countries, there is no bargaining power to be gained by offering to pay cash in dollars or another currency.

Foreign exchange

Travellers' cheques and foreign currency notes of all major currencies can be exchanged at any commercial bank or Rennies Foreign Exchange bureaux, and most of the better hotels also have exchange facilities for guests. New rates are posted daily.

If you have trouble locating an exchange bureau or have a related enquiry then contact Rennies Foreign Exchange on 011 407 3211; fax 011 339 1247, or American Express 011 403 0052; fax 011 403 7437, or Diners Club 011 358 8400; fax 011 482 6993.

Credit cards

Cards are accepted just about everywhere on the tourist trail and at many places off it. Visa and Mastercard are the standards, Diners Club and American Express less so, especially in the remoter regions. If you travel on plastic, keep an emergency cash stash for those late night arrivals in towns like Upington.

Budgeting

For some years South Africa has been a very cheap area to visit for tourists from Europe or North America but, in the way of these things, it is not as cheap as it used to be, but that is what happens when tourism booms. I am reluctant to give budgets because they are highly subjective. At the bottom end, staying in backpackers' accommodation and cooking your own food, you could get by on around R60 a day for basics, excluding transport and sightseeing.

By European or North American standards, train tickets, eating out and accommodation are excellent value, but the bigger costs, such as visiting game parks and long trips on luxury trains, tend to inflict wallet pain, no matter what currency you are using. There are bargains, however, especially in some of the state-run game parks where prices have been kept down to make them affordable to more than just wealthy whites.

SECURITY

The rapid changes in South Africa have caused some trauma. The police state mentality has faded but there is a severe unemployment problem, poverty is rampant in places and crime has risen sharply in some areas. Daylight muggings are frequent in downtown Johannesburg but, generally, violent crime specifically directed against tourists is rare.

Basic precautions apply in South Africa's cities as they would in any large town anywhere. There are a number of places you should avoid such as deserted areas and streets, and poorer areas, especially at night. Busy streets and well-used parks are normally safe enough, but do not walk around either in the city or suburbs at night – take a taxi. Ask the staff wherever you are staying for advice if you are unsure. Do not carry large amounts of cash around with you. Leave your valuables in a safety deposit box, not in your hotel room. Do not openly wear obviously bulging money belts. Blending in and not looking too much like a tourist helps. I have found that walking as if I know exactly where I am going, even if I do not, generally deters trouble.

The political violence which tore the country apart in the 1980s and 1990s has all but disappeared. However, the townships are still dangerous places and you should not venture into one alone or without someone you can trust to show you around and see you safely on your way home.

GETTING AROUND

Go by train if you can. It is cheap, efficient and safer than any road transport. The trains, sadly, do not go everywhere and there will be times when you are forced to go by bus or plane. Or bike. Public transport can be sparse away from the major centres for, as a rule, the car is king. Even in Johannesburg public transport can be a nightmare. Taxi services in the smaller towns are difficult to find, while local bus services in the same centres can be unreliable.

By air

Deregulation has resulted in a much more competitive domestic flight market, although fares are still not overly cheap. There are regular connections between all major centres, with feeder airlines serving some of the smaller towns. Domestic carriers include SAA, SA Express, Comair, Air Link and Sun Air. If you have your own pilot's licence, bring it with you – local plane hire rates are among the cheapest in the world.

By bus

The major towns have fairly reliable bus services but usability varies. Durban has one of the best city bus services in the country; Johannesburg's is fair, although much of the city is not covered. The biggest drawback is that the buses stop running in the early evening in all the cities.

There are a number of inter-city bus services run by companies such as Greyhound, Intercape, and Translux, an attempt by the railway operators to capture some of the bus-riding public.

By taxi

There are two kinds of taxi, the normal passenger cars one sees worldwide, and minibuses. The former are confined to the bigger cities and are expensive to use. One is denied the pleasure of hailing a taxi, too. They are not allowed by law to cruise for business, so can only be found at designated taxi ranks at hotels, airports and railway stations.

The minibus taxi industry is something else altogether. The result of abysmal public transport from the cities to the townships, the sector has grown at a staggering rate since deregulation into a multi-million rand business. It has brought transport to people who otherwise would have spent hours commuting to and from work by foot and municipal bus. It is a fiercely competitive business and fares are low.

Minibuses tend to work set routes in the cities. They can be hailed, using what seems to be a complicated variety of hand signals which indicate to the driver where you want to go, and they will basically stop anywhere to pick up or set down, causing massive amounts of road rage on the part of drivers behind them. Long-distance minibus taxi services run between the major centres and to and from the border towns.

Warning There is a more sinister aspect to the taxi business. While the taxis should be administered by one of the various taxi associations, many operators are fly-by-nighters, using unroadworthy vehicles and sometimes, unlicensed drivers. A good deal of the carnage on South Africa's roads involves overloaded minibuses or sheer bad driving by taxis. Use your discretion – if the vehicle or the driver looks dodgy, walk away. Turf wars are also fought between taxi operators and, too often, it is the innocent commuters who are quite literally caught in the crossfire.

Car rental

There are plenty of car rental firms and this is a good way to get around areas where rail services are sparse. In some cases, like visiting the Kruger National Park, it is basically the only option – unless you are in a vehicle you will have to be charming and brilliant at cadging lifts, or you will be spend a lot of time outside the park gates.

To hire a car, the driver should hold a valid South African or International Driver's Licence. Licences from the UK, USA, Canada or Australia will usually be accepted also. The driver must be over 25. Cars can be hired at any of the major airports or through a travel agent. Rentals start around R65 per day plus R0.99 per kilometre at the low end for a little car, rising to R2,300 per week for a luxury saloon. You may be better off, however, choosing an 'unlimited mileage' rate. Some agencies offer weekend or other specials.

Major operators include:
Avis, tel: 08000 21111 (national), or 011 923 3660.
Budget, tel: 0800 016 622 (national), or email: <bracsacr@mccarthy.co.za>.

Driving in South Africa

South Africa has a fantastic road network, a gift from a former government which wanted and built wide, hard roads in order to be able to transport the army at speed around the land. Despite curbed spending on road maintenance, the country's roads are wide and in good condition. Outside of the towns, roads can be almost disturbingly traffic-free. Even on the main Cape Town-Johannesburg road, driving through the Karoo can be an intensely satisfying solitary experience. Unfortunately, the country also has one of the world's worst accident rates, a combination of high speed limits and reckless driving, often on the part of lethal minibus drivers.

Major roads are tarred as are most secondary roads. Most of the country is reachable in an ordinary two-wheel drive car, the exceptions being some of the game reserves and many mountainous areas.

South Africa drives on the left.

Fuel

At the time of writing (mid-1998), the country's chemical workers were on strike and South Africa's petrol pumps were running dry. When the pumps are running, which is most of the time, petrol costs around R2.40 per litre (R10.91 per Imperial gallon; R9.08 per US gallon). You can use all major credit cards to pay for fuel.

Bike and camping equipment hire
Johannesburg

It's not easy to hire bikes or camping gear here or in Pretoria. Try asking at your hotel or backpackers' hostel. The ever-helpful Pete at the Explorers' Club in Yeoville, Johannesburg, advises it normally works out cheaper and is certainly safer to take organised trips. But if you do want to be independent contact Camping Africa, tel: 011 728 4207, fax: 011 728 3008 or email <cdt@gem.co.za>. They also have a website which you may wish to visit <http://www.icon.co.za/~campafrica>. They have a large hire division for everything from tents to water bottles.

Cape Town

In a city where so much life is directed at outdoor activities, hiring equipment is pretty straightforward and worth considering. Rent-a-Tent, tel: 021 557 4336, is helpful and reasonable. Two-people tents for hiking are R15 per day, large two-person tents (big enough to stand up in!) are R30 per day. They also hire out backpacks at R15 per day.

Haro Adventures, tel: 021 54458, hires out 15-speed mountain bikes for R40 per day but owner John Peiser offers reduced rates for longer hire periods. You will have to leave a R200 deposit. Haro also has a shop in Hermanus, the whale-watching capital, tel: 0283 76 3142.

ACCOMMODATION
Camping

South Africans love camping and there are sites everywhere, although you will often have to share with the caravanning fraternity. Prices naturally vary according to the facilities on offer as well as the location. Generally sites will have some kind of ablutions' block with either flush or long-drop toilets and showers, sometimes hot ones. You can often camp in the grounds of backpackers' hostels, if they have a garden, that is.

Budget

Ten years ago there were almost no youth hostels or backpackers' hostels in the country, basically because no one was visiting. Now there are backpackers' hostels everywhere, even in small Karoo towns. Dorm beds cost from R25 a night, doubles start around R45 per person. Some are good, some are revolting, and the situation is in constant flux with places opening and closing all the time. Many places will send someone to pick you up from the station or airport, but phone ahead to check.

The *BUG* book (sold in all good backpackers' haunts) is a pretty comprehensive guide to just about every bit of budget accommodation in South Africa as well as in Mozambique, Zimbabwe, Namibia, Botswana, Swaziland and Lesotho. Regular updates on its content can be picked up at travel agencies aimed at independent travellers.

Moderate and up

Hotels are mostly good by international standards, although hoteliers still have much to learn. Hotels are star-graded on a voluntary basis; ratings range from one to five stars. The industry is dominated by a few hotel groups – Sun International, Southern Sun/Holiday Inns, Karos and Protea. The chains are much like any other hotel chain in the world – you know what you are getting and you will probably pay for it.

Game and nature reserves

As opposed to game lodges where the accommodation is usually highly luxurious and dollar heavy, accommodation in game reserves is generally in huts, chalets or bungalows. Facilities are basic but usually spotless. Ablution facilities may be en suite but often there will be communal shower and washing blocks. There may be a restaurant but the emphasis tends to be on self-catering.

Bed and breakfast

Also quite a new trend, the B&B idea has spread rapidly across the country, especially in the tourist regions. B&Bs are generally highly visible but Satour or a travel agent will be able to recommend some.

Self-catering

A huge range of options here and an inexpensive way of enjoying your trip. If you want a seaside apartment or a cottage in the hills, get hold of Satour or speak to a travel agent. Remember, prices will rocket in season, especially around December/January, and apartments overlooking Cape Town's Clifton beach on the Atlantic seaboard will always be let out at extortionate rates.

EATING AND DRINKING

For a country with such an incredible multicultural history, it is a surprise that overall South African cooking is mostly fairly bland. There are one or two tasty exceptions – *bobotie*, a Cape Malay dish made with mince and eggs, infused with turmeric, curry and herbs, and *waterblommetjie bredie*, a mutton and spice stew whose main vegetable ingredient is water lilies.

Potjiekos – a stew made in a cast-iron pot over an open fire – is a traditional Afrikaner dish as is *boerewors* (farmer's sausage) – never ask what goes into it – and *biltong*, salted, air-cured meat. This is a meat oriented society and the *braai* (barbecue) is at the centre of it all. The *braai* is an institution, where the women hang out in the kitchen, making salads (if there are any to be made) and the men gather around the fire, beers in hand, ostensibly to cook the meat, but often charring it instead. Fat fires are doused with beer, giving the meat a not-unpleasant ale taste. There will be *mieliepap*, savoury porridge made from maize meal, to go with the piles of meat. The staple diet of much of Africa, *mieliepap* – also known as *sadza*, *nsima*, or *samp* – is found everywhere.

Drinking is taken seriously here. Beer brewing is almost a monopoly but no one is complaining too loudly. Lager rules since the climate is really too hot for warm ales. At least the lagers are cheap and plentiful. Look out for Castle (almost the national drink), Lion, and Black Label, as well as independent brands such as Windhoek Lager and Mitchell's Draft.

The country's wine industry started in the 18th century and some of the product is superb. There are too many estates to single any out here. Instead why not simply hire a car in Cape Town and go cruising the Wine Route for a day or two. Take one non-drinker to handle the car.

Look out for *mampoer*, sometimes called *witblits* (white lightning), a spirit usually distilled from peaches, pears or raisins, which will bring tears to your eyes. It used to be made illegally in the hills of the western Transvaal and all sorts of bases including chillis and potatoes have been tried. The hangovers are wicked, so approach with care.

SHOPPING

US-style shopping mall culture is big here, and, along with crime, is one of the reasons behind inner-city decay. As one would expect in a Westernised shopping environment, there are not a lot of uniquely African goods available in the malls other than in the curio shops which suck in the unwary.

If it is curios you want, rather try the flea markets. Since the borders have opened, traders from as far away as Mali, Ghana, Congo and Zambia have begun heading south in a steady stream, bringing carvings, beadwork, jewellery, drums, and all sorts of stuff from throughout Africa. You will see them if you ride any of the trains south from the Zimbabwe border. And they will definitely see you! Prices are much lower than in the mall curio shops and you can try and bargain further.

Johannesburg's best flea market happens on Sundays on the roof of the Rosebank shopping mall; most of the curio traders line the streets outside and fill the parking lot opposite the centre. Johannesburg's original market still happens on Saturdays in the parking lot opposite the Market Theatre complex near the western end of Bree St in downtown Johannesburg. Much of the stuff on sale is curios and crafts from far-away African countries and prices here can be better (depending on how effectively you are able to bargain) than the curio market at Rosebank where there are loads more affluent white people for the traders to sell to.

The inner city crime wave and competition from other markets really hammered the original market but a recent visit there was happily beggar-free and there was no sign of any trouble. If you do want to go to that market, use your common sense – the market area and theatre complex itself are safe during the day, the surrounding area much less so. Take a taxi to get there.

Cape Town's Greenmarket Square market happens daily in a cobbled square in the heart of the city. Those carved malachite chess sets have had to come a lot farther, and there are more tourists in Cape Town, so prices are higher. Bargain hard.

Trading hours for most shops are from 09.00–17.00 Monday to Friday, and 08.00–13.00 on Saturday. Shops in the malls are usually open all day on Saturdays and sometimes on Sunday.

If you are looking for bargains, stay away from the sprawling shopping malls which infest South Africa's towns and cities. One exception is Johannesburg's Oriental Plaza at the top (west end) of Bree St in Fordsburg. As its name implies, the Oriental Plaza is a rambling complex of Indian-owned shops where you can buy anything from spices to really sharp suits (I know, I got married in one!) Prices are generally lower than in the suburban shopping malls and the buzz of people and smell of spices and *samosas* cooking generates something more of an experience than your average sterile suburban mall.

South Africa, it is no secret, is well-blessed with precious minerals and stones. Gold jewellery is generally cheaper to buy here than overseas – after all, the country has almost half the world's known gold reserves. For jewellery, the Oriental Plaza is not a bad place to start, but your best bet might be to approach jewellery sellers at the flea markets. If they do not have whatever your heart desires, they will be able to recommend shops off the beaten path.

Photographic supplies

All kinds of films are available and a full range of processing services from one-hour labs to fully professional outfits. Import duties are high so photographic equipment is quite expensive but most of the better brands are readily available. X-ray machines at all airports are film-safe.

VAT refunds

All foreign nationals are eligible for VAT (sales tax) refunds on goods purchased in South Africa and taken home. However, you must make sure the dealer fills out the necessary form at the time of purchase. You then take the form, your receipt and passport and claim the VAT back at the airport when you leave the country. If travelling overland or by sea, VAT refunds are done at the border post of exit.

MEDIA AND COMMUNICATIONS

The local media industry is strong and vibrant and often controversial. There are plenty of newspapers, magazines and radio stations. The South African Broadcasting Corporation controls the bulk of TV and radio services and programming is multi-lingual. M-Net is a subscription entertainment television service.

Post

The service is fairly reliable although many South Africans will warn you not to send anything valuable by mail. Airmail to the UK takes around one week, a little longer to the US. Rates are low. There are 24-hour, door-to-door speed services. For postal information call 0800 02 31 33.

Phone

The telecommunications network is quite sophisticated. International calls are simple to make and are half-price between 20.00 and 06.00 weekdays and from 20.00 on Friday to 06.00 on Monday. To make an international call dial 09 followed by the country code and number in the usual way.

The country code for calls to South Africa is 27.

To contact the emergency services dial 10111 for police, 1022 for fire service, 999/998 for ambulance.

Internet cafés have mushroomed, and phone cards and cellular phones are widely available – if you have a GSM phone, you will be able to use it here, should you wish to.

Local time

South African Standard Time is two hours ahead of GMT, one hour ahead of Central European Winter Time and seven hours ahead of the USA's Eastern Standard Winter Time. Australia is 6-9 hours ahead of South Africa and New Zealand 11 hours ahead.

South Africa's Railways

South Africa has the best-run and, with 21,244km (13,201 miles) of track, the largest railway system on the continent. Steam locomotives were widely used until the late 1980s, until they were ousted as a total dieselisation and electrification programme, implemented in 1972, was completed. The huge operation is state-owned and it is the biggest single employer in the country.

A commercialisation process – read privatisation without the state actually letting go completely – in the last few years has resulted in dramatic cut-backs in passenger trains on all but the main routes. While it is now difficult to reach some parts of the country by train, the passenger service as it is still allows fairly comprehensive coverage.

HISTORY

The story of railway development in southern Africa is largely the story of the opening up of the continent itself. At the turn of the 20th century there was no road network to speak of – ox-wagons moved across the country at a pitiful pace, while trains on the newly built railways were already hauling substantial quantities of freight at speeds of around 30km/h (20mph). As in the rest of Africa, the development of railways in South Africa was largely driven by the need for transport into the interior and as a means of getting mineral and agricultural wealth out. A look at any map of the region will show how the railways tend to run from port to interior and, in many cases, do not interconnect.

The first railway in the country was a short line from Durban to Point, opened in 1860 and running a distance of about three kilometres (two miles). This was followed in the Cape with the opening of a 93-km (58-mile) railway from Cape Town to Wellington in 1863, but after that the government of the Cape seemed to have had no interest in doing any more with its railway. The discovery of diamonds in 1869 at a place later to be called Kimberley changed everything. News of the Kimberley diamond strike spread across the world and prospectors began pouring into Cape Town. From there they had to make their way north by ox-wagon, horse-cart or on foot, across some of the harshest terrain in the country, on a journey which took around two weeks.

The Cape Government moved slowly to take advantage of the commercial prospects – only in 1872 did Cape House pass legislation placing the railway in government hands and authorising it to extend the line northward to the diggings. The Cape Government Railway was formed and the line inched over the mountains and into the Karoo. Eleven years later, the line had reached the banks of the Orange River, still about 100km (80 miles) short of Kimberley. Many of those years were spent finding a way through the Hex River Mountains, a 2,250m (7,300ft) high barrier which effectively cuts the Western Cape off from the hinterland.

By the time the railway reached Kimberley in 1885, the furore surrounding the diamond strike had settled down. However, by this stage the imperialist visionary Cecil Rhodes was beginning to increase his already considerable power. He had founded the De Beers Mining Company in Kimberley in 1880 and, crucially, was a member of the Cape Parliament.

So far the railway had been built entirely in British territory. To the west, the two Boer Republics – the Zuid-Afrikaansche Republiek (ZAR), formerly the Transvaal, and the Orange Free State – were agricultural economies and fiercely independent, and would perhaps have remained so were it not for the discovery of gold in the Transvaal in 1886. That gold strike altered the entire history of South Africa. Diggers rushed for the Witwatersrand, and a mining settlement called Johannesburg rose out of the dirt. Rhodes formed the Goldfields Company, but he knew the key to development was to extend the railway from Kimberley into the Transvaal.

Paul Kruger, the authoritarian president of the ZAR, would have none of it. He resented the influx of foreigners into the republic. Kruger wanted nothing to do with a railway from the British-ruled Cape Colony. Instead he had been developing the idea of a railway from his capital Pretoria to Delagoa Bay in Portuguese East Africa (now Maputo in Mozambique), which would give the republic access to a non-British sea port. The Zuid Afrikaansche Spoorweg Maatschappij (ZASM), formed in 1887, found construction of the line extremely difficult, however. Disease and wild animals took their toll on the track gangs down in Mozambique, while pushing the line over the Escarpment from the lowveld to the highveld was also phenomenally difficult.

While the line inched over the veld, Rhodes, taking advantage of a friendly Free State government, had begun pushing the Cape Government Railway towards the ZAR border. Kruger was unhappy with the prospect of the railway from the south reaching his border before the ZASM line was completed. However, more money was needed to finish the Delagoa Bay line, and Rhodes, carrying a measure through Cape Parliament, provided the £600,000 needed to do the work. In return Kruger allowed the line from the south to proceed, and the first train steamed into Johannesburg on September 15 1892, nearly three years before the ZASM line was finished. The railway to Delagoa Bay was not opened until January 1895, and even then the opening festivities were somewhat marred by thieves who broke into the banqueting hall the night before and stole all the food.

By that time further lines had been built; one from Port Elizabeth, in the Cape, joined the Cape Town–Johannesburg line at De Aar, while the Natal Government Railway, built to transport coal from the Natal coalfields to Durban, had reached Ladysmith by 1886. Rhodes, meanwhile, figuring that if there was gold in the Transvaal then maybe the stories of an 'El Dorado' in the country to the north were true, had begun to build a line north from Kimberley toward the land of the Matabele. The Cape-to-Cairo dream, a trans-continental railway serving the interests of the British Empire across British-ruled Africa, was alive.

Development in the 20th century was rapid. As the country rebuilt after the ravages of the Boer War, railways criss-crossed the country, built to tap the vast resources of the land. Electrification began in the 1920s in Natal – today more than two thirds of the network is electrified. The demands of the mining industry as well as the once-strong agricultural sector were catalysts for the rapid growth of railways in South Africa. Modern economics has, however, seen a lot of branch lines close as their traffic has been lost to road transport.

GEORGE PAULING

George Pauling was the greatest railway contractor of his day, a legendary figure in the history of southern Africa's railways. His achievements were remarkable. When Pauling set off into unmapped bush to survey a new route he was accompanied by a French chef and 300 native carriers. The 'chop' boxes contained rare foods and champagne, and entertainment in the wilds rivalled the best a civilised hotel could have offered, according to Lawrence Green in his book *A Decent Fellow Doesn't Work*. Pauling built the railway north from Victoria Falls to the Belgian Congo border – one stretch of this line runs arrow-straight for 116km (72 miles), at the time a record for Africa, and only recently surpassed by the long desert straights on Spoornet's Sishen–Saldanha Bay ore railway. Pauling's men also once laid nearly 10km (six miles) of track through the Rhodesian bush in just 12 hours.

RIDING SOUTH AFRICAN RAILS

The country's passenger trains are run by Main Line Passenger Services (MLPS), an autonomous business unit within Spoornet, which runs the railway network as a whole. MLPS has to negotiate track use with Spoornet as well as hire locomotives from the Spoornet division which leases locomotives. It has been suggested that there are many railwaymen in Spoornet who would like to see the passenger train become extinct in South Africa, as they are seen as loss-makers and a drain on resources. This is quite a change, for, not long ago, passenger trains were regarded as a matter of strategic national interest.

In addition to the MLPS trains there are various steam, luxury and other specialised services. These are discussed separately in Chapters 9 and 10. The remainder of the this chapter deals with MLPS and the commuter rail systems.

Almost all MLPS trains have three classes of accommodation: first, second, and third or economy,. Sleeper accommodation is standard in first and second but less common in third which tends to have open seater coaches.

There is little difference between the accommodation in first and second class – compartments in both are fitted out as six-berth cabins or two-berth coupés. However, there is a maximum of four people in a first class cabin and, if you are travelling in a first class coupé, you will not be required to share with a stranger.

Third class compartments are strictly six people only, but there will be all sorts of visitors and hangers-on to make a truly crowded experience. Most third class accommodation is in open seater coaches. Over holidays or at month-ends, a mass of humanity will be packed in. All passengers, irrespective of class, are allowed 50 kilograms (110 pounds) of personal luggage. In third class this will spill over from the overhead racks into the aisles and onto seats, if any are vacant, as the journey continues.

Segregation of sexes is enforced and men and women may not share a compartment unless they book the whole compartment, or book as a group. This is fine if two of you share a coupé, but it can get quite expensive if you are booking but not filling an entire six-berth compartment between Johannesburg and Cape Town.

Name trains

South Africa is served by eleven 'name' passenger trains as well as a few regional services. These are summarised below. All are discussed in detail in later chapters, beginning on the pages shown. All services are return workings.

A NEW TRICK

For the people of Calvinia, a hot little town at the edge of the Great Karoo, the arrival of the circus was a huge event, if not the biggest, most exciting thing to happen to the town every year. Pagel's Circus was the big name in 1905 and he and his entourage would amble around the country by train. Calvinia lies at the foot of a series of little hills called the Pramberge but the climb to the top from the other side is a long slog for Calvinia-bound trains. At the front of Pagel's train was a well-used and ailing Class 6 locomotive, a hand-me-down from the former Cape Government Railways. The little engine made run after run at the bank, getting only part of the way up before, wheels slipping furiously, it shuddered to a stop. Pagel, tiring of the driver's exertions, told him to run the train as far up the hill as he could and slam on the brakes. This done, the circus master dropped a ramp out of one of the boxcars and led his elephants off the train. Marshalling them behind the guard's van, he signalled the driver to release the brakes. With calls and exhortations, Pagel's elephants leaned their bulk into the train. The engine was barking, wheels slipping and flaming embers shot into the sky. But the train held and, almost painfully, inched forwards. The elephant handlers shouted louder, the elephants leaned harder and the Circus Train dragged itself up the hill and down the other side into the town. Pagel became a hero, at least in Calvinia.

Trans-Natal (page 119) Overnight sleeper train between Johannesburg and Durban. Runs daily.

Trans-Karoo (page 63) Overnight sleeper express linking Pretoria and Johannesburg with Cape Town. Runs daily.

Trans-Oranje (page 134) Weekly service between Durban and Cape Town. Departs Cape Town Mondays, returns Wednesdays. Takes two nights/one day.

Southern Cross (page 101) Weekly train between Cape Town and Port Elizabeth at the eastern extremity of the Garden Route. Departs Cape Town Friday evenings, returns Sunday mornings.

Bosvelder (page 80) Overnight sleeper train from Johannesburg to Messina on the Zimbabwe border. Runs daily.

Bulawayo (page 84) Weekly train between Pretoria, Johannesburg and Bulawayo in Zimbabwe. Runs via Gabarone, capital of Botswana. Departs Johannesburg Tuesdays, returns Thursdays.

Diamond Express (page 137) Overnight service linking Pretoria and Johannesburg with Bloemfontein, via Kimberley. Runs daily except Saturdays.

Komati (page 85) Overnight sleeper service between Johannesburg, Pretoria and Komatipoort on the Mozambique border with onward connection to Maputo, Mozambique. Runs daily.

Trans-Lubombo (page 129) Twice-weekly second class sleeper service between Maputo, Mozambique, and Durban, via Swaziland. Departs Durban Tuesdays and Fridays, returns Thursdays and Sundays.

Amatola (page 69) Overnight sleeper train between Johannesburg and East London, via Bloemfontein. Runs daily.

Algoa (page 72) Overnight sleeper train between Johannesburg and Port Elizabeth, at the eastern end of the Garden Route. Runs daily.

Other services

Other services of interest to the tourist (all return workings) are:

Grahamstown–Alicedale (page 75) Service to settler city of Grahamstown in Eastern Cape. Connects with *Algoa*. Runs weekdays only.

East London–Cape Town (page 114) Weekly overnight service. Runs Sundays only.

Cape Town–Klawer (page 111) Overnight train from Cape Town to Namaqualand. Weekends only; departs Cape Town Fridays, returns Sundays.

The Doily (page 80) Overnight service from Beitbridge in Zimbabwe to Johannesburg. Runs daily. Accommodation in second and third class only.

The Taxi (page 91) Daily service between Mafikeng and Kimberley. All classes.

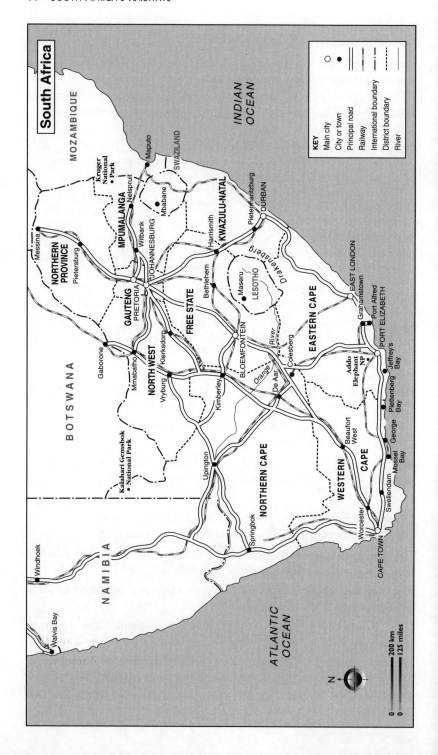

Johannesburg–Bloemfontein–Zastron (page 78) Monthly overnight train, with second and third class accommodation only. Usually runs on the Friday nearest the end of the month.

Pretoria–Nelspruit–Kaapmuiden–Hoedspruit (page 89) Weekly train, leaving Pretoria on Fridays, returning Sundays. On weekdays, there is a **Kaapmuiden–Hoedspruit** return service which connects with the daily *Komati* trains.

Johannesburg–Kimberley, via Mafikeng (page 91) Weekly overnight train, second and third class only, leaving Johannesburg on Friday, returning on Sunday. On the Friday nearest month-end, a special train runs from Johannesburg to Mafikeng and returns on Sunday.

Broadly speaking, the main 'hubs' for South African passenger train traffic are Johannesburg/Pretoria (which I will call the 'Reef'), Cape Town and Durban. Port Elizabeth, East London, Bloemfontein and Kimberley are served by fewer trains as a whole but are useful cities to build itineraries around. Just three normal passenger trains (this excludes the luxury *Blue Train*, see page 145) begin or end their journeys in Pretoria and pass through Johannesburg. These are the *Trans-Karoo* to Cape Town, the *Diamond Express* to Bloemfontein via Kimberley and the weekly *Bulawayo*. All other trains heading south from the Reef, including the *Trans-Natal*, the *Amatola* and the *Algoa*, begin and terminate in Johannesburg. The services north to Messina and Beitbridge and west to the Mozambique border start and end in Johannesburg.

Three trains head east from Cape Town – the weekly *Southern Cross* to Port Elizabeth, the weekly *Trans-Oranje* to Durban and the weekly un-named service to East London (No. 14255 and return working No. 41256).

There are just three passenger trains from Durban – the daily *Trans-Natal* to Johannesburg, the weekly westbound *Trans-Oranje* to Cape Town and a twice-weekly service to Maputo in Mozambique via Swaziland.

With a bit of judicious planning, one can use this network to cover the country's main points by train without too much hassle.

Four passenger trains (two north–south, two east–west) start in or pass through Bloemfontein, and three go through Kimberley. If you end up in Port Elizabeth or East London, you have a choice of two trains from each of those cities, one northbound, one westbound.

Itineraries
Some possible itineraries follow:
Itinerary 1
Cape Town–Port Elizabeth on the *Southern Cross* (breaking the journey at George to explore the Garden Route and ride the *Outeniqua Tjoe-Choo* steam train to Knysna), **Port Elizabeth–Johannesburg** on the *Algoa*, **Johannesburg–Nelspruit** on the *Komati* to visit the Kruger National Park and then on to **Maputo** in Mozambique via Komatipoort. From Maputo take the twice weekly *Trans-Lubombo* to **Durban**, then *Trans-Natal* to **Johannesburg** or *Trans–Oranje* back to **Cape Town**.

Itinerary 2
Johannesburg–Maputo on the *Komati* and Mozambique Railways daily shuttle, **Maputo–Durban** on the *Trans-Lubombo*, **Durban–Cape Town** on the *Trans-Oranje*, *Southern Cross* to **Port Elizabeth** then on the *Algoa* from Port Elizabeth to **Johannesburg**.

Itinerary 3
Johannesburg–Port Elizabeth on the *Algoa*, **Port Elizabeth–Cape Town** on the *Southern Cross*, **Cape Town–Johannesburg** on the *Trans-Karoo*, **Johannesburg–Bulawayo** on the weekly *Bulawayo*. A variation on this journey would be to get off the *Trans-Karoo* at **Kimberley** and take the daily train to **Mafikeng**, No. 22007, otherwise known as the *Taxi*, and pick up the *Bulawayo* there. There are two things to watch out for here. Firstly, the northbound *Trans-Karoo* arrives in Kimberley at 01.53 while the *Taxi* doesn't leave until 06.57 – that can be a long, miserable wait in winter. More importantly, the *Bulawayo* runs just once a week, with the northbound service rattling through Mafikeng late on a Tuesday night. Get the days wrong and it's the bus for you.

Clearly, just about any variation can be tailored from the above. But you have to watch out for the days on which trains run. With four trains passing through, Bloemfontein is a good place to change direction but, I have to say, not the most exciting place to spend a week waiting for the the *Trans-Oranje* going in your direction. Kimberley is the same, although there are trains running through every day.

Also be aware that late running is commonplace. This is something to remember if you are planning a tight connection such as changing trains at Kimberley from the northbound *Diamond Express* ex-Bloemfontein to the Cape Town-bound *Trans-Karoo*. The *Diamond* arrives in Kimberley at 19.50 while the southbound *Trans-Karoo* comes through at 20.51 and stops for 20 minutes. But if the *Diamond* is late, well…

Full timetables are given in the relevant sections.

Reservations and information
Contact information for local reservation and information offices is given in the various city descriptions later in the book. However, if you need to contact MLPS before your arrival in South Africa the Johannesburg office can be reached on (+27) 11 773 2944, or 11 773 8920, or 11 774 2082; if dialling from inside South Africa add a 0 at the start to complete the Jo'burg 011 area code.

The reservations service has improved dramatically in recent years. No more endlessly ringing telephones or disinterested staff. Telephone booking can be done from anywhere, the only stipulation being that you pick your ticket up at least a few hours before departure, if you still have to pay for it. When making a telephone booking, the reservations clerk will quote you a reference number, which you should note carefully. When you actually come to get the ticket, this makes the process much easier. Credit card bookings are welcomed. I have found it a good idea to confirm bookings the day before departure, especially in the holiday season when space on trains is limited.

Tickets

The trains are run as a service for the people and fares are correspondingly cheap, especially by European and US standards. Even budget travellers can enjoy the benefits of first or second class without having to cash too many travellers' cheques. Whatever class you do choose, your travelling companions are bound to be interesting. All fares quoted in this and later chapters, unless otherwise specified, are for single/one-way journeys, including sleepers in first and second class; economy may be either seater or sleeper fare. There is no difference in price between coupé and compartment fares in first and second, and no difference either between a seat and a compartment berth in economy.

Sample fares

	first class	*second class*	*economy*
Johannesburg–Cape Town:	R326	R227	R137
Johannesburg–Durban:	R164	R108	R67
Johannesburg–Bulawayo:	R212	R152	R95

Rail passes

South Africa is the only country in the region offering any sort of rail pass. There are five options of Spoor Pass. (*Spoor* is Afrikaans for 'rail'.)

5 days travel in 21 days	R990
8 days travel in one month	R1,510
12 days travel in one month	R2,150
16 days travel in two months	R2,720

The passes are available for both first and second class travel. Since most services are overnight, accommodation on that leg is also taken care of, Spoornet suggest helpfully. In addition the Spoor Pass holders get guaranteed bed and breakfast hotel rates at more than 150 hotels in Southern Africa through the Tourlink Hotel Pass. Accommodation can be reserved before departure. Preferential car hire rates are offered by Avis, and Tourlink can also arrange various day and half-day tours from Cape Town, Durban and Johannesburg.

Though passes are available some train staff do not seem to know much about them. I heard one rail pass holder complain on the *Bulawayo* train that he was having to pay for his food even though his travel agent in the UK had assured him that all meals were included in the fare.

These passes can only be booked outside South Africa, although you may book them abroad and collect them when you arrive. The Johannesburg agent is Tourlink, tel: (+27) 11 404 2617. There are also agents in the UK and US.

UK	**UK Leisure**, tel: 01733 335599.
US	**Tatum International**, tel: 602 867 4500.
	Design and Travel Tours, tel: 708 530 8135.

Bedding

Bedding is not normally provided automatically in the sleeper compartments. The bedrolls with their crisp white sheets and thick royal blue blankets are good value at R18, however, especially in winter when the trains can get disturbingly cold. A bedding attendant will start knocking on the compartment doors to distribute bedding as the train gets under way, and will make the bed up for you later in the evening. For backpackers it makes a nice change from a malodorous sleeping bag, and it is a lot more pleasant for everyone than toughing it out in just your clothes, despite the promise of a warm summer night outside.

Corridor etiquette

One of the best things about these corridor trains is passing the hours standing in the corridor, back resting on the bulkhead and leaning on the conveniently placed hand-rail which runs the length of the coach. It is a good way to meet fellow travellers or just escape from your compartment for a while. Train crew will knock on the hand-rail when they need to squeeze past.

Eating and drinking

Most of the name trains have dining cars, while all other long-distance services have catering cars. Anyone seeking a dose of old world train eating is likely to be disappointed, although, until recently, food was served on china and eaten with silverware in the traditional style. However, MLPS has decided to focus its service on the bulk of its clients, the economy passengers, and the emphasis in catering is now more on fast-food arrangements.

The menu is reasonably varied but fairly bland. Dishes include tomato cream soup, grilled sirloin steak and chips, fried hake, hamburgers, beef curry and more traditional combinations such as beef stew and pap (maize meal porridge). Most train meals arrive in a polystyrene box, complete with plastic knives and forks and sachets of vinegar and tomato sauce, but the food is reasonably filling if a little pricey for what you get. There have, however, been plenty of complaints from the public about the new direction and it is possible that MLPS will think again. Indeed, some train meals have reverted to table service, with meals served on real plates with proper cutlery. Every train's dining car is now franchised out to independent caterers, and the quality of food and service varies greatly.

Each dining car has its own bar selling a pretty wide range of South African beers and spirits.

Catering cars are coaches which have a full kitchen but no seating. You place your order through a hatch and go and eat in your compartment. The menu is basically the same as that in full dining cars. Passengers can also elect to have their meals delivered to their compartments – a roving steward makes his way down the train soon after departure taking orders. There is also a trolley service, selling snacks and alcohol, and you can order tea and coffee. The old tradition of ordering your wake-up cuppa still continues – be prepared for the rattle of the steward's key in the pre-dawn darkness.

A BRIDGE TOO DEAR

The Kraai River bridge would have been the highest railway bridge in Africa, spanning a 300-foot deep gorge on the railway line between the Eastern Cape towns of Aliwal North and Barkly East. The engineers had planned the bridge in detail – a tunnel had been bored through the rock on one side of the gorge, opening out on the edge of the drop.

Meanwhile, construction of the line continued while they waited for the steel girders to arrive. It is a hilly route and reverses (giant zig-zags up the mountainside) were built to take the railway through the valley of the Kraai River. It takes a while for trains to negotiate the section. There is plenty of stopping and starting and with a heavy train on a steep grade and the rails wet from rain or frost in the winter, it is a tremendous struggle to run trains at all. The bridge across the valley would have solved everything.

Years passed and the line was finished, and still there was no bridge. The stories grew wilder. One, which has become fact in its repeated telling, is that the ship carrying the steel from England in 1915, was torpedoed by a German submarine somewhere in the Atlantic Ocean.

It took years for the truth to come out and perhaps the people of Barkly East still don't like it. The minister of transport visited the town one day and people complained to him about the reverses and how it took trains so long to travel the 130km from Aliwal North. The bridge would have cost £60,000 to build, but there was no money for it, said the minister. 'What did you expect? It's just a little branch line, after all.'

As with all African trains, supplementing train fare with your own *padkos* – literally 'road food' – is a good idea. In third class you will find passengers eager to share their food with you.

Unlike elsewhere in Africa, there are relatively few vendors selling food from the trackside, possibly because the trains run mostly at night. There are exceptions however – Messina station near the Zimbabwean border is overrun with people selling ice cold drinks, boiled eggs, corn on the cob (*mielies*), and plenty of dodgy-looking sandwiches.

Showers and facilities

First and second class coaches have shower rooms, generally with hot water and pleasantly under-utilised. Toilets are at each end of the coach. They flush right onto the track – you will be exhorted not to use them while the train is in a station. Their cleanliness degrades rapidly through the journey.

Fresh, safe, drinking water is available in every coach from large, plastic, wall-mounted bottles at each end of the corridor. They are refilled at every major stop.

Commuter trains

South Africa's main cities have reasonable commuter train services, all run by a separate company called Metro Rail. For many years, starting in the late 1980s, the trains became killing grounds – gunmen would often walk through the coaches while the trains were moving and indiscriminately open fire on innocent people. Motives were apparently political, although the violence continued past the elections.

New commuter trainsets have been put in service; these have closed circuit security cameras and new windows which prevent terrified passengers from jumping out. Policing on the trains running into certain hot spots like outlying townships was also heavily increased, along with the number of armed security guards at major urban stations. The trains are much safer today, but you should still avoid travelling on township routes either alone or at night. Your best assurance is to go with someone you trust and who knows the area. Also check in advance whether there are any security problems.

Specific commuter services of interest to the visitor are discussed under the relevant city headings later in the book. The following are among the most scenic or interesting, or have the most useful routes:

Cape Town–Simonstown (page 98) Classic, sea-front train ride along Cape Peninsula.

Cape Town–Stellenbosch (page 99) Through winelands to a famous university town.

Cape Town–Wolseley (page 100) Ride into wheat and wine country. Great scenery in winter.

Cape Town–Strand (page 100) Strand is a beach-front town at the eastern end of False Bay.

Johannesburg–Pretoria (pages 55 and 61) Regular connections between the capital and the country's economic heart.

Durban–Kelso (page 128) Seaside run down part of Natal's South Coast.

Pretoria and Johannesburg

Pretoria and Johannesburg are in effect South Africa's two capitals, the former the seat of government, the latter the heart of the economy and the most energetic city in Africa. They are, officially, 56km (35 miles) apart, and certainly on different planets as far as the state of mind in each is concerned, but because Johannesburg has been sprawling northward for decades, the cities have become one vast conurbation. Both are in Gauteng province, the smallest province in the republic but home to over 10 million of its people and accounting for about 65% of its GDP. It is likely that many travellers coming to South Africa will pass through one or both of them at some stage of the journey (most international flights to South Africa arrive at Johannesburg), and both cities have some charm, although you may have to look for it. But they are certainly not holiday centres, very definitely so in parts of Johannesburg.

This chapter is not designed as a stolid account of what there is to do, but rather to give an idea of what lies behind the brashness (Johannesburg) and somnambulance (Pretoria).

PRETORIA

Pretoria, the official seat of government, was founded first. It was named in 1854 as the *kerkplaas* (church place) for the central Transvaal and became the capital of the new independent Voortrekker republic in 1860. The settlement was named after trekker leader Andries Pretorius, who had prevailed over the Zulu army at the gory Battle of Blood River in 1838. Pretoria was never much more than a sleepy farming town, at least until the Anglo–Boer War when it became the focus of nationalist fervour. Even today it has the feel of a town which became a capital city by accident – there never seems to be much urgency about the place, possibly because of the heat, which can be dreadful in summer, or maybe that is just the way administrative cities are.

Pretoria lies in the valley of the Apies River, somewhat lower and warmer than Johannesburg. The warm climate is ideal for well-known and exotic plants – people were crazy about roses here in the early days. The arrival of jacaranda trees in 1888 altered the city forever and, in late spring, the overriding impression of the city is a spread of purple haze from the estimated 70,000 of them lining many of the streets.

Pretoria is a major rail centre, with lines radiating in all directions, including the main lines to the eastern coalfields and Mozambique, and north to

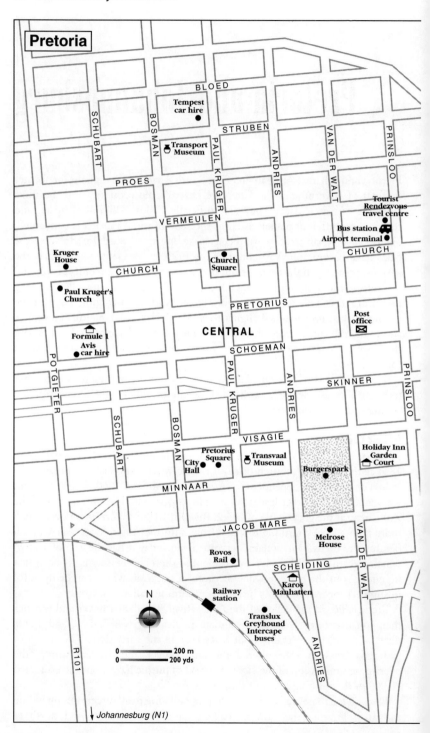

Pretoria

BLOED

SCHUBART

BOSMAN

Tempest
car hire

STRUBEN

Transport
Museum

PAUL KRUGER

ANDRIES

VAN DER WALT

PRINSLOO

PROES

VERMEULEN

Tourist
Rendezvous
travel centre

Bus station
Airport terminal

CHURCH

Kruger
House

CHURCH

Church
Square

Paul Kruger's
Church

PRETORIUS

CENTRAL

Post
office

Formule 1
Avis
car hire

POTGIETER

SCHOEMAN

PAUL KRUGER

ANDRIES

SKINNER

PRINSLOO

SCHUBART

BOSMAN

VISAGIE

Pretorius
Square

Transvaal
Museum

Holiday Inn
Garden
Court

City
Hall

Burgerspark

MINNAAR

JACOB MARE

Melrose
House

VAN DER WALT

Rovos
Rail

SCHEIDING

Karos
Manhatten

N

Railway
station

Translux
Greyhound
Intercape
buses

ANDRIES

R101

0 ——— 200 m
0 ——— 200 yds

↓ Johannesburg (N1)

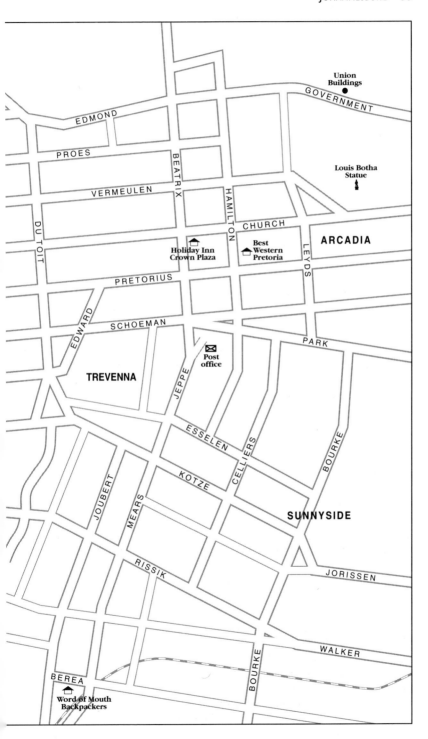

Messina and the Zimbabwe border. Three of the country's 11 state-run name trains are based here and two others pass through on their daily journeys. Rovos Rail's *Pride of Africa* (see page 143) is also based here.

Its having been the seat of government more or less since 1854, means that Pretoria is overrun with civil servants, soldiers and diplomats. In the 1980s, the streets would be packed with military personnel at lunch times as the city was then full of headquarters buildings, military depots and bases, but the steady stream of brown has all but disappeared as the defence budget has dwindled. The civil servants are still there, though, and the city would sink without them. The foreign embassies, usually lovely residences in acres of green grass, lurk behind high walls in quiet tree-lined streets east of the centre.

Once a very white city, Pretoria is slowly adapting to Africa and there is a much looser feel to the place than there was five years ago. That said, a deep conservative aura remains, and the city is nothing like Johannesburg for general energy and street life. However, the taxi ranks already throb with vitality, and the hawkers are gradually edging their way up the city's pristine pavements.

Some of Pretoria's colonial buildings survive, most notably **Paul Kruger**'s modest single-storey house, now a **museum**, where he would sit on the verandah and hold court, ruling the country from his own chair. On the whole, however, the dominant architectural theme seems to be 1970s government-inspired blandness. Apart from Kruger's house, other buildings worth looking at are **Melrose House** (275 Jacob Mare St), a neo-Baroque mansion where the treaty ending the Anglo–Boer War was signed, and the impressive **Union Buildings**, South Africa's parliament, east of the city centre on Church St.

The red sandstone Union Buildings were designed and built by Sir Herbert Baker (the man behind many of South Africa's better looking constructions) and are utterly perfect for a seat of government, commanding a view across a huge expanse of well-trimmed lawn and gardens into Pretoria. Stand on the grass below the buildings and imagine nearly a million people cheering the crowning of their new president, just as it was in May 1994.

The skyline just south of the city is dominated by two incredible structures. To the east is the ugly University of South Africa administration block, to the west a towering slab of sandstone called the **Voortrekker Monument**. The monument, six km (four miles) south of the city centre, is the one to visit. Built in 1938 in lasting memory of the Voortrekkers, it reflects a time when Afrikaner nationalism was surging. Over 250,000 people came to the opening ceremony and it is an intense symbol of the Afrikaner people. The inside walls are a detailed bas-relief history of the Great Trek and the Battle of Blood River. On December 16, the day of that battle, a shaft of sunlight falls through the roof and lights up the inscription *Ons Vir Jou Suid Afrika* ('We for You, South Africa') on a cenotaph in the basement of the monument. The views from the dome and the roof are awesome.

The **Museum of Natural History** on the corner of Paul Kruger St and Boom St is worth a look, not least for the massive whale skeleton excellently

mounted outside. The **Transvaal Museum** (Paul Kruger St) boasts a fine
fossil collection among its various attractions.

Two superb art museums are the **Pierneef Museum** (Vermeulen St), a
tribute to the man who painted the landscapes you might see in some of the
railway dining cars, and the **Pretoria Art Museum** (Schoeman St), which
contains the works of South Africa's finest.

Practical details

Phone
The area code for Pretoria is 012.

Railway station and rail information
The station is on Paul Kruger St, 800m south of the city centre. For
information, tel: 012 315 2401.

Airport transfer
Johannesburg International serves both Johannesburg and Pretoria, and a
couple of bus operators run between Pretoria and the airport. The fare is
around R35 to R45, depending on who you go with. It takes up to an hour to
travel the 40km, depending on traffic conditions. Operators include: Impala,
tel: 012 323 1429; or Pretoria Airport Shuttle, tel: 012 323 0904.

Tourist information
The **Pretoria Information** bureau is at the corner of Prinsloo and
Vermeulen Streets, or tel: 012 313 7694. **Satour**'s head office is also in
Pretoria, on Rigellaan (Rigel Av), or tel: 012 347 0600.

Getting around
Once again the echoes of the apartheid economy ring clear. Most white people
remain firmly wedded to their cars, one person per car, while the
municipalities scratch around for the funds to keep their bus fleets going.

There is a reasonable municipal **bus service** with the main terminus at the
south-east corner of Church Square in the centre of the city. Fares are quite
low but the services are not as frequent as one would like. However, the bus
to Sunnyside, east of the city, runs until 22.30, which is a miracle in South
African municipal bussing.

If you are brave, you can use the minibus **taxis**. The industry mushroomed
as black commuters, stuck far out on the fringes of the city, clamoured for
better transport. Normal saloon taxis are expensive, but if it is after dark and
especially if you are lost, do not hesitate to use one.

The city centre is quite small so getting around on foot is easy. If you have
a bike, take care – South Africa's urban drivers do not win any prizes for being
nice to cyclists, or to each other, for that matter.

There is a regular **commuter train** service with trains running from
Pretoria to the outlying townships and to Johannesburg, a 1½-hour journey
which costs about R10 in first class (there is no second).

Do not go to the townships, nor on the trains unless you are with someone you trust and who can show you around and see you safely home. Trains to Johannesburg run every half-hour early in the morning, and then hourly until 22.00 during the week and 1½-hourly on weekends. The Pretoria–Johannesburg trains are safe, but do travel in first class, not economy.

Safety

Pretoria seems to have escaped the crime wave which hit Johannesburg and other parts of the country in the early 90s, largely because this is, after all, a military city. Many from Johannesburg have set up home here, preferring the living purgatory of the daily commute to uncertainty in the Golden City. However, criminals have followed the money (diplomats' luxury saloons seem to be a favourite target) and standard precautions apply. Try not to walk around after dark in the city centre or around the railway station, and do not wear money-belts openly. If you arrive at night, take a taxi from the station or airport.

Accommodation

Orange Court Lodge 7 Orange Court, 540 Vermeulen St, tel: 012 326 6346. All sorts of rates – pick one. Singles start at R120, or R300 for six people in a three-room flat.

Kia Ora 257 Jacob Mare St, tel: 012 322 4803. Near station and offers free lifts. Singles and doubles R75 per person, dorm room R25.

JOHANNESBURG

People who live here will tell you it is Africa's most vibrant city and the continent's second-most-populated after Cairo. Since the 1994 elections, and the opening of the country's borders as a result, Johannesburg has become the intense focus of much of Africa. If you dare to go downtown, the babble in the streets is now French and Portuguese and the unfamiliar lilt of Swahili. Home to about 10 million people, Johannesburg is the pot and it is cooking.

The city is built on the Witwatersrand – the Ridge of White Waters – a low range of rocky hills where George Harrison discovered gold in 1886. The area is known locally as the Reef, after the line of rich, gold-bearing ore which runs east–west, from Springs to Randfontein. The city owes its existence to gold and greed, something which has tainted its soul. Two things stand out – it is one of the world's few major cities not built near or on a body of water, and it apparently has more trees (mostly exotics, planted to beat the heat on the otherwise bare expanses of veld) than any other city on the planet. It is also the country's undisputed crime centre, and with some tourists finding themselves at the wrong end of a gun or knife, you might want to spend as little time here as possible.

The city started out as a shabby mining camp, a lawless, rough place in keeping with mining camps everywhere. It is pretty lawless these days, too, or at least that is what people will delight in telling you. Its redeeming features are its incredible climate, energy and money. Jo'burgers work hard and relax hard and testosterone and adrenalin levels are high. It can be a fascinating place to visit, even if just to see how people live. It is not much good for a relaxing holiday, though.

Unlike most of the world's cities, Johannesburg's social and cultural life is patchy. The city centre itself has been abandoned as shopkeepers, restaurateurs and businesses flee rising crime and head for the sprawling shopping malls of the suburbs. The suburbs themselves are like suburbs in any developed country, though here the walls are all generally higher, the dogs more highly-strung, and the people quite hyper-tense. Restaurants are often located inside antiseptic shopping malls, although you can sit 'outside' under an umbrella.

Should you find yourself here for a few days, a likely event as the city is still the region's airline hub, there are a few diverting things to do. The **Market Theatre complex** at the bottom of Bree St in downtown Johannesburg now houses a few bars and restaurants, a theatre, drama and music workshops, the **Africana Museum**, a jazz bar called Kippies, and a heaving flea market in the parking lot on Saturdays. The museum has excellent displays on townships and Sophiatown, a legendary multi-racial suburb which was bulldozed in the 60s as the Group Areas Act came into force.

The Chamber of Mines (tel: 011 498 7204) arranges tours down **working gold mines** for around R250 – it is well worth doing one of these if you want to get any sense of what built Johannesburg. The trips last all day, largely because there are no longer any working gold mines in Johannesburg itself. The **University of the Witwatersrand** in Braamfontein has an art gallery, the city's Planetarium and one of the friendliest travel agents in the universe. Non-student courses and programmes are also offered (tel: 012 716 1111).

If you want to see what the **townships** look like, rather take a tour than wander off there on your own – walking around these places looking lost or wearing a backpack or money-belt is asking for trouble. Do not stray into the townships or squatter camps at all unless you are with someone you trust and who can deflect any unwanted attention. The tours to various townships may sound discomfiting but these are apparently not as zoo-like as one might expect. Various residents offer tours.

Suburbs

Choose your base in the city with some care. The northern suburbs are safe but sterile, and can be a nightmare to get around if you do not have your own transport. The downtown hotel- and high-rise-flat-land that is **Hillbrow** is unsafe, both to stay in and walk around.

Hillbrow was the first of the country's 'grey areas' that appeared when black people began braving the state and moved into previously 'white' districts. They rented apartments from slumlords who, knowing they could blow the whistle on complaining tenants at any time, often charged extortionate rents and let the buildings decay. Hillbrow was always a prostitution and drugs centre, and is even more of one now that the borders are open. The life on the streets is wild and absorbing, but take extreme care if you wander around here.

Yeoville, a bohemian suburb a few blocks east of Hillbrow, is a much

Johannesburg

AMESHOFF

University of the Witwatersrand

Jan Smuts House

Rosebank, Pretoria

Civic Theatre

Civic Centre

Wits   Wits Theatre

JORISSEN

BRAAMFONTEIN

BERTHA

MELLE

BICCARD

SIMMONDS

LOVEDAY

SMIT

SMIT

QUEEN ELIZABETH

WOLMARANS

HARRISON

RISSIK

Rotunda Coach terminal

Johannesburg Publicity Association

N

0 — 200 m
0 — 200 yds

Africana Museum

BREE

WEST

SAUER

JEPPE

SIMMONDS

Stock Exchange

DIAGONAL

PRITCHARD

HARRISON

KERK

RISSIK

PRESIDENT

Africana Geological Museum

City Hall

MAIN

WEST

SAUER

MARKET

John Vorster Square

REEF

BEZUIDENHOUT

COMMISSIONER

FOX

HUBERT

MAIN

MAIN

Vanderbijl Square

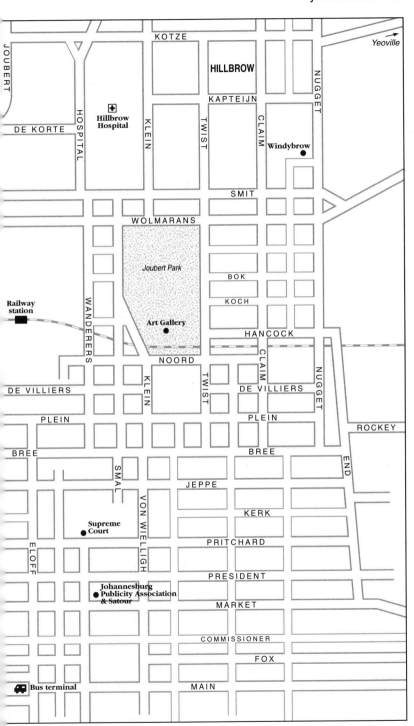

mellower place although there is a significant underworld vibe. It was another early multi-racial suburb and retains a lot of its anti-establishment aura. There are quite a few youth hostels around here and the place still buzzes at night, a rare thing in South African towns and cities. Most of the action happens along Rockey St with its line of sleepy coffee shops, bars and restaurants – take a slow walk down and look for something that appeals. Be careful at night. Recommended are House of Tandoor (sit on the roof terrace in summer) which has great, cheap Indian food and live bands, and Ba Pita at 5b Rockey St, a long-standing bar of mixed repute. For outstanding curries, try Poly-Poly in Hunter St, one block north of Rockey.

Melville is a trendier suburb than Yeoville with a vibrant and safe nightlife. It is probably the most happening place in the city as far as after-hours goes and is overrun with restaurants, coffee shops and bars. Some places have live music.

Practical details
Phone
The area code for Johannesburg is 011.

Airport transfer
Shuttle buses run the 25km–30km between Johannesburg International Airport and various hotels in the northern suburbs, Johannesburg railway station and the adjacent Rotunda coach terminal. The area around the Rotunda is unsafe and you should phone from here to organise a lift. The station was recently refurbished and has a few bars and restaurants where you can relax between trains. Stay inside and you will be fine.

For shuttle or taxi information, ask at the Info Africa desk on the ground floor of the airport's international arrivals hall.

Tourist information
Johannesburg Publicity, tel: 011 883 4033. The youth hostels and hotels are probably the best sources of information for the independent traveller.

Railway station and rail information
The station is on Rissik St, about 500m north of the city centre. For information, tel: 011 773 8920, or 011 774 2082. These numbers are good for country-wide enquiries.

Accommodation
Luxury
Rosebank Hotel Corner of Tyrwhitt and Sturdee, tel: 011 447 2700. Good safe location at 4-star hotel. Doubles R605 Single R538, all en-suite. Room only.
Karos Indaba Hotel William Nicholl Drive, at the corner of Peter Weinning Road, Fourways, tel: 011 465 1400. Thatch roofs and rustic white washed walls, 30 minutes from downtown Jo'burg. All rooms en-suite and air-conditioned. Doubles R470, singles R420. Breakfast included.

Mid-price:
Misty Hills Country Hotel Plot 69, Drift Boulevard, off DF Malan Drive,
tel: 011 957 2099. It's 25 minutes from Jo'burg and Pretoria and set in the foothills of
the Swartkop. Good value. From R154pp sharing, and from R264 single. Includes
breakfast.
Hamilton House Guest House 43 Niven Avenue, Douglasdale, Sandton,
tel: 011 462 3277. Stone and thatch lodge set in 4 acres. Double 225pp, single R225.
There is also a suite for R265pp. Full breakfast is included.

Budget
Bruma Lake Lodge 41 Hans Pirow Road, Bruma, tel: 011 615 1092. East of city
centre, quite near airport and next to Bruma Flea Market. Good facilities.
Recommended. Dorm R30, double R120 per room with bathroom, and R80 without.
Breakfast R15.
Pink House 73 Becker Street, Yeoville, tel: 011 487 1991. Well-established
backpackers in the centre of Yeoville. Dorm R40, double R50pp.
Explorers Club Lodge and Safaris 9 Innes St, Observatory, tel: 011 648 7138,
fax: 011 648 4673. A lovely, friendly backpackers' hostel. Ticket and booking agents
for Spoornet trains. Free pick-ups from station. Owner Pete Kirchoff is a travel guru.
Doubles R45 per person, dorm room R30.

Getting around
Johannesburg is a pain to get around unless you have your own wheels. The
city's inhabitants are besotted with their cars and public transport spending has
been neglected as a result. There are municipal **buses** which run from the
centre of town into most of the suburbs but the service is often sparse – no
buses late at night or on Sundays – and the size of Johannesburg means that
many areas are just not adequately covered. On some routes buses run only
infrequently and you can expect to wait an hour or more during off-peak
times.

People without their own transport make use of the vibrant **taxi** industry,
but be aware of the safety issues. Metered cabs can be found at designated taxi
ranks, usually outside hotels or at the railway station, and cannot be hailed in
the street.

There are **commuter train** services to the West and East Rand and to
Pretoria. Other than the service to Pretoria (details earlier in this chapter), the
trains are unlikely to be of much use to most travellers as they serve only
dormitory towns and do not go anywhere else. The trains are generally pretty
safe although you should ride in first class – muggings and assaults are rife in
third.

Safety
Johannesburg has the highest crime rate of any city in the country, but if you
take precautions, it is unlikely to affect you. Unsafe areas include most of
downtown (including the area around the railway station), Hillbrow and
Berea, and all townships and squatter camps. Walk with confidence, and on

the street side of the pavement. Always be aware of what is going on around you. Daylight muggings in Hillbrow and downtown are rampant. Looking like a tourist will attract unwelcome attention – do not display cameras, money-belts and such like openly. Leave money, air tickets and passports in your hotel/hostel safe, and do not carry anything with you that cannot be easily replaced. If you must take your camera, carry, and use it, discreetly.

If you arrive after dark, take a taxi or arrange for someone to pick you up. Walking around with all your gear late at night is silly. If you do get mugged, do not resist but be unthreatening and cooperative.

There is a lot of paranoia in Johannesburg and locals will entertain you all the time with horror stories. If you take care, it probably won't happen to you. Common sense is everything.

Routes from Johannesburg and Pretoria

PRETORIA TO CAPE TOWN – *THE TRANS-KAROO*

The *Trans-Karoo* is the only train which covers the complete distance between Pretoria and Cape Town via Kimberley, but there are other trains which run part of the way and which connect with onward services.

The journey is mostly overnight, which is a pity as some of the country's most dramatic scenery is traversed in darkness. However, dawn finds the southbound train at the edge of the Karoo and the slow amble out of this semi-desert, down through the mountains into the Western Cape, is one of railroading's greatest experiences. The northbound train is equally good on this section since the timings mean that it is well into the Karoo by the time darkness falls.

Timetable

Distance: 1,530km.
Frequency: Daily.
Classes: First, second, economy.

Pretoria–Cape Town Trans Karoo 81008 Southbound			Cape Town–Pretoria Trans Karoo 81007 Northbound	
dep	10.10	Pretoria	arr	11.48
dep	11.08	Germiston	dep	11.00
dep	12.30	Johannesburg	dep	10.30
dep	13.16	Krugersdorp	dep	09.31
dep	14.10	Oberholzer	dep	08.32
dep	15.14	Potchefstroom	dep	07.38
dep	16.11	Klerksdorp	dep	06.56
dep	16.24	Orkney	dep	06.33
dep	17.09	Leeudoringstad	dep	05.49
dep	17.34	Makwassie	dep	05.27
dep	18.26	Bloemhof	dep	04.43
dep	19.13	Christiana	dep	03.56
dep	19.53	Warrenton	dep	03.12
dep	21.10	Kimberley	dep	02.12
dep	21.47	Modderrivier	dep	01.14
dep	22.30	Belmont	dep	00.32

dep	23.01	Oranjerivier	dep	00.03
dep	23.21	Kraankuil	dep	23.38
dep	00.54	De Aar	dep	22.28
dep	01.55	Merriman	dep	20.56
dep	02.38	Hutchinson	dep	20.14
dep	03.40	Nelspoort	dep	19.08
dep	04.55	Beaufort West	dep	18.25
dep	06.03	Leeu-Gamka	dep	17.00
dep	06.42	Prince Albert Road	dep	16.26
dep	07.59	Laingsburg	dep	15.14
dep	08.26	Matjiesfontein	dep	14.47
dep	09.30	Touwsrivier	dep	14.00
dep	10.17	De Doorns	dep	13.15
dep	11.02	Worcester	dep	12.45
dep	11.36	Wolseley	dep	11.57
dep	12.24	Hermon	dep	11.13
dep	12.51	Wellington	dep	10.48
dep	13.05	Huguenot	dep	10.32
dep	13.50	Bellville	dep	09.50
arr	14.15	Cape Town	dep	09.20

Fares

Single fares, per person:

First   R326
Second   R220
Economy   R137

Leaving Pretoria, the train hustles to Johannesburg, sharing the line with packed commuter trains. There is a lengthy stopover in the golden city before the *Trans-Karoo* heads west then south-west and finally south into the gold mining and farming country. Unless you like maize fields or mine dumps, this is not the most rivetting section of the route, but there is a certain pleasure in standing in the corridor at sunset and watching the rows of neatly tended maize rush by.

The towns along the way, with names like Krugersdorp, Potchefstroom, Klerksdorp, Christiana and Bloemhof, exist because of gold mining or farming, and are often strongholds of Afrikaner nationalism. The vast areas of maize fields gradually give way to the first signs of the desert near Warrenton, as the landscape becomes increasingly dominated by thorn trees and scrubby bushes.

Kimberley

South Africa's diamond capital is a small city with a clump of high-rise buildings rising sheer out of the flatness of the surrounding landscape. Kimberley has a rich history. It grew rapidly when the first diamonds were found here in 1868 and large scale diamond mining still takes place – it remains the headquarters of global diamond mining conglomerate De Beers. Kimberley and its population of diggers, diamond kings and whores was besieged by Boer forces for four months during the Anglo–Boer War. Tying up Kimberley was vital to the Boer war effort as the town effectively controlled the railway north and south.

Although a bland town in many ways, much of the mining town flavour remains. The original open cast mine, the **Big Hole**, has been turned into a tourist attraction, well at least as attractive as a 365m (1,200ft) deep hole can be. It was a remarkable act of desperation or greed that enabled men with spades and picks to dig this far down. The diamond strike was originally made on a small hill called Colesberg Koppie. With thousands of prospectors digging frantically for stones, the hill became a hole.

There are other similar working mines here as well as the **Kimberley Mining Museum**, situated just beside the Hole. The museum is connected to the town centre by a restored, turn of the century electric tramcar. It is one of the country's best mining museums and includes a preserved mining town of 48 typical houses and other features.

Most passenger trains run through Kimberley late at night. The exceptions are the southbound *Trans-Karoo* and northbound *Trans-Oranje* which arrive in the early evening. For those alighting Kimberley is a placid town, with almost none of the security risks of the larger cities.

There is also a railway museum at the station, by the south end of the main platform. It is open from 10.00–16.00 on weekdays only.

Tourist information 0531 82 7298.
Rail information 0531 88 2631.
Satour 0531 31434.

De Aar

This is the premier railway junction where the Cape Main Line meets the railway from Namibia and Port Elizabeth. Unfortunately there is no longer a passenger service to Namibia although negotiations were in progress at the time of writing to change this. See Chapter 18, page 272.

De Aar had one of the finest steam depots in the country, a place which was revered as a steam shrine by enthusiasts. Steam has now all but gone apart from the occasional special train operated by Steamnet 2000 (see Chapter 9 page 140). Its other claim to fame is being the central ammunition and ordnance storage depot for the South African Defence Force. A place to dally only if life in very small towns intrigues you.

Tourist information 0536 36 0891.
Rail information 0536 382 0314.

Beaufort West

A railway town in the heart of the Karoo. It is a very quiet, although pretty enough, place with Victorian houses looking onto the tranquil streets. This is the spot to jump off if you are heading for the nearby Karoo National Park.

Tourist information 0201 3001.
Rail information 0201 492176.

Laingsburg

Like Beaufort West, this quiet town really owes its existence to sheep and goat farming. However, the town is now more famous for being mostly obliterated in 1981 when a wall of mud and rock smashed through the sleeping streets after heavy rains in the Karoo saw the Buffels River burst its banks. The water level lapped the tops of the arches of the graceful railway bridge south of the town.

Tourist information 0201 3001, as Beaufort West.
Rail information 0235 511249.

Matjiesfontein

This town, whose name translates rather romantically as 'fountain of mat rushes', is the site of the well-known **Lord Milner Hotel** and not much else, apart from a cluster of restored Victorian houses and a collection of sad-looking railway coaches. Matjiesfontein was a vital watering point for steam locomotives heading to and from the arid Karoo. The founder was a Scot named James Logan, who carved a farm out of the surrounding country and gradually developed the little hamlet. A spring on the farm provided his income. Logan found that the dry crisp air of the Karoo helped cure him of a chronic chest ailment and he accordingly decided to develop Matjiesfontein as an international health resort.

Since all trains stopped at Matjiesfontein, the canny Scot opened a dining room on the station platform for the hungry passengers, as there were no dining cars on the trains in the early years. When the Anglo–Boer War broke out, the hamlet was used as a field hospital and a staging post for troop trains heading north. Author Olive Schreiner spent much time in the locality and raved about the purity of the air. The hotel, named for the Boer War-era British high commissioner in South Africa, has become an institution following a full restoration in the 1970s. It is a rambling Victorian building set in well tended gardens with shade trees and a cool covered courtyard with splashing fountains.

Matjiesfontein is a good place to break your journey in either direction, especially if you are looking for a dose of Victorian desert culture. The hotel is quite pricey but there is the cheaper **Losieshuis** (boarding house) a little farther down the street. The restaurant on the station platform has long since gone.

A popular way of getting to Matjiesfontein is to take the *Trans-Karoo* from Cape Town, spend a night or two in town and then catch the down train back.

Tourist information 02372 5203.

Accommodation

Lord Milner Hotel 36 rooms, all with bath, tel: 023 5513011. Doubles R160pp, single R210, breakfast included.
Losieshuis (attached to the hotel) R105pp double, R145 single, no breakfast.

Touwsrivier

A railway marshalling yard at the top of the pass through the Hex River mountains. In steam days, this was a vital yard where downhill trains were divided up into shorter lengths to allow the locomotives to cope with the steep Hex River Pass.

In later years the yard was the site of a large steam locomotive graveyard – called a 'strategic reserve' – where hundreds of steam locomotives rusted away their last years. The idea was to store retired steam engines all over the Karoo where they would rust slowest in the desert air. If there was ever a repeat of the 1973 oil crisis, the railways would have had a massive supply of coal-burning engines just needing minor attention to be put back into service. In reality, these reserves were just dumps and, by the late 1980s, most of the locomotives in them had been cut up and turned into spoons.

The Hex River Pass

The range of high, granite mountains which effectively cuts the Western Cape off from the interior was the biggest single obstacle facing railway builders. From De Doorns in the heart of the Hex River valley, the railway climbs to 959m (3,145ft) above sea level, an altitude gain of 482m (1,589ft) in just 25km (15 miles). Surveyor Wells Hood laid out a line which twisted savagely through the high looming walls of granite, on a ruling gradient of 1-in-40 uncompensated. The pass was completed in 1875 at a cost of £500,000.

Running trains up the Hex River was an arduous business. Trains were banked (pushed) by a helper engine attached to the rear and a stud of powerful locomotives was maintained at tiny De Doorns shed for just this purpose. The line was electrified in the 1940s, however, and the steam bankers retired.

The pass itself is now closed, replaced by a series of long, dark tunnels. The ruling grade is an easier 1-in-66 and the route seven kilometres shorter. The longest tunnel is 12km (7.5 miles) long. It is quicker and smoother but the magic of a ride over the mountain pass has been lost.

The Valley of the Hex

The Hex River runs down a beautiful, narrow valley, with the rail line closely following the twisting river. The first Europeans settled here in the early 1700s. Some of the world's finest grapes now come from this valley – vineyards spread across most of the valley floor. The valley ends with a narrow defile and the railway line squeezes between a sheer rock face and the river, before passing out into a wide plain. After some fast running, the train glides into **Worcester**, a fairly large town which spreads out at the foot of the mountains.

After Worcester, the line heads straight across the plain before two converging mountain ranges – the Hex River and Nuweberg Mountains – force the tracks into the tortuous Tulbagh Kloof. The most dramatic view is on the right hand side (looking in the direction of travel) of southbound trains, left on the northbound services.

The countryside opens up again at the foot of the kloof into the wheat-lands and vineyards of the Boland. The train runs through wine farming towns such as Wellington and Paarl. Once clear of these towns, the pace picks up and before long, Cape Town's dormitory towns – Kraaifontein and Bellville – are reached. After Bellville, the line heads straight for Cape Town, with its famous mountain now the centrepiece of the view. Clicking over the points and through marshalling yards, progress into the Mother City is sedate all the way into Platform 24.

JOHANNESBURG TO THE EASTERN CAPE

From Algoa Bay to the Great Fish River is a 300-km (186-mile) wide band of bush-covered hills; harsh land in the dry season, beautiful and lush in the wet. This was the land given by Britain to the 4,000 or so 1820 Settlers, many of them returned veterans from the Napoleonic Wars, who were allocated farms in the frontier districts of the Cape. Between the Fish River, which was the frontier, and the Kei River was more fertile country in which nine bitter frontier wars would be fought between the black tribes and the British settlers and army.

This really was frontier country. There were wild animals to contend with, the *Zuurveld* (Sour Fields) – you would have thought the name would have been a warning – where most of the settlers were allocated farms, proved unsuitable for agriculture (the first three wheat crops were destroyed by rust), and there was pressure from the black settlers, the Xhosas, moving southward through what was later known as the Transkei. There was a lot of bitter fighting and at one stage, Britain had thousands of soldiers deployed on the frontier, struggling to protect the settlers from Xhosa raids.

There were few farmers among the settlers; most of them had been drawn from the cities and had little idea of how to work the land. Of the 1,004 men who arrived in the *Zuurveld* in 1820, only 438 remained by 1823. After the first crops failed, many had packed up and headed for Grahamstown, the settler city. However, the area remains uniquely English, with town names like Cradock, King William's Town, Bathurst, Beaufort, Jamestown, Cathcart and Alexandria.

The Eastern Cape Province is served by two trains each from Johannesburg and Cape Town (for the services from Cape Town, see pages 101–111). The Johannesburg services are the *Amatola* and the *Algoa*. The *Amatola* runs from Johannesburg to East London, and the *Algoa* goes to Port Elizabeth. Both trains run daily in each direction, with sleeper accommodation in all classes and a full dining car service.

It is difficult to recommend many of the places along the route as tourist attractions because, mostly, they are not. The towns close to Johannesburg, Vereeniging, Sasolburg and so on, are industrial towns. One of them is basically a steelworks, the other a chemical plant. Farther south, after crossing the wide, slow Vaal River near Vereeniging, the train begins crossing the wide, flat maize fields of the Free State province.

What you will notice is how much space this country has. The farms are big, rolling into a flat horizon. This is South Africa's Big Sky country.

Kroonstad, the first major Free State town, is a thriving farming town. Its location on the main road between Johannesburg and Cape Town is an added bonus. It is also a town I once tried to have my ailing car mended in but without much success, not least because of distinct apathy on the part of various mechanics. Go by train and pass straight through.

Both the *Amatola* and *Algoa* pass through **Bloemfontein**, South Africa's judicial capital. The city is more fully described on page 136.

After crossing the Orange River, the railway plunges into the Eastern Cape Province, Settler Country. Once more, the towns along the way, with evocative English names like Cradock, Cookhouse, Alicedale, names brought by English settlers in the 1820s, are farming towns or, in the case of Cradock, decaying, former railway towns. The countryside here at the eastern edge of the Karoo is dramatic, dry, craggy hills covered with aloes and sunbaked river beds. The southbound trains rush through in the darkness but the northbound trains cover the section in daylight.

The Amatola
Distance: 1,023km.
Frequency: Daily.
Classes: First, second, economy.

Jo'burg–East London *Amatola* 74013 Southbound		East London–Jo'burg *Amatola* 47014 Northbound	
dep 12.45	Johannesburg	arr 08.15	
dep 13.09	Germiston	dep 07.53	
dep 14.08	Vereeniging	dep 06.48	
dep 14.31	Sasolburg	dep 06.22	
dep 14.39	Wolwehoek	dep 06.09	
dep 14.56	Dover	dep 05.52	
dep 15.19	Koppies	dep 05.30	
dep 15.45	Heuningspruit	dep 05.05	
dep 16.25	Kroonstad	dep 04.39	
dep 17.07	Hennenman	dep 03.48	
dep 17.29	Virginia	dep 03.26	
dep 17.59	Theunissen	dep 02.55	
dep 18.32	Brandfort	dep 02.20	
dep 19.48	Bloemfontein	dep 01.33	
dep 20.59	Edenburg	dep 23.53	
dep 21.35	Trompsburg	dep 23.13	
dep 22.30	Springfontein	dep 22.46	

dep	23.22	Bethulie	dep	21.14	
dep	01.00	Burgersdorp	dep	19.51	
dep	02.00	Molteno	dep	18.37	
dep	02.45	Sterkstroom	dep	17.52	
dep	04.00	Queenstown	dep	16.55	
dep	05.17	Cathcart	dep	15.10	
dep	06.13	Toise	dep	14.20	
dep	06.42	Stutterheim	dep	13.55	
dep	07.05	Amabele	dep	13.30	
dep	07.45	Berlin	dep	12.46	
dep	08.04	Mount Ruth	dep	12.26	
arr	08.30	East London	dep	12.00	

Fares
Single fares, per person:

First	R215
Second	R149
Economy	R96

Johannesburg to East London – *The Amatola*
East London is the jumping off point for the southern part of the Wild Coast in the former 'independent homeland' of the Transkei. There is a beautiful hiking trail along the coast, and it is significantly safer than it has been in recent years thanks to a strong effort by local communities to improve their tourism prospects.

Aside from some excellent hiking country, there is not a lot to tempt the average traveller out of a speeding train between Bloemfontein and East London. Most of the towns are nice enough but focused on farming. If you like fly-fishing, though, the rivers around Maclear and Barkly East are thick with trout. The area is tough to get to – car hire in Queenstown or even East London is probably the way to go.

Queenstown
A settler town founded in 1847, this prosperous community is noted for being built around a hexagonal central fort and street pattern, the idea being that this gave defenders a clear field of fire down all the streets. As it was, Queenstown was never actually attacked by anyone and the hexagon is now a garden.

The town's **Frontier Museum**, stocked with 1820 Settler artefacts, is worth a look, as is the municipal art gallery. The fishing in the dams around the town is supposed to be excellent. Otherwise, not a whole lot going on.

Tourist information 0451 2265.
Rail information 0451 682004/5.

East London

This port on the Buffalo River has the charm of an English seaside town, without the weather. Its economy tends to fluctuate wildly but the port is generally busy these days, while tourist prospects are looking better than they have done in years. From as early as 1688 European sea captains had commented on the river's suitability as a place to land supplies, but the port was only founded in April 1847 when Fort Glamorgan was built at the start of the Seventh Frontier War. Until the river was dredged it remained a difficult place to land; most ships would anchor at sea and passengers used to be lowered in wicker baskets and brought ashore by lighter.

East London's most famous idea is the dolos, a unique inter-linking concrete block designed by Eric Merrifield, the port engineer, and which is now used in harbour construction and breakwaters all over the world. Named after the knuckle bone used by witch doctors in divination, the shape of the dolos ensures it gets entangled with other dolos blocks, forming an unbreakable barrier against the waves.

The **beaches**, Orient Beach especially, are lovely and there is great surfing at Nahoon. Orient is just one side of the harbour breakwater, close to the city centre.

One of the city's best attractions is the **East London Museum**, on the north end of Oxford St, whose exhibits include the world's only dodo egg and a coelacanth, a primitive fish with stumpy fins. The coelacanth was believed to have been extinct for about 80 million years until this one was caught by a fishing trawler in 1938. Others have since been found, but this was the first and East London is proud of it. The displays of Xhosa and Fingo culture are terrific.

East London is a reasonably mellow place during the day, but it has a thriving nightlife in the many bars and few clubs. There are plenty of restaurants.

Tourist information 0431 44 2719.
Rail information 0431 442719.

Accommodation

Esplanade Hotel Clifford St, tel: 0431 22518. Singles R155 with breakfast; doubles R199 (week), R176 (w/end).
East London Backpackers 128 Moore St, tel: 0431 23423. Dorm beds R25, camping R15 per person.
Sugarshack Backpackers Eastern Beach, tel: 0431 28240. Right on the beach. Call for free lift from station. Dorm beds R25.

Johannesburg to Port Elizabeth – *The Algoa*

From Springfontein, the *Algoa* heads south over the original Midland Main Line to Port Elizabeth. The route was opened in 1875 as railway builders pushed to link the seaports with the diamond fields to the north.

The Algoa

Distance: 1,112 km.
Frequency: Daily.
Classes: First, second, economy.

Jo'burg–Port Elizabeth *Algoa* 73011 Southbound		Port Elizabeth–Jo'burg *Algoa* 37012 Northbound	
dep	14.30	Johannesburg	arr	09.00
dep	14.54	Germiston	dep	08.40
dep	15.53	Vereeniging	dep	07.40
dep	16.17	Sasolburg	dep	07.14
dep	18.00	Kroonstad	dep	05.34
dep	18.42	Hennenman	dep	04.46
dep	19.04	Virginia	dep	04.24
dep	19.35	Theunissen	dep	03.53
dep	20.09	Brandfort	dep	03.18
dep	21.20	Bloemfontein	dep	02.33
dep	22.33	Edenburg	dep	01.10
dep	23.09	Trompsburg	dep	00.37
dep	23.58	Springfontein	dep	00.12
dep	00.52	Norvalspont	dep	23.02
dep	01.37	Colesberg	dep	22.29
dep	02.50	Noupoort	dep	21.39
dep	03.33	Rosmead	dep	20.38
dep	04.53	Cradock	dep	19.11
dep	06.09	Cookhouse	dep	17.59
dep	07.31	Alicedale	dep	16.26
dep	07.42	Eagle's Crag	dep	16.10
dep	08.03	Paterson	dep	15.47
dep	08.35	Addo	dep	15.14
arr	09.25	Port Elizabeth	dep	14.30

Fares

Single fares, per person:

First	R240
Second	R162
Economy	R101

Colesberg

One of the first towns after Springfontein, Colesberg is an unlikely rail destination but worth stopping in if you want to soak up some of the daily excitement of a true Karoo town. Colesberg straddles the N1 national road between the highveld and Cape Town and tends to be an overnight place for motorists on the long journey. Its main street is lined with lovely examples of Victorian Karoo architecture and it has enough trees to make it feel like a true oasis.

Colesberg is an easy place to spend a day or so in, but beware of the pounding midsummer heat and the terrifyingly cold mid-winter nights.

Tourist information 051 7530777.

Accommodation

The Central Hotel On the main road through Colesberg (the N1), tel: 051 753 0734. Singles from R120–R195, doubles from R150–R295, family rooms R250–R400 (depending on season). Security parking available.
Colesberg Backpackers Kerk St. Dorm bed R35.

Port Elizabeth

Situated in the beautiful sweeping curve of Algoa Bay, Port Elizabeth is the country's fifth largest city. From 1799 until 1820, the lonely British outpost of Fort Frederick was the only settlement but the arrival of the British settlers changed everything. Cape Governor Sir Rufane Donkin named the wind-blown settlement after his wife who had died of fever in India.

It should be a beautiful place – there are scores of **Victorian buildings**, some impressive monuments (including the fort and the campanile, the unmistakable bell tower on the foreshore) – but its outlook has been trashed by a high-level freeway running between the city and the seafront.

PE, as it is known everywhere, has also been hard hit by the ills of the national economy. Its industry is largely based on motor manufacturing and any economic downturn means that fewer cars are sold. The city centre has degenerated somewhat as businesses have been driven away to the suburbs by rising rates of crime (an insane practice which has been echoed in just about all South Africa's cities).

The notorious wind, for which PE is famous, does not help. It can blow for weeks without letting up, driving people to despair and craziness.

Despite its problems, PE deserves its nickname, 'the friendly city', because its people genuinely are friendly. The presence of the University of PE means there is a good crowd of young people and a happening nightlife, too. The main attractions are the **beaches**, an **oceanarium** where dolphins perform daily, and the large **Port Elizabeth Museum**, which has excellent archaeological and anthropological exhibits. The two main beaches, Kings and Humewood, are sheltered from the prevailing wind. More or less.

PE's position at the eastern end of the Garden Route will hopefully inspire its revival. Communications links to the Western Cape and

Johannesburg are good – as well as the two passenger trains described in these pages there are flights to all major domestic destinations.

Tourist information tel: 041 558884 (24-hours); or email: <pepa@iafrica.com>.
Rail reservations and information 041 507 2400.

Accommodation
Luxury
Edward Hotel Belmont Terrace, tel: 041 586 2056. An Edwardian building in the historical part of town. Many rooms have views over the bay. Single R285 and double R350, for bed and breakfast. Room only is R250 single and R300 double. Many rooms recently refurbished.

Protea Marine Hotel Marine Drive, Summerstrand, tel: 041 532 101.39. About 7 minutes drive from centre. Across the road from the beach – many rooms are sea facing, all are en-suite. From R450 single and double R540, room only.

Mid-price
Country Club 39 Church Road, Walmer, tel: 041 51 5099. A ten-room luxury guest house close to the beach. Has tennis, a putting green and pool. From R300–R450pp sharing. Includes breakfast.

Lemon Tree Lane 14, Mill Park Road, tel: 041 334 103. Self-catering apartments, although friendly owner will cook if you want to be lazy! Set in a lush garden. R115pp sharing, single R150.

Budget
Jikeleza Lodge 44 Cuyler St, tel: 041 56 3721. A quiet backpackers' lodge with a large garden to hide in. Dorm bed R25, singles R50, doubles R35 per person.

Kings Beach Backpackers Windermere Road, tel: 041 55 8113. On the beach with free pick-up available. Dorm R40, double R100, camping R20pp. Free tea and coffee and toast in the morning.

Port Elizabeth Backpackers 7 Prospect Hill, tel: 041 56 0697. Central location. Well established, well run hostel. Dorm R40–R45, double R120, family rooms (3–6 people) R50pp.

Connections with the *Algoa*

Grahamstown is served by a branch line which joins the main Port Elizabeth–Bloemfontein line at Alicedale. A weekdays-only return train connects with the *Algoa* train at Alicedale. This is a new service; until recently, Grahamstown had not seen a passenger train for years.

Times

Distance: 57km.
Frequency: Weekdays, one train each way.
Classes: Economy only.

	Grahamstown–Alicedale Train 33792 Westbound		Alicedale–Grahamstown Train 33793 Eastbound	
dep	08.00	Alicedale	arr	16.11
dep	08.33	Stonehaven	dep	15.41
dep	08.52	Highlands	dep	15.25
dep	09.10	Atherstone	dep	15.10
dep	09.27	Coldspring	dep	14.55
dep	09.35	New Cemetery	dep	14.46
arr	09.50	Grahamstown	dep	14.30

Fares

Economy   R8.00 per person one way.
Seater coaches only.

The Grahamstown railway won an award from the State President's Award Panel last year in recognition of its role in creating jobs in the region. For years Grahamstown had been without any sort of rail passenger service, despite the town having many schools and a university which were eager to provide human traffic.

This has now been turned around, with two economy class coaches attached to the daily goods train from Alicedale on the Johannesburg–Port Elizabeth main line. First and second class coaches may be reinstated if traffic levels warrant.

Growing tourism in the Eastern Cape is sure to boost tourism numbers in the little town. The annual Grahamstown Arts Festival already draws significant numbers of people and the development of a hiking trail, which hikers would reach by train, is another looming attraction in a town whose citizens mean business.

The connection is only good for passengers on the southbound *Algoa* who want to get to Grahamstown, or travellers from Grahamstown wanting to catch the northbound *Algoa* (see *Algoa* times above). If you are heading to or from Port Elizabeth from Grahamstown, then you are better off going by bus.

While the branch line continues through Grahamstown to the seaside town of **Port Alfred**, there are no longer any passenger services on this section. The line, finished in 1879, was the first to be built by George Pauling, the railway contractor who later had a constructive hand in much of the country's early railway building. Pauling wanted to tap into the potential traffic from the new harbour at Port Alfred, and accordingly extended the railway to the sea and formed the Kowie Railway Company. The port, however, was a total loss – the estuary on which it was built silted up faster than it could be dredged, and the railway found itself without any traffic. Stubbornly, operations continued until a train derailed and fell off the high Blaaukrantz Bridge in 1911, killing 31 people. The resulting claims from what is still one of the country's worst train smashes, bankrupted the company.

Port Alfred is a pretty holiday town. There is a lot of tourist potential and passenger trains may run down to the sea again one day. Right now, the only option is to catch a minibus taxi. These go from outside the Grahamstown station entrance.

Grahamstown

The original frontier town, it was founded in 1812 as a fort to garrison the troops sent to protect the settlers from marauding tribes pressing down from the east. Colonel John Graham selected the site, an old burned-out farmhouse lying in the lee of some hills and near the headwaters of the Qoyi (Rushing) River. Grahamstown was a struggling military base until the 1820 Settlers arrived and turned the town into a trading and hunting centre. There were still large herds of wild animals moving through the frontier territory and the town thrived on the hunting trade. At one time, there were 174 registered ivory traders vying for the many tons of tusks passing through every year.

The town has a distinctly English feel, reflected in the **Settlers cottages**, Victorian buildings and churches, of which there are said to be 52. The most imposing building is the **cathedral** of St Michael and St George which was built bit by bit from 1828.

The country's only camera obscura can be seen in the Observatory Museum, one of four parts of the **Albany Museum**, on Bathurst St. The device projects a panoramic view of the town onto a screen in a darkened room. The first diamond from the Kimberley strike was valued here by Dr W. Atherstone, sparking off the frantic rush for the diamond fields. Unfortunately for Grahamstown the diamond rush ended its rule as the colony's second city. The railways bypassed the town and many of its own citizens joined the rush to the north. The Albany's other parts are the 1820 Settlers Memorial Museum, Fort Selwyn, and the National History Museum. Grahamstown has South Africa's second coelacanth, caught and stuffed in 1952.

If you like real nostalgia, try the ancient Odeon cinema. This a classic of its kind where the seats and sound have not changed since it was opened. Take blankets, a six-pack and pizza. Smoking is allowed in the gallery.

Grahamstown is a university and school town now – there are at least six senior schools, and a university population of about 3,000 students. The town gets awfully quiet during school and university holidays. The only annual event of any significance is the **drama and arts festival** which happens during the July vacation. It is a good opportunity to get to grips with South African culture, but you need to book well in advance as accommodation gets scarce. It can also be bitterly cold then, but there are enough pubs to keep winter at bay.

Tourist information 046 23241. The helpful bureau is on Church Square.
Rail information 046 6361134.

Accommodation
Hotel Graham High St, tel: 046 6222324. R299 single, R359 double, breakfast included.
Backpackers Barn 4 Troupe St, tel: 046 29720. Phone for a free pick-up from the station. Dorm bed R30, double R40 per person.

Nightlife
There are a few worthwhile places, mostly aimed at the 3,000 students. The Rat and Parrot on New St, a general drinking pub, has the student vote. The Monkey Puzzle, in the botanical gardens (be careful in the gardens at night) is much more of a locals' hang-out. It has live bands on Sundays. The cheap food includes kudu steaks. You can also pay R15 and sit outside for a *potjie*. The Vic is a rough-edged bar in the Victoria Hotel.

Shamwari Rail Safaris
The specialist travel operator African Rail Safaris uses the *Algoa* train for trips from Johannesburg to the Shamwari Game Reserve. More details are given in Chapter 10.

The *Apple Express* and Langkloof Narrow Gauge
The *Apple Express* is a national treasure, constantly threatened with closure and yet being saved every time. The train runs on part of the 285-km (177-mile) two-foot (61cm) gauge railway which runs from PE up the valley of the Langkloof (Long Gorge) to Avontuur (Adventure). The line was built at the beginning of the century to serve the fruit farmers who had settled in the valley and desperately needed a quick means of getting their produce to the port. Fruit was the line's staple traffic for decades, along with limestone from nearby quarries. Much of the fruit traffic has now been lost to road transport and half the line is effectively closed, although the rails are still in place and occasional special trains run to Avontuur and back.

The *Apple Express*, however, just keeps on steaming. Now operated by the Apple Express Society, rather than by Spoornet who still own the line and run everything else on it, the passenger train runs over holiday periods from Humewood Road, PE's narrow gauge station, to Thornhill. The train crosses the 250-foot high Van Stadens River bridge, the highest narrow gauge bridge in the world. The train stops short of the bridge so passengers who like scaring themselves can walk over the spindly iron structure and then take photos as the train eases over afterwards. A barbecue is held at Thornhill.

Longer trips are occasionally run to Avontuur and back; these are aimed at railway enthusiasts. There isn't a better way of travelling up the valley. For bookings, tel: 0426 40 0619, or 041 507 2333, or fax 041 507 3233.

Getting into the Garden Route

There is no direct rail link from PE down into the Garden Route. The mountainous terrain and the many rivers which have cut deep canyons into the coastline would have made this a prohibitively expensive exercise. The rails were instead pushed into the Little Karoo which lies behind the mountains which dominate the Garden Route. Only the narrow gauge railhead at Avontuur comes close; Knysna, at the end of the branch line from George, is just 40km (25 miles) away, separated by the rugged Little Langkloof Mountains.

If you want to head into the Garden Route along the coast, you will almost certainly have to go by road. There is a remote chance of getting a ride on one of the few freight trains going up the Long Kloof but I have not heard of anyone doing this for years, though there are still regular freights to Humansdorp from PE. If you want to try, beg at Humewood Road station in PE – you may just get lucky.

JOHANNESBURG TO ZASTRON

The Zastron train from Johannesburg is one of the those little railway weirdnessses. It is a train which reflects a sadder side of South African life, aimed at workers in Johannesburg who want to visit their families down in the north-eastern Cape and southern Lesotho once a month. The migrant labour system is one of apartheid's echoes. Black people were banished to their so-called 'homelands', often pieces of wasted, dry earth which they had never seen in their lives, and most of which had been granted 'independence' by Pretoria with one or other corrupt puppet 'government' in power. Meanwhile, cheap labour was still needed in South Africa's mines and factories, most of which were in the rich Pretoria–Johannesburg–Vereeniging triangle, and so the migrant labour classes were created. Workers could get temporary residence in Johannesburg, but their families would have to stay behind in the homelands. At month end – pay day – special trains would be laid on to take people back to their families. The Zastron train is a reminder of this.

Zastron

Sociology and political science students will love this train for its own sake. But the real reason for going to Zastron, an otherwise unremarkable town which nestles down in the far south-east corner of Free State province, is to see its exquisite **Bushman paintings**. The caves in the surrounding sandstone hills were natural galleries and strongholds for the Bushmen. The Hoffman Cave is one of the best galleries, containing a perfectly preserved 4.5m long and 1.5m wide frieze depicting Bushmen hunting eland, the large, magnificent antelope which figures in so much of their work.

Tourist information 05542 18.

Rail information There are no passenger staff here. Buy your ticket on the train.

Accommodation

Maluti Hotel Hoofd St, tel: 05 673 1379. Singles R135, doubles R195. Breakfast R15–28 depending on what you eat.

The Zastron train

Distance: 609km.

Frequency: Once a month, usually on Friday closest to month end, returning following Sunday.

Classes: First, second, economy.

Jo'burg–Zastron Train 75283 Southbound (Friday)			Zastron–Jo'burg Train 57284 Northbound (Sunday)	
dep	18.00	Johannesburg	arr	06.18
dep	18.28	Germiston	dep	06.00
dep	19.26	Vereeniging	dep	05.00
dep	19.50	Sasolburg	dep	04.33
dep	20.00	Wolwehoek	dep	04.22
dep	20.20	Dover	dep	04.05
dep	20.45	Koppies	dep	03.40
dep	21.50	Kroonstad	dep	02.45
dep	22.30	Hennenman	dep	01.50
dep	22.50	Virginia	dep	01.27
dep	23.20	Theunissen	dep	00.56
dep	23.53	Brandfort	dep	00.19
dep	00.20	Glen	dep	23.47
dep	01.05	Bloemfontein	dep	23.25
dep	01.16	Shannon	dep	22.50
dep	01.23	Bloemspruit	dep	22.27
dep	02.06	Sannaspos	dep	22.02
dep	03.33	Dewetsdorp	dep	20.40
dep	04.47	Wepener	dep	19.17
dep	06.02	Boesmanskop	dep	18.06
arr	07.00	Zastron	dep	17.00

Fares

Single fares, per person:

First	R125
Second	R90
Economy	R51

JOHANNESBURG TO THE ZIMBABWE BORDER

The line north from Johannesburg and Pretoria opens up South Africa's bushveld. This part of the country probably has the greatest proliferation of provincial and private game parks and nature reserves of anywhere in Africa. It is beautiful country, too, with rolling savanna and distinctive flat-topped acacia trees stretching to the horizon. One thickly forested mountain range, the east–west Soutpansberg, divides the highveld from the lowveld. If you wish, you can travel through the mountains in daylight, truly one of the world's most stunning train rides.

The *Bosvelder* and the *Doily*

There are two daily trains from Johannesburg. The *Bosvelder* ('Bushveld'), a daily, all-class sleeper, runs as far as the copper mining town of Messina, just short of the Zimbabwe border. A second train, known to railwaymen and merchants as the *Doily* actually crosses the Limpopo River into Zimbabwe and is an option if you are heading out of South Africa.

The *Doily* owes its survival to the traders from Zimbabwe and farther north who bring a staggering array of curios and goods to sell in South Africa. At the end of the month, matrons with heavy carrier bags of the eponymous doilies virtually commandeer the train at Beitbridge, heading for the flea-markets of Johannesburg. If a doily does not take your fancy, then there are Zambians with malachite chess sets, or Zairoise with carved hardwood masks. Sellers will roam the train, trying to flog their goods. Some of the stuff is beautiful, some ugly beyond belief.

Of the two trains, the *Doily* is much more of a genuine African rail experience. It is an overnight service with second and third class accommodation only and a catering car which serves light take-away meals.

Timetables

Distance: 633km (655km to Beitbridge).
Frequency: Daily.
Classes: First, second, economy (*Bosvelder*); second, economy (*Doily*).

Jo'burg–Messina–Beitbridge			Beitbridge–Messina–Jo'burg	
Bosvelder	*Doily*		*Doily*	*Bosvelder*
78089	78281		87282	87090
Northbound			Southbound	
dep 18.50	dep 18.07	Johannesburg	arr 08.45	arr 05.30
dep 19.17	dep 18.29	Germiston	dep 08.25	dep 05.10
dep 20.19	dep 19.29	Pretoria	dep 07.02	dep 03.59
dep 20.42	dep 19.52	Pretoria-Noord	dep 06.40	dep 03.37
dep 21.30	dep 20.40	Hammanskraai	dep 05.49	dep 02.49
dep 21.55	dep 21.00	Pienaarsrivier	dep 05.28	dep 02.26
dep 22.33	dep 21.34	Warmbad	dep 04.53	dep 01.51
dep 23.07	dep 22.07	Nylstroom	dep 04.20	dep 01.17
dep 23.34		Boekenhout		dep 00.48

dep 23.55	dep 22.59	Naboomspruit	dep 03.30	dep 00.32
dep 01.05	dep 23.58	Potgietersrus	dep 02.44	dep 23.22
dep 02.45	dep 01.40	Pietersburg	dep 00.50	dep 22.05
dep 03.29	dep 02.36	Solomondale	dep 23.46	dep 21.00
dep 03.50	dep 02.57	Dikgale	dep 23.14	dep 20.45
dep 04.16	dep 03.23	Munnik	dep 22.49	dep 20.25
dep 04.59	dep 04.06	Soekmekaar	dep 22.09	dep 19.50
dep 05.14	dep 04.21	Groot-Spelonke	dep 21.54	dep 19.37
dep 05.36	dep 04.43	Mannamead	dep 21.32	dep 19.20
dep 05.59	dep 05.06	Bandelierkop	dep 21.14	dep 19.06
dep 06.29	dep 05.48	Madombidzha	dep 20.26	dep 18.34
dep 07.06	dep 06.16	Louis Trichardt	dep 20.12	dep 18.20
dep 07.26	dep 06.36	Schoemansdal	dep 19.52	dep 18.00
dep 07.35	dep 06.45	Cilliersrus	dep 19.38	dep 17.19
dep 07.50	dep 07.00	Mara	dep 19.29	dep 17.10
dep 08.31	dep 07.41	Waterpoort	dep 18.51	dep 16.30
dep 09.18	dep 08.28	Mopane	dep 18.01	dep 15.46
arr 10.16	dep 09.40	Messina	dep 17.00	dep 14.45
	dep 10.56	Limpopo River	dep 15.10	
	arr 11.10	Beitbridge	dep 13.00	

Fares

Single fares, per person:

First	R139 (*Bosvelder* only)
Second	R95
Economy	R56

The *Doily* is aimed at travellers coming to and from Zimbabwe and actually crosses the border to the terminus at Beitbridge. There are unfortunately no onward rail connections to elsewhere in Zimbabwe – the nearest rail connection is at the junction at Rutenga where you could pick up the daily mixed train between Bulawayo and Chiredzi (see page 206 for details). It is a late-night connection, though, and there are loads of cheap bus and taxi services from the border to Bulawayo, Harare and elsewhere.

Of course, if you are coming from the other direction, taking the *Doily* is an easy option, especially if you have a five-foot wooden giraffe named Geraldine travelling with you, like we did. We were frantic to cross the border in time to catch the *Bosvelder* from Messina. Our bus was late and we were faced with the sweaty mission of clearing customs, schlepping all our gear across the 475-m bridge over the Limpopo River on foot and then taking another taxi into Messina to catch the *Bosvelder*. A kind Zimbabwean trader overheard our panic and told us to de-bus at Beitbridge station, about 10km north of the border. You clear Zimbabwean customs there while South African officials board the train on the other side. Panic over!

If you are heading south and do not mind settling for the, admittedly scant, difference between first and second class then the *Doily* is the train to catch as it arrives in Pretoria and Johannesburg at a really civilised hour compared to the *Bosvelder* – in the grip of a crisp highveld winter, the difference will be appreciated.

Having said that, the *Bosvelder*'s earlier departure time means the train crosses the Soutpansberg during the day – magnificent scenery as the track twists alongside a river in the bottom of a deep valley. Facing the direction of travel, the best view is on the right; the scene on the other side is often just a sheer rock face whizzing by just centimetres away.

On the northbound *Doily*, the train is usually held at Limpopo River station for a considerable time to allow immigration officials to stamp passports while customs officers look deep into people's bags. The southbound train is often delayed at Beitbridge as Zimbabwean customs officials have a reputation for unpacking the entire train and carting away anything – or anyone – without the proper documentation. It can be tiresome, but then you should not expect to be in a hurry.

The southbound *Doily* also has a long layover in Messina. If you are hungry, there are a few take-away places in the main road opposite the station. The platform itself is thronged with hawkers selling icy drinks, corn-on-the-cob, boiled eggs and even maize meal and sausage.

The journey north

Leaving Johannesburg, the trains run on the main line via the busy junction at Germiston to Pretoria and then into the bushveld. This part of the country is either farmland or undeveloped bush country, sprinkled with a few agricultural towns. It is also traditionally the last refuge of conservative whites – many of whom have not adjusted well to the change of government.

Warmbaths

The first town of any size after Pretoria, Warmbaths – called Warmbad in all train timetables – is named after the hot springs which have made the town famous. The spa is reckoned to be the best in the world after Baden-Baden's legendary waters. The provincial nature reserve is next to the spa.

Tourist information 014 7363694.

The railway now runs through a vast thorn scrub covered plain, saved from being pure bushveld country by the large amount of farming that goes on here. The towns are largely unremarkable save for the deeply conservative atmosphere which prevails in most of them. Most are farming towns founded by the descendants of the Voortrekkers and named for the trek leaders. Old white attitudes die hard here.

Heading north, the first town after Warmbaths is **Nylstroom** (Nile Stream) named by the trekkers who, having been on the wagon for years, thought they had come to the source of the Nile. The next town is **Naboomspruit**, known for its mineral waters and prolific bird life kept in a vast bird sanctuary.

Potgietersrus, a town of shaded avenues and wide, empty streets, is named after a Voortrekker family who were murdered by a local chief called Makapan in 1854. Revenge on the chief was swift.

Pietersburg is the major town of the Northern Province. Founded in 1886, it is another town of wide streets, shaded by jacaranda trees – vaguely beautiful in spring, less so otherwise.

Louis Trichardt, which lies at the foot of the impressive Soutpansberg range, is named after one of the original trek leaders, who having got this far, decided in September 1837 to trek eastwards to Delagoa Bay (now Maputo). Trichardt and his followers were systematically felled by malaria.

The Soutpansberg range – 'salt pan mountains' is 130km long, rising to 1,753m high at its highest point. At the summit of the range is a fertile, cool and wet plateau, dotted with the pretty huts of the Venda people. It is a sacred place to the Venda, full of enchanted waterfalls and haunting forests. The magnificent Soutpansberg hiking trail cuts across part of the range. If you like hiking, this is the trail to do. Book at the Department of Forestry, tel: 01551 51152.

Messina

Messina is a copper mining town which has found a new lease of life now that the borders have opened up fully. There are buses (from the Zimbabwean side) north to Bulawayo and Harare. One legendary company to look out for is Shu Shine Bus Services who charge Z$60 per person to take you in relative comfort to Bulawayo from the border. You could also get to Rutenga and catch the daily train to Bulawayo, although late timings might make this a somewhat unattractive journey for some travellers.

Tourist information 01553 40211.
Rail information 01553 47225.

Game parks and nature reserves

There are too many reserves reasonably close to this route to describe in full. Most of the smaller nature reserves are well stocked with antelope, zebra, wildebeest, giraffe and smaller mammals. Others may have resident rhino and even buffalo, elephant, lion and leopard. The following is a list of some of the reserves closest to the line of rail. Getting there could be a problem late at night – your best option is to call in advance and have someone meet you at the station. Alternatively, hire a car in Pietersburg and spend a few days touring the region.

Mabula Game Lodge, tel: 014 734616. Big Five country, this is a stunning private reserve. It is over 120km (75 miles) from Warmbaths though – ask to be met.
Malati Park Nature Reserve, tel: 014 7430340. A luxury, private reserve. Mammals include white rhino and the beautiful, and rare, sable antelope.
Potgietersrus Nature Reserve and Game Breeding Centre, tel: 0154 4914314. Divided by the railway line, the breeding centre boasts exotic mammals like Madagascan lemurs and Asian hog deer, as well as indigenous varieties such as rhino, sable and herds of antelope. There is a three kilometre (1.8 mile) walking trail.

Nylsvley Nature Reserve, tel: 014 7431074. The province's biggest reserve, Nylsvley is 20km (12.5 miles) south of Naboomspruit. Its main attraction is its prolific bird life, drawn by the 4,000 hectares (9,900 acres) of wetland.

Percy Fyfe Nature Reserve, tel: 0154 4515678. This famous reserve is 35km north of Potgietersrus. There are walking and mountain biking trails. Difficult to get to, though.

Pietersburg Game Reserve, tel: 015 2952011. A large game reserve just south of the town, boasting 21 species of game including white rhino, eland, springbok – a national animal facing difficult times in real life – and the amazing gemsbok (oryx). Walking trails.

Ben Lavin Nature Reserve, tel: 015 5164534. A beautiful reserve 12km (7.5 miles) east of Louis Trichardt. Game includes giraffe, zebra and wildebeest. Black-backed jackals howl at night to make for a truly soulful bush experience. Walking trails.

Messina Nature Reserve, tel: 01553 3235. Famous for its baobab trees, around 12,000 of which grow in the reserve. The Bushmen believe these trees are upside down, having been thrown down from heaven. Game includes sable antelope and giraffe. Walking trails may be arranged.

Sheldrake Game Ranch, tel: 01553 2958. A hunting reserve with lots of game including predators like cheetah and leopard. Walking trails available.

PRETORIA TO BULAWAYO – *THE BULAWAYO*

The *Bulawayo* is the last remaining train connecting South Africa with Zimbabwe. The *Limpopo* overnight train to Harare was withdrawn in April 1998, because of low ridership figures and more than a few operating problems. Both trains used to go through Beitbridge, and both were notorious for horribly late running. The *Bulawayo* now runs to Bulawayo via Botswana in an effort to minimise time spent on NRZ track. It seems like an awfully long way around but in fact the journey time is about the same. This route also offers travellers the distantly pleasant opportunity of spending time in Gaborone or Francistown (or any of Botswana's other trackside towns).

The *Bulawayo* does drag along a full service dining car and those beers will be welcome when the heat comes rolling through the windows.

Frequency: Weekly, one each way.
Classes: First, second, economy.

			Pretoria–Bulawayo Northbound	Bulawayo–Pretoria Southbound	
	dep	09.00 Tue	Pretoria	arr	13.24 Fri
	dep	09.55	Germiston	dep	12.37
	dep	10.32	Johannesburg	dep	12.15
	dep	11.43	Krugersdorp	dep	11.10
	dep	15.29	Zeerust	dep	07.34
	dep	17.10	Mafikeng	dep	06.20
	dep	19.52	Lobatse	dep	03.00
	dep	21.15	Gaborone	dep	23.43
	dep	00.57	Mahalapye	dep	19.20

dep	02.08	Palapye	dep	17.55
dep	03.34	Serule	dep	16.37
dep	06.07	Francistown	dep	14.53
dep	09.00	Plumtree	dep	12.21
arr	11.00 Wed	Bulawayo	dep	09.00 Thu

Fares
Single fares, per person

First	R212
Second	R152
Economy	R95

For information on **Botswana** and the Botswana section of the route, see Chapter 17; for information on **Zimbabwe** generally, see Chapters 11, 12 and 13, and specifically for **Bulawayo** see page 184.

JOHANNESBURG TO MAPUTO
The route east from Pretoria to Mozambique is one of the most exciting journeys in southern Africa, involving a somewhat shocking transition from the relative calm of South Africa to the vibrant chaos of Mozambique.

The Komati
The *Komati* train runs between Johannesburg and the border town of Komatipoort daily in each direction. It travels overnight with the standard sleeper accommodation and a full dining car. The train takes about 12 hours to cover the 530km (330 miles) from Johannesburg to the border.

The eastbound train's timings are such that they give you a miserable early morning start if you want to get off at places like Nelspruit or Malelane, but the westbound train is a much more comfortable option for people coming from the game parks or trout country.

Timetable
Distance: 530km.
Frequency: Daily.
Classes: First, second, economy.

Jo'burg–Komatipoort
Komati 78091
Eastbound

Komatipoort–Jo'burg
Komati 87092
Westbound

dep	17.45	Johannesburg	arr	06.12
dep	18.12	Germiston	dep	05.53
dep	19.15	Pretoria	dep	04.56
dep	19.57	Eerste Fabrieke	dep	03.35
dep	20.22	Rayton	dep	03.11
dep	20.37	Forfar	dep	03.01
dep	20.50	Bronkhorstspruit	dep	02.46

dep	21.54	Witbank	dep	01.55
dep	22.46	Middelburg	dep	01.12
dep	22.58	Derwent	dep	01.02
dep	23.46	Sunbury	dep	00.22
dep	00.15	Belfast	dep	00.06
dep	00.49	Machadodorp	dep	23.16
dep	01.00	Goedgeluk	dep	23.06
dep	01.24	Waterval Boven	dep	22.56
dep	02.17	Ngodwana	dep	21.44
dep	02.51	Schagen	dep	21.08
dep	02.59	Alkmaar	dep	20.59
dep	03.30	Nelspruit	dep	20.41
dep	04.31	Kaapmuiden	dep	19.38
dep	04.43	Rockvale	dep	19.18
dep	04.58	Malelane	dep	19.01
dep	05.12	Impala	dep	18.49
dep	05.27	Hectorspruit	dep	18.38
arr	06.00	Komatipoort	dep	18.07

Fares
Single fares:

First	R121
Second	R85
Economy	R48

The journey
From Pretoria, the *Komati* heads west into the coal belt, a landscape littered with power stations and with horrific smoke pollution in winter. Luckily you will not see this because it will be dark outside. East of Witbank, an industrial and coal mining town, the countryside starts opening up. The area around **Belfast** is one of the country's premier trout-fishing regions. The landscape is very similar to that in parts of the UK with rolling green hills, cut with icy cold trout streams and dams. It is hardly surprising that it has become a weekend retreat for mostly affluent Jo'burgers. It is also good cycling country and offers many fine places to stay.

The trout fishing centres around **Machadodorp**, a little farming town which would have imploded until wealthy, trout-crazy city folk flooded in and revitalised the regional economy. The fishing, however, is expensive unless you are well-connected and have access to one of the numerous fishing syndicates. Two places worth looking at are Critchley Hackle Lodge and Gateways (tel: 011 803 8669, email: <getaways@iafrica.com>). Both are near Belfast and will pick you up from the station – arrange a lift in advance though.

Waterval Boven is an uninviting railway town at the lip of the escarpment. It was formerly a vital coaling and watering point for steam locomotives needing replenishment after the long slog up from the lowveld. The route has been electrified now but it is still an impressive journey – the line falls into the valley like a piece of unruly spaghetti. It is all horseshoe and reverse curves and tunnels – wild stuff, if you are still awake.

A steam train, the *Oosterlyn Express*, runs down the escarpment line to Waterval Onder and back on most Sundays. The depot has three steam locomotives, cared for by a dedicated bunch of enthusiasts. Phone 013262 and ask for 14. Business hours only.

Nelspruit

A hot little town and the capital of Mpumulanga province. There is not a lot to do here – some locals have taken to relieving the intense boredom by having their buddies drive their pick-up trucks at high speed through underground parking garages while they lie on the cab roofs and watch the concrete whizz by just inches from their faces.

Even so there are people who believe that Nelspruit, which is surrounded by the country's finest game parks and something of a tourist centre as a result, will become the country's second city. It is certainly a good jumping off point to get to Kruger National Park and other game parks in the region. Nelspruit has all the usual amenities, including a good tourist office, and various car hire companies. It is not really a place to dally in though. Instead I would suggest you rent a car, and either go up to Kruger or into the beautiful forest country around Sabie and Graskop.

Nelspruit Publicity 013 7551988
Rail information 013 7529256

Attractions near Nelspruit

There is a railway line which winds its way up from Nelspruit, through the forests, to Graskop. Its passenger trains are history, however. In fact, most locals cannot even remember when they last saw a passenger train on these tracks. Hopefully a more tourist-oriented MLPS will see the potential in operating even a limited service up this line. Right now, however, you are on your own.

Sabie is a forestry town on the edge of the escarpment. Its main attractions are its hiking trails into the surrounding hills and a few stunning waterfalls. This is amazing cycling country, although if you are planning the long slog up from Nelspruit, take plenty of water and courage.

Graskop perches on the edge of the Escarpment, literally looking over the lowveld all the way to Mozambique. Not a lot to divert one here though. Most people head for God's Window, a natural lookout point on the very edge of the Escarpment – the view is stupendous. God's Window is about 10km (6 miles) from Graskop.

Accommodation

Panorama Rest Camp just outside Graskop itself, tel: 013 767 1091.
Merry Pebbles Resort at Sabie is one of the finest camping grounds out of season, tel: 013 7642266. Once you have moved away from the caravan area and its power supply, you can camp in a clump of trees at the edge of the bubbling Sabie River.

Pilgrim's Rest is a preserved mining town about 15km (9 miles) over the hills from Graskop. Founded during the 1870s' gold rush, the town became a centre for the hunters, prospectors and adventurers who were wandering around the region. Gold mining stopped in the 1970s but the town is preserved as a national treasure.

Accommodation
Royal Hotel A full-on colonial relic, tel: 01315 81221. There is almost sawdust on the saloon floor. Singles R250, doubles R270. Restored miners' cottages cost R120 per night.

Malelane has a little station near the main southern entrance to Kruger National Park. There is not much here other than a restaurant in train carriages. The *Komati* does stop here and it might be an option if you are heading for Kruger. Remember the transport hassles that start inside Kruger (see below).

Getting around
You'll need a car to get into the the area. The best option is to hire one in Nelspruit and go exploring for a few days. You will need a car anyway if you want to go into the Kruger National Park (see below)

Komatipoort
Quiet town on the banks of the Crocodile River, just 10km (6 miles) from one of the Kruger entrances, and the terminus for the *Komati* train. Travellers heading for Mozambique have to wait for the Mozambican railways shuttle to come over the border and pick them up.

The onward journey into Mozambique is described in the Mozambique section of Chapter 17.

Kruger National Park
'Kruger', as it is colloquially known, is a South African institution, unmatched in its diversity of animal life and geography. Some people hate it for its tarred roads and mass-transit appeal, yet nowhere in southern Africa does game viewing of this variety and quality come as cheaply as it does in Kruger.

The park comprises two million hectares (8,000 square miles) of wilderness, home to 174 species of mammal, 500 species of bird, 114 reptile species, 49 species of fish and 39 species of amphibian. It is bordered by the Limpopo River in the north, the Crocodile River 350km (220 miles) to the south, Mozambique to the east and a stout fence in the west. Much of the park is easily accessible with 2,624km (1,630 miles) of tarred and gravel roads. You can drive in for a day, or stay over in one of the 26 lodges or rest camps, which do, however, get heavily booked in the holidays. Accommodation varies from the intensely luxurious to basic self-catering rondavels.

Warning All overnight visitors have to stay in one of the camps and it is

Above left Spotted hyena, *Crocuta crocuta* (AZ)

Above Leopard, *Panthera pardus* (AZ)

Left Hunting dog, *Lycaon pictus* (AZ)

Below Cheetah, *Acononyx jubatus* (AZ)

Above Prehistoric rock art in the suburbs of Harare, Zimbabwe (AZ)

Right Elephants, *Loxodonta africana*, mating (AZ)

Above Crowned crane,
Balearica regulorum,
South Africa (AZ)

Left Livingstone's lourie,
Touraco livingstonii (AZ)

Below Burchell's zebra,
Equus burchelli (AZ)

Next page Bushbuck,
Tragelaphus scriptus (AZ)

imperative that you reach your intended camp before the gates close, usually around sunset. Never leave your vehicle unless at a place where you are clearly permitted to. This is raw Africa. You are in the territory of many animals with whom close interaction is usually painful. Kruger, and the surrounding lowveld is also a malaria area. Do not forget your pills or repellent.

The best way to see the park is by car although there are seven guided wilderness trails which cost around R800 per person – these must be booked in advance. These walks take three days and equipment is provided. For bookings or general **information**, tel: 012 222810, or fax 012 246211.

Getting there

You can get to Kruger's front doorstep by train. Be warned, however, that you cannot just walk through the gates of the park. At some stage, unless you are doing a walking trail, you are going to have to get inside a vehicle. Hire cars are available at Skukuza, the largest camp in Kruger, and at Phalaborwa which is near Hoedspruit. You might try bumming a lift at the Park gates, especially since entry is charged per person. However, once in the park, you can only hitch at the rest camps and this is likely to be a frustrating experience. Cycling is not allowed, mainly because you would be such an easy target for a passing carnivore or irascible buffalo.

Train options

The nearest stations to Kruger are Malelane, and Komatipoort which are served by the daily *Komati* train.

There is also a weekday train from Kaapmuiden to Hoedspruit which is close to a number of private reserves. This train connects with the daily *Komati* at Kaapmuiden, leaving at 05.11 and arriving in Hoedspruit at 08.34. It returns from Hoedspruit at 15.34, arriving at Kaapmuiden at 19.08, in time for the westbound *Komati*. The connection is quite tight so late running could mean a long wait.

On Fridays, there is a train all the way from Pretoria to Hoedspruit, leaving the capital at 18.45 and arriving at 08.06 the next day. This service returns on Sunday, leaving at 14.17 and arriving in Pretoria at an unfriendly 03.17. Take the *Komati*.

Timetable

Distance: 556km.
Frequency: Weekly.
Classes: First, second, economy.

	Pretoria–Hoedspruit Train 78091 Eastbound		Hoedspruit–Pretoria Train 87092 Westbound
dep	18.45 Fri	Pretoria	arr 03.17 Mon
dep	19.18	Eerste Fabrieke	dep 02.24
dep	19.44	Rayton	dep 01.58
dep	19.57	Forfar	dep 01.45

dep	20.11	Bronkhorstspruit	dep	01.24
dep	21.09	Witbank	dep	00.21
dep	22.05	Middelburg	dep	23.34
dep	22.17	Derwent	dep	23.20
dep	23.03	Wonderfontein	dep	22.42
dep	23.15	Sunbury	dep	22.31
dep	23.28	Belfast	dep	22.20
dep	00.16	Machadodorp	dep	21.46
dep	00.26	Goedgeluk	dep	21.37
dep	00.41	Waterval Boven	dep	21.28
dep	01.54	Ngodwana	dep	20.18
dep	03.20	Nelspruit	dep	19.04
dep	04.40	Kaapmuiden	dep	18.01
dep	04.58	Luphisa	dep	17.31
dep	05.07	Gutshwa	dep	17.21
dep	05.16	Legogote	dep	17.12
dep	05.28	Phomeni	dep	17.02
dep	05.36	Numbi	dep	16.53
dep	05.54	Hazyview	dep	16.38
dep	06.04	Mkhuhlu	dep	16.27
dep	06.14	Fayini	dep	16.18
dep	06.25	Ireagh	dep	16.09
dep	06.32	Murotso Halt	dep	16.02
dep	06.37	Matshaye	dep	15.59
dep	06.43	Mthuthi	dep	15.50
dep	06.49	Hokwe	dep	15.44
dep	06.57	Rolle	dep	15.36
dep	07.07	Mbumba	dep	15.26
dep	07.17	Cottondale	dep	15.16
dep	07.25	Maswing Halt	dep	15.08
dep	07.30	Acornhoek	dep	15.01
dep	07.41	Klaserie	dep	14.50
arr	08.06 Sat	Hoedspruit	dep	14.17 Sun

Fares

Single fares:

First	R121
Second	R85
Economy	R48

Timetable

Distance: 165km.
Frequency: Weekdays only.
Classes: First, second, economy.

Kaapmuiden–Hoedspruit Train 88252 Northbound		Hoedspruit–Kaapmuiden Train 88251 Southbound	
dep 05.11	Kaapmuiden	arr 19.08	
dep 05.29	Luphisa	dep 18.48	
dep 05.38	Gutshwa	dep 18.38	
dep 05.47	Legogote	dep 18.29	
dep 05.57	Phomeni	dep 18.19	
dep 06.07	Numbi	dep 18.10	
dep 06.24	Hazyview	dep 17.55	
dep 06.33	Mkhuhlu	dep 17.44	
dep 06.42	Fayini	dep 17.35	
dep 06.52	Ireagh	dep 17.26	
dep 06.59	Murotso Halt	dep 17.19	
dep 07.04	Matshaye	dep 17.14	
dep 07.10	Mthuthi	dep 17.07	
dep 07.16	Hokwe	dep 17.01	
dep 07.24	Rolle	dep 16.53	
dep 07.34	Mbumba	dep 16.43	
dep 07.44	Cottondale	dep 16.33	
dep 07.52	Maswing Halt	dep 16.25	
dep 07.59	Acornhoek	dep 16.18	
dep 08.10	Klaserie	dep 16.07	
arr 08.34	Hoedspruit	dep 15.34	

JOHANNESBURG TO KIMBERLEY, VIA MAFIKENG

This is a long way round but there may be good reason to use these three trains. Mafikeng, while not the prettiest town in the world, has some history to it. It is also a minor railway hub. The weekly *Bulawayo* between Johannesburg and Bulawayo passes through here. Travellers coming south who do not wish to go through Johannesburg can change here for the daily train to Kimberley, the *Taxi*, and pick-up further southbound or eastbound trains there. The *Taxi* – a somewhat ironic name given that the minibus-taxi industry has decimated rail travel in Africa – is aimed at travellers from Mafikeng and farther north who are heading for Cape Town. The countryside between Mafikeng and Kimberley is arid wasteland. However, the *Taxi* is a 'milk train' which means it stops at every siding where there might be life, taking nine hours to cover the 350-odd kilometres.

Another possibility is to catch a minibus taxi from Kimberley to Upington to connect with the train service from there into Namibia. For Upington see page 116, and for the connection to Namibia pages 236–7.

The weekly train from Johannesburg, the only one of the three trains covering the full route, allows access to the small farming towns of the north west province. There is not a lot to see, although one exception might be the little town of Groot Marico, a sleepy bushveld community which the noted South African writer Herman Charles Bosman turned into a legend.

Groot Marico

Not a lot goes on in Groot Marico but if you want an insight into South African farming town life, this is the place to get it. It is a pretty place, spreading along the banks of the Groot Marico river, life source for the tobacco and wheat farmers which line its banks. The town is better known – perhaps unjustly – for its *mampoer* or *witblitz*, moonshine brewed in the surrounding hills. It is wicked stuff but thankfully legal so there is no danger of lead poisoning or worse from it being brewed in rusting car radiators. There are only a few licensed brewers but a scary number of sources – peach is one of the most popular bases, chillies and tomatoes less so. For the sober there is some great mountain biking in the hills surrounding the town.

The friendly **Groot Marico Hotel** on Paul Kruger St is the only place to stay, tel 014252 45. Singles R85, doubles R150, breakfast included.

Timetable Southbound
Distance: 665km.

Train 72242 Monthly 2nd, 3rd	Train 72244 Weekly 1st, 2nd, 3rd		*The Taxi* 22008 Daily 1st, 2nd, 3rd
dep 18.00	dep 19.00 Fri	Johannesburg	
dep 18.29	dep 19.29	Roodeport	
dep 18.47	dep 19.47	Krugersdorp	
dep 19.29	dep 20.29	Magaliesburg	
dep 20.29	dep 21.29	Derby	
dep 20.50	dep 21.50	Koster	
dep 21.27	dep 22.27	Swartruggens	
dep 22.07	dep 23.07	Groot Marico	
dep 23.01	dep 23.52	Zeerust	
arr 00.11	dep 02.00	Mafikeng	dep 07.00
(terminates)	dep 02.00	Sethopo	dep 07.10
		Vryhof	dep 07.33
	dep 02.46	Mareetsane	dep 07.54
		Badibua	dep 08.11
	dep 03.13	Kraaipan	dep 08.23
	dep 03.35	Madibogo	dep 08.46
	dep 03.52	Wirsing	dep 09.04
		Kameel	dep 09.21
		Curnow	dep 09.36
		Devondale	dep 09.51
		Paradise	dep 10.06
	dep 05.07	Vryburg	dep 10.46
		Tierkloof	dep 11.08
		Brussels	dep 11.22

	De Beers	dep 11.35
dep 05.54	Dry Harts	dep 11.50
dep 06.07	Pudimoe	dep 12.03
	Magopela	dep 12.16
dep 06.36	Taung	dep 12.32
dep 06.50	Magogong	dep 12.48
dep 07.06	Hartswater	dep 13.04
	Tadcaster	dep 13.16
dep 07.28	Jan Kempdorp	dep 13.29
	Dawlish	dep 13.43
dep 07.56	Veertien Strome	dep 13.56
dep 08.40	Warrenton	dep 14.27
	Content	dep 14.43
	Windsorton Road	dep 15.02
	Riverton	dep 15.25
	Macfarlane	dep 15.34
	Dronfield	dep 15.42
	Kamfersdam	dep 15.52
arr 10.02 Sat	Kimberley	arr 16.00

Timetable Northbound

The Taxi 27241 Daily 1st, 2nd, 3rd	Train 27243 Weekly 1st, 2nd, 3rd		Train 22007 Monthly 2nd, 3rd
dep 06.57	dep 15.30 Sun	Kimberley	
dep 07.06		Kamfersdam	
dep 07.16		Dronfield	
dep 07.27		Macfarlane	
dep 07.39		Riverton	
dep 08.03		Windsorton Road	
dep 08.22		Content	
dep 09.03	dep 16.46	Warrenton	
dep 09.13	dep 16.59	Veertien Strome	
dep 09.41	dep 17.25	Jan Kempdorp	
dep 09.51		Tadcaster	
dep 10.05	dep 17.47	Hartswater	
dep 10.20	dep 18.00	Magongong	
dep 10.36	dep 18.16	Taung	
dep 10.49		Magopela	
dep 11.03	dep 18.44	Pudimoe	
dep 11.12	dep 18.54	Dry Harts	
dep 11.28		De Beers	
dep 11.41		Brussels	
dep 12.03		Tierkloof	
dep 12.44	dep 19.45	Vryburg	

dep 13.01		Paradise	
dep 13.20		Devondale	
dep 13.30		Mnyani	
dep 13.38		Curnow	
dep 13.55		Kameel	
dep 14.12	dep 21.02	Wirsing	
dep 14.35	dep 21.18	Madibogo	
dep 14.59	dep 21.39	Kraaipan	
dep 15.11		Badibua	
dep 15.31	dep 22.09	Mareetsane	
dep 15.52		Vryhof	
dep 16.14		Sethopo	
arr 16.26	dep 23.25	Mafikeng	dep 22.25
	dep 00.43	Zeerust	dep 23.46
	dep 01.23	Groot Marico	dep 00.25
	dep 01.58	Swartruggens	dep 01.00
	dep 02.42	Koster	dep 01.44
	dep 03.00	Derby	dep 02.02
	dep 03.56	Magaliesburg	dep 02.58
	dep 04.44	Krugersdorp	dep 03.46
	dep 05.01	Roodepoort	dep 04.03
	arr 05.28	Johannesburg	arr 04.30

Note that Trains 72242 and 27241 are month-end specials, taking workers from the Reef to home and back in the course of a heady, often liquid, weekend.

Fares

Single fares, Johannesburg–Kimberley:

First	R136
Second	R98
Economy	R55

Single fares, Kimberley–Mafikeng:

First	R78
Second	R57
Economy	R32

Routes from Cape Town

CAPE TOWN

For thousands of years, the Khoikhoi and San people roamed the rich game country stretching north from the foot of Table Mountain into the interior, with the San gradually being displaced by the pastoralist Khoikhoi. The Portuguese navigator Bartolomeu Dias was the first recorded European to make landfall in Table Bay in 1487. He named it Cabo da Boa Esperanca (the Cape of Good Hope). While the place had abundant fresh water and plenty of fresh meat roaming the countryside, the Portuguese were evidently little impressed and sailed on round the coast. They wanted a victualling station to supply ships bound for the Far East and settled firstly on Ilha de Moçambique and later Delagoa Bay, today Maputo, to the south.

It was roughly another 150 years before any Europeans settled permanently at the foot of Table Mountain, when three Dutch ships, commanded by Jan van Riebeek arrived in the bay in 1652. The settlement they founded was to serve as a supply point for ships of the Dutch East India Company on their long journey to Asia and back.

Vegetables were grown in the company gardens, a hospital and fort were built and animal bartering with the Khoikhoi flourished. Table Bay became a crossing point for ships from all over the world, a role which has diminished somewhat this century. The harbour remains an important centre for fruit and grain exports, and its ship repair facilities are impressive. However, it has now been mostly eclipsed as a bulk cargo port by Richards Bay and Durban, both on the KwaZulu-Natal coast.

Cape Town can be a bizarre place. It is a mixture of African and European but not really one or the other – too western to be African and too African to be fully European. It is a fully cosmopolitan city and was often regarded as the most liberal of South Africa's cities. However, the gulf between white and black is disturbingly pronounced here. The city's affluent suburbs spread up into the trees at the foot of the mountains, but a few miles away lie the densely-packed, wind- and sand-swept townships of the Cape Flats. Nowhere else in the country is the division so shatteringly visible.

That said, it is a wonderful city to spend time in. A week would be barely adequate – most people need a lifetime. The city is dominated by the 300m (1,000ft) high flat-topped slab of Table Mountain, and surrounded by beautiful beaches and vineyards. Superb paths wind up out of the city onto the mountain, and deer graze in the forests of its slopes.

Until recently Cape Town was the parliamentary capital of South Africa but that function will move to Pretoria at the beginning of 2000. Tourism is its key industry and yet Cape Town has so far avoided the tackiness that usually comes with a booming tourist trade.

Practical details
Telephone code
The area code for Cape Town is 021.

Information
Satour tel: 021 21 6274, fax: 021 419 4875.
Captour tel: 021 418 5214, fax: 021 418 5227.
National Parks Board tel: 021 22 2810, fax: 021 24 6211.
Flight information tel: 021 934 0407.
Rail information SA Rail, tel: 021 405 3871.

Accommodation
Luxury
The Bay Hotel Victoria Road, Camps Bay, tel: 021 438 4444. All 70 rooms have sea or mountain views. It overlooks beautiful Camps Bay beach. From R390 to R1,450 pp sharing an en-suite room, with private lobby.
Clifton House 1 Clifton Road, Clifton, tel: 021 438 2308. Intimate hotel with five rooms, on the slopes of Lions Head. All rooms are en-suite with sea or mountain views and private balcony/terrace. R300–R600pp sharing, singles from R350. Includes breakfast.

Mid-price
The Ashby Manor Guest House 242 High Level Road, Fresnaye, tel: 021 434 1879. This rambling old Victorian house is situated on the side of Signal Hill. Great sea and mountain views. Singles From R90, doubles from R150, two-bed fully equipped apartment from R280 (sleeps 4-5). All self catering.
City Lodge corner of Dock and Alfred Roads, tel: 021 419 9450. At the entrance of the Waterfront complex. Double R390, single R309.

Budget
City Slickers on the corner of Rose and Hout, in the city centre, tel: 021 22 2357. It has a rooftop bar, with super view of Table Mountain for sundowners. Dorms R35pp, doubles R90 for the room. Bedding is R5.
Green Elephant 57 Milton Road, tel: 021 448 6359. Popular backpackers' hostel in lively studenty suburb. Free 24-hour pick-up from airport and city centre. Dorm bed R35, double R50pp, and you can fill up on breakfast for just R9.
St Johns Waterfront 4/6 Braemer St, Greenpoint, tel: 021 439 1404. On Atlantic coast, with self catering kitchen, bar – and two swimming pools! Dorms R50pp, doubles R135–180.

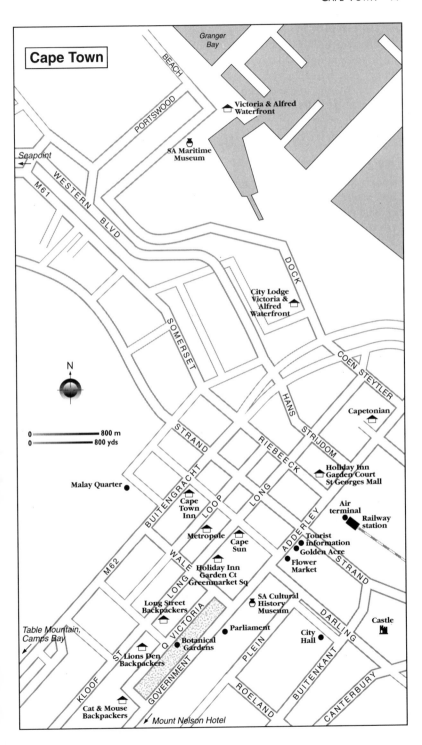

Cape Town

Granger Bay

Victoria & Alfred Waterfront

SA Maritime Museum

Seapoint

BEACH

PORTSWOOD

WESTERN BLVD

M 61

SOMERSET

DOCK

City Lodge Victoria & Alfred Waterfront

COEN STEYTLER

N

0 ——— 800 m
0 ——— 800 yds

STRAND

RIEBEECK

HANS STRIJDOM

Capetonian

Malay Quarter

BUITENGRACHT

LOOP

LONG

Holiday Inn Garden Court St Georges Mall

Cape Town Inn

Air terminal

Railway station

Metropole

Cape Sun

ADDERLEY

Tourist information

Golden Acre

STRAND

M 62

WALE

LONG

Holiday Inn Garden Ct Greenmarket Sq

Flower Market

Long Street Backpackers

VICTORIA

SA Cultural History Museum

Table Mountain, Camps Bay

Parliament

City Hall

DARLING

Castle

ST

Lions Den Backpackers

Botanical Gardens

PLEIN

KLOOF

GOVERNMENT

ROELAND

BUITENKANT

CANTERBURY

Cat & Mouse Backpackers

Mount Nelson Hotel

Getting around

Cape Town probably has the best-run public transport in the country, with a substantial commuter rail service radiating out of the city into the suburbs and beyond, a reasonable bus network and ubiquitous mini-bus taxis which reach places other forms of transport do not.

The Atlantic seaboard is pretty hard to get to unless you use the minibuses and, even then, these often do not go all the way. Car hire is a good, fairly inexpensive option, especially if you are paying in hard currency.

COMMUTER TRAINS

The commuter rail network covers most of the city except the Atlantic seaboard and the suburbs directly north of the city along the shores of Table Bay. The commuter trains are a good way of getting to Stellenbosch, Strand on the False Bay coast, and Simonstown, the naval base and resort town on the Cape Peninsula.

Cape MetroRail Enquiries tel: 021 403 9080.

Cape Town to Simonstown

The Simonstown line is a dramatically beautiful route, at least for the second half of the journey. From Cape Town, the trains run through the leafy southern suburbs before swinging west at Muizenberg and literally picking their way over the rocks along the shore to Simonstown. The railway line is jammed between the sea and the shore and sea spray floats through the train windows on blustery days. The line skirts the pretty fishing village of Kalk Bay and the seaside resorts of Muizenberg, St James and Fish Hoek.

It is worth taking a slow trip along the line and getting off to explore these little places. **Muizenberg** sits at the western end of a fine, endless white beach. Reminiscent of an English seaside town, it has faded in recent years, although there is a strong local push to restore its amenities. **St James** and **Fish Hoek** also have excellent beaches. St James is famous for its brightly painted Victorian bathing huts.

You can buy fish and chips wrapped in newspaper in the best British style at **Kalk Bay** harbour and sit on the quayside and watch the boats come and go as you eat. Kalk Bay also has the Brass Bell, one of the world's best sited pubs. Perched on the edge of a tidal pool, on the sea side of the railway line, the pub has an open-air courtyard where you can sit and be overwhelmed by the sweeping view of False Bay. The front door of the upstairs restaurant opens right onto the station platform, a useful trick.

Simonstown

Simonstown is the terminus of the 90-minute ride from the city. The Royal Navy's Atlantic Squadron developed the town as a naval base from 1814, building workshops and a dry dock. The town is still a naval base and dockyard, with a definite naval atmosphere. There are a couple of historic buildings and South Africa's only standing **Martello Tower** which now houses a small museum. The brass statue of a Great Dane in the main street is in honour of Able Seaman Just Nuisance, a dog of no fixed address who, among other things, used to escort drunken sailors off the train and to their ships during World War II. AB Just Nuisance was a formal member of the Royal Navy and received full pay to the end.

Incredible views and a reasonably sheltered position have pushed local real estate prices through the roof, but a lot of well-off pensioners have made this their last anchorage. Nearby **Boulders Beach**, named for the distinctive rounded rocks which surround it, is a penguin sanctuary. There is a fee to get onto the beach, and the money is partly used to pay the penguin watchman who is there to make sure people do not abuse the birds.

Trains run on the Simonstown line around every 20–30 minutes, starting at 05.00 and with last trains at around 22.30 in both directions. Some of the trains do not run through to Simonstown, however; many services now terminate in Fish Hoek. Try and ride in a coach with fully opening windows. Many of the newer coaches have sealed, tinted windows of which only the top third opens.

Single (one-way) fares for the full distance are R7.50 in first and R3.50 in third.

If you are hungry on the train, or need a beer to fight the heat, look out for **Biggsy's Restaurant Carriage**, the country's only daily commuter carriage and eatery which is attached to one of the sets running between the city and Simonstown. Biggsy's makes five return trips a day, starting at 06.15, while the last departure is from Simonstown at 19.00. The full English breakfast is an outstanding way to start the day if you are heading for the city. You can also book in advance: tel 021 405 3870.

Into the winelands
There are two commuter services into the winelands, one from Cape Town to the beautiful university town of Stellenbosch, and one to Wolseley on the Cape main line.

Wine Route Information tel:021 886 4310.

Cape Town to Stellenbosch
The first trains leave Cape Town for Stellenbosch at 05.58 and the last at 18.30. Coming the other way, the first train of the day from Stellenbosch is at 05.16 and the last at 19.19. There are later trains in the evening from Bellville to Stellenbosch and vice versa, and then later connections from between Bellville and Cape Town, but you will have to change at Bellville.

Single fares are R10 in first, R5.00 in third.

Stellenbosch
The ride to Stellenbosch takes little over one hour. The route is through industria for a few miles out of Cape Town and then through rolling hills and vineyards for the rest of the trip. Tickets cost R9.50 in first and R4.50 in third, one way.

Stellenbosch is situated in the shadow of the Helshoogte mountains. It is a peaceful place. *Sloots* (ditches) with running water line the shaded streets, helping create a cool and restful feeling. The town's university is important for Afrikaners who regard it as one of the guardians of their distinctive language and culture. There are a number of good museums and galleries and plenty of restaurants. The surrounding mountains are cut with superb hiking and mountain biking trails. The university, though, provides the town's pervasive atmosphere. The railway station is about ten minutes walk from the centre of the town.

Stellenbosch Publicity Association   36 Mark St, tel: 021 883 3584.

Wolseley
Wolseley is little more than a small farming town but the train ride out there is beautiful, especially in winter when the countryside is green and there is snow on the surrounding mountains. Single tickets cost R9.50 in first and R4.50 in third.

Safety
There are occasional reports of muggings on both the Simonstown and Stellenbosch trains. Try and ride in a carriage with other passengers and you will be fine. The lines to avoid, unless you have a local friend escorting you, are any of the lines to the townships on the Cape Flats. Criminal activity is rampant on these trains.

Spier Wine Train
Another, pricier way of getting into the winelands is on the steam-hauled **Spier Wine Train** which runs from Cape Town to the Spier estate near Stellenbosch. The train used to run on Wednesdays and Saturdays from Cape Town station right to a dedicated Spier siding opposite the estate. However, only charter operations are being run at the moment so you will have to hire the whole train plus locomotive, R15,000 for a vintage electric, R18,000 for steam. The bi-weekly trips may be reinstated during the peak holiday season in December. Phone 021 419 5222 for information.

If you cannot afford that, take the commuter train to Stellenbosch and get off at Lynedoch. It is a ten minute walk from the station to the estate. Watch out for the traffic.

Cape Town to Strand
A further commuter train runs from Cape Town to Strand, a seaside dormitory town at the far eastern end of the Cape Flats. You could sit on the beach at Strand – just about its only attraction – but my advice would be to head for the next door village of **Gordon's Bay** which huddles in a crook of False Bay under the towering Hottentot's Holland mountains. It is an attractive place with a fine stretch of beach with luxury holiday houses clinging onto the mountainside and overlooking a small, pretty harbour. The residents

have one of the finest views in the Cape, all the way across the heaving blue of False Bay to the distant mountains of the Cape Peninsula.

It is a long, long walk from Strand, though; get a bike in Cape Town and take it with you on the train. The trains run regularly, starting from Cape Town at 05.43 with the last train from Strand at 19.19. Single fares in first are R10.00, R5.00 in third.

Warning The Strand service skirts the Cape Flats and there have been reports of muggings on the trains. Travel in first class and avoid travelling at night. As always, use common sense.

INTO THE GARDEN ROUTE AND LITTLE KAROO

The Garden Route is an exquisite piece of the country, running 227 km (141 miles) from Mossel Bay to the Storms River, near Port Elizabeth. It is a narrow strip of land, jammed between a looming mountain range and a string of beaches and bays on an often wild, rocky coast. The Outeniqua mountains are its life source. Some 2,500cm (98in) of rain falls annually on their peaks, supplying the coastal strip with abundant water. It is one of the lushest parts of South Africa, embracing wide, placid freshwater lagoons, mountains and hills covered with flowering plants, and huge tracts of thick rainforest. The water is warmed by the Mozambique Current, and the climate is mild all year round. The nearest big towns are Cape Town itself and Port Elizabeth in Eastern Cape Province. The romantically-named *Southern Cross* provides a weekly service between the two cities.

The *Southern Cross*

Distance: 1,070km.
Frequency: Weekly.
Classes: First, second, economy.

Cape Town–Port Elizabeth *Southern Cross* 13051 Eastbound (Friday)			Port Elizabeth–Cape Town *Southern Cross* 31052 Westbound (Sunday)	
dep	18.15	Cape Town	arr	08.40
dep	18.45	Bellville	dep	08.16
dep	19.26	Huguenot	dep	07.32
dep	19.39	Wellington	dep	07.19
dep	20.40	Wolseley	dep	06.19
dep	21.27	Worcester	dep	05.47
dep	22.32	Robertson	dep	04.21
dep	22.53	Ashton	dep	03.59
dep	23.21	Bonnievale	dep	03.32
dep	00.34	Swellendam	dep	02.10
dep	01.48	Karringmelk	dep	01.12
dep	02.30	Heidelberg	dep	00.09
dep	03.30	Riversdale	dep	23.07

dep	04.22	Albertinia	dep 22.16
dep	05.47	Hartenbos	dep 21.02
dep	06.58	George	dep 19.50
dep	09.14	Oudtshoorn	dep 17.40
dep	09.34	Hazenjacht	dep 16.50
dep	10.17	Vlakteplaas	dep 16.19
dep	11.04	Barandas	dep 15.32
dep	12.18	Willowmore	dep 14.17
dep	14.18	Klipplaat	dep 12.31
dep	17.15	Uitenhage	dep 09.20
arr	17.50	Port Elizabeth	dep 08.45

Fares
Single fares:

First	R212
Second	R152
Economy	R87

From Cape Town, the train travels over the Cape Main Line to Worcester where the electric locomotives are swapped for diesels which then pull the express eastwards along the Langeberg overnight to the Garden Route. Construction of the railway east from Ashton began in 1894 when the New Cape Central Railway took over the former Cape Central Railway which had bankrupted itself running the line from Worcester to Ashton.

In an early incident of southern African corruption, the new company managed to wangle a government subsidy of £2,000 per mile for extending the line to Voorbaai, near Mossel Bay. The subsidy was granted under certain conditions, one of which was that there should be no ruling gradients steeper than 1-in-40. A number of the grades were – and still are – steeper than that but the gradient posts were painted 1-in-40 to appease government inspectors.

It is mountainous country, especially around Ashton and Bonnievale where trains almost double back on themselves on the 5-chain (100m) reverse curves. The *Southern Cross* runs over this section at night but the swaying of the coach, the squealing wheel flanges and the string of fairy lights winding through the darkness will leave you in no doubt about what kind of terrain you are in.

Swellendam
It is a hard-hearted person who does not like Swellendam. This little town, South Africa's third oldest, huddles at the foot of the Langeberg in a tree-shaded jumble of quiet streets and lush gardens. Swellendam, founded by the Dutch East India Company, was a capital city for a heady three months in 1795 when the townspeople fired the company's magistrate and declared the town an independent republic. It did not last; British occupation followed and the town's expansionist ambitions were crushed.

Swellendam is an agricultural town, but a brilliant place either to chill out

NO TRICKLE DOWN FOR SOUR VOMIT

Swellendam's tourist boom has not gone altogether smoothly. The nearby town of Suurbraak (whose name very loosely translated means 'Sour Vomit') is also an old settlement, populated mostly by Cape Coloureds who rely on Swellendam for employment. It is a hard place where alcoholism is common and prospects are low. The good folk of Swellendam would rather Suurbraak got swallowed up as it is such a painful echo of recent history. Suurbraak was recently highlighted in press reports as an example of how the tourist boom's supposed trickle-down effect is not actually trickling down. The implication is that the old colour lines are still there and in some places they are.

This is not active racism, though, but rather the way the economy is still skewed towards whites. Travellers are more likely than locals to notice the imbalances and the divisions which still exist between black and white. All the well-meaning government programmes are not going to solve the problem, at least not in the short term.

for a few days or use as a base for walks in the mountains. The 74-km **Swellendam hiking trail** – a real tough bastard – starts at the forest station just outside town, climbs over to the other side of the mountain range and runs along the far side before circling back to the start. Call 0291 41410 for advance bookings. There are also mountain bike trails, day walks and canoeing and white-water rafting on the lovely Breede River in winter.

Diversions in town include the fine **Drostdy Museum** complex, housed in the magistrate's old residence, which contains period furniture and other intriguing bits and pieces. There are plenty of historic buildings making it well worth taking a walk around the town generally.

Information

The tourist information office (tel: 0291 42770) is on Voortrek St, open from 09.00–12.30 and 14.00–16.00, 09.00–12.30 on Saturdays.

Accommodation

The B&B industry is booming here, so there is plenty of choice.

Roosje van der Kaap 5 Drostdy St, tel: 0291 43001. Four guest rooms. Singles R85, doubles R150
Waenhuis Backpackers' 5 Buitekant St, tel: 0291 42281. Run by friendly people who will meet you at the station. Bike hire. Dorm bed R25, double R50 per person, campsite R15 per person.
Swellendam Backpackers' Lodge 5 Lichtenstein St, tel/fax: 0291 42648. Can organise rafting trips and horse riding. Dorm bed R30, camping R25 per person.

Into the Garden Route

It is a pity that some of the country's best scenery – the ride along the foot of the Langeberg mountains, through little farming towns like Ashton, Bonnievale and Robertson – is lost in the darkness. However, eastbound trains reach George, at the western edge of the Garden Route, early on Saturday morning, before climbing the terrific Montagu Pass over the formidable barrier of the Outeniqua mountains to Oudtshoorn, the main town of the Little Karoo. The early morning arrival is convenient if you want to continue ambling along the Garden Route, some of which can be done on the country's only regular scheduled steam-hauled train, discussed later in this chapter.

The Little Karoo

The coastal terrace and the dry but beautiful land of the Little Karoo are separated by the Outeniqua mountains, a harsh sweep of high, jagged uplands. The Little Karoo is a 250km-long, 60km-wide (155 miles by 37 miles) valley, wedged between the Outeniquas and the harsh etch of the Swartberg range to the north. It is a stunning but arid place, although not as harsh a landscape as its bleak namesake to the north. The region is known for its ostrich farms. These birds used to be bred for their feathers, which looked outrageous on ball gowns across Europe at the turn of the century. Latterly their meat has been a bigger selling point.

The change in scenery is dramatic as the lush green of the Garden Route gives way to the sandstone cliffs and arid scrub of the Little Karoo. Both west- and eastbound trains traverse this beautiful landscape during the day, although the westbound run climbs Montagu Pass in the early evening. It took almost nine years to build the line between George and Oudtshoorn. The engineers had to hack out eight long tunnels and blast numerous cuttings through rock. The ruling grade is 1-in-36 compensated, hard work for any train but especially so for steam locomotives.

Oudtshoorn

Oudtshoorn is the largest town in the little Karoo. It was built on the staggering profits from ostrich farming which boomed at the beginning of the century on the back of the seemingly insatiable demand for ostrich feathers in Europe and north America. The boom spawned ostrich barons, many of whom built wildly ostentatious palaces. Many of these multi-roomed, balconied, turreted houses are still standing, wildly flamboyant and overstuffed follies and another chapter of South African weirdness. Alas, feather capes, fans and boas slipped into history and, along with government control of the industry, this cost the country its edge in ostrich farming. Oudtshoorn almost disappeared. Only one palace, at **146 High St**, is formally open to the public.

Ostrich farming is still a major industry although these days it is the meat that people want. The town has become an agricultural centre for the region, while the nearby School of Infantry, one of the army's most hard-core training bases, ensures a little more cash for the town's coffers. It is a punishingly hot

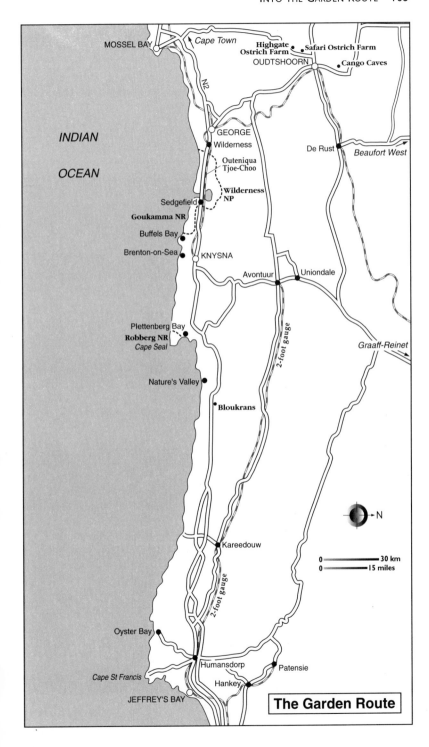

The Garden Route

place as any recruit from the army base will tell you; summer temperatures are often over 40°C (104°F), as air is trapped in the valley and effectively superheated.

There is a **museum**, housed in the old Boys' High School, with exhibits of firearms, and the history of the ostrich industry. The bizarre and wonderful **Cango Caves**, once used by the San as a refuge, are nearby. Although the chambers are mostly lit up and packed with humanity during school holidays, the displays of stalactites, stalagmites and helictites are worth the hard 30-km (19-mile) slog from town.

Tourist information Seppie Greef Buildings, Voortrekker Rd, tel: 044 222221.
Rail information 044 2032203.

After Oudtshoorn, the railway winds its way past looming sandstone cliffs near Barandas and into the tightness of the Toorwaterpoort. Here the railway shares the canyon floor with a notoriously temperamental river, criss-crossing from side to side. The rail bed had to be carved out of the rock face in many places. Flood damage is a constant threat to the survival of this section of the railway. Floods in 1996 destroyed a whole chunk of the railway in the poort and it was only reopened early in 1998. Go now!

The little stations along the way serve isolated farming communities but there are few people to be seen. There were many more wayside halts in steam days, where locomotives could re-coal and water, but diesels, and a general slump in freight levels have seen train services over this line shrink dramatically. The train joins the old main line to the north at Kliplaat and then swings south for Port Elizabeth, arriving at 17.50.

For **Port Elizabeth** information, see Chapter 6 above, page 73.

Steam along the Garden Route

The branch railway which runs from George to Knysna is the country's official museum railway but is run by Transnet Heritage Foundation as a genuine working line, complete with revenue-generating steam-hauled freights as well as passenger trains, which have been given the hideous but catchy appellation *Outeniqua Tjoe-Choo*. The 46km (29-mile) line was an inspired choice for a working museum. The area is thriving in South Africa's tourist boom and the countryside is exquisite. The railway drops down from George through thick forest to the coast, hugs the seaside briefly and then gallops over bridges and causeways through what is fittingly known as the Lake District.

Spoornet is committed to maintaining the railway as a steam-operated line and a diverse collection of restored engines is kept at George and at the railway workshops in Voorbaai close by, near Mossel Bay. This is also the country's last depot to train steam crews and fitters. The sheds can be visited by appointment. Ask the station-master at George for details.

There is one passenger service from Knysna to George and back every day except Sunday. There are other trains but these are usually freight only. The schedule does change – check with the operating office at George to see what trains are running. For bookings and information call 0445 21361.

STEAM OVER THE OUTENIQUAS

In steam days, the trek over the Outeniqua Mountains was tough on the engine crews. Slogging uphill with the throttle full open meant that the long tunnels became filled with thick, choking, hot smoke, forcing engine-men to cover their faces with wet cloths and lie on the floor of their cabs. Two engines were needed to pull trains over the pass and it was not until 1947 and the arrival of the GEA class Garratts – articulated locomotives which have two engine units, supplied by a single boiler in the centre – that one locomotive was sufficient. The Garratts improved conditions a little. Since it made little difference which way the engine was facing, they were usually worked 'backwards' with the chimney trailing. This did not help passengers much, but it made life tolerable for the crew.

Life was still unpleasant for the firemen though. On heavy, uphill trains, keeping the steam-pressure up on the GEAs, with their huge fire-boxes, was back-breaking work in the violent heat of a loco cab. The unfortunate firemen on these hand-stoked locomotives would shovel solidly from the start of the climb, all the way to the summit. The first GMAM Garratts with their mechanical stokers were welcomed with relief. Today, it is diesel all the way unless you find yourself on one of the special trains which regularly hammer over the pass. One GEA has been restored and is based at George. To feed it, the fitters down at the locomotive depot at Voorbaai have welded two shovels side-by-side to make a mega-implement. Interestingly, whenever the GEA is rostered to work a special train, Voorbaai's stokers start booking off sick.

There are also a couple of expensive tour operators offering this trip with the option of going one way by train and returning by minibus. Local travel agents will have details.

Rovos Rail's *Pride of Africa* (see page 143) also does a return trip from Cape Town to Knysna twice a month. It is expensive but sitting in the sun-drenched air on the observation car balcony, drink at hand, while rolling across the lakes, is worth a rand or two.

The Outeniqua Tjoe-Choo
Times

dep Knysna 09.35	dep George 13.00
arr George 12.30	arr Knysna 15.30

Fares
R50 round trip, R40 one way.
Under threes travel free; children under 16 pay R30 return, R20 one way.

George

Lying at the foot of the towering Outeniquas, George is now a bustling town. The first town to be proclaimed after the British occupation of the Cape in 1806, it was named after King George III, who donated a bible to the local church. The town is a fairly important economic centre. It is still important in the timber trade, though rampant logging almost wiped out the indigenous hardwood trees, yellow-wood and stinkwood especially, that once covered the region. In 1936 the government banned harvesting of indigenous hardwood trees for 200 years, allowing some of the species to grow back. The town streets are lined with trees and the place has a pleasant feel about it.

Until recently George was quite a conservative town, but the tourist boom has done a lot to change attitudes. The **airport** is served by domestic flights from Cape Town, Johannesburg and Port Elizabeth. The airport is about 15km (10 miles) out of town but there are usually cabs hanging about to meet the flights. George is not known for its nightlife, though the normal pubs and hotel bars abound and there is a small cinema showing reasonably up-to-date films. And there are plenty of restaurants.

George Tourist Information Centre tel: 044 801 9295.
Garden Route Tourist Information Centre tel: 044 873 6355.

Accommodation

Outeniqua Hotel 123 York St, tel 0441 874 7130. Singles R90, doubles R150.
George Backpackers' Hostel 29 York St, tel: 0441 74 7807.

The nearby beach villages of **Herolds Bay** and **Victoria Bay** have great swimming although accommodation is a bit limited, unless you dig camping. Victoria Bay has its own little station perched high on the hill above the village, but you have to tell the conductor in advance if you want to alight there. The train hugs the hill before rolling across the stunning curved viaduct over the Kaaimans River, said to be the most photographed bridge in the country. Lean out the window and you look straight down into the sea. It can be sobering.

Wilderness is the first of the main beach resorts, a popular honeymoon destination with a sprawl of holiday homes and a couple of hotels. Aside from being a breathtaking piece of coast, it is also famous for being the home of P.W. Botha, the second-last white state president, who occasionally breaks his self-imposed silence to lambast the new order.

The railway now heads into the Lake District proper, skirting lagoons and forest-covered hills and passing the **Fairy Knowe** halt just 2km (1.2 miles) past Wilderness. Fairy Knowe Backpackers, one of the world's greatest such places, is hidden in a clump of trees two minutes walk from the station. Ask the conductor to stop the train if you want to get off; wave it down if you want to get on. Fairy Knowe's managers Chris and Monica can arrange canoeing, cycling, abseiling, paragliding, hiking, horse-riding, fishing – the place is a mini Outward Bound centre, without the brutal instructors. They also get discounted tickets for the steam train. Dorm beds are R45 per person, doubles R60pp sharing. Breakfast is R15. To book, call 044 877 1285.

The railway line passes a number of lakeside settlements and resorts at Swartvlei, Bleshoender and Sedgefield. Crossing the Goukamma River, the track doubles back violently as it climbs over the hills which overlook the Knysna Lagoon. After coasting down through forests, the train rolls across the long bridge over the lagoon into Knysna.

Knysna

Knysna used to be a sleepy village with a disproportionate number of resident hippies, who have now either moved on or cashed in on exploding tourism. Its surroundings are awesome. The town rolls back from the huge lagoon into the indigenous forest behind. The lagoon is sheltered by hills standing between it and the sea, and the Knysna Heads, two steep sandstone cliffs, guard the entrance to the lagoon. The wind and currents are treacherous here and many boats have come to grief in the passage, one of the reasons why Knysna never really took off as a port.

Before tourism, its main industry apart from timber was a little boat-building. Both timber yards and the boatyard are still in business, although on a much smaller scale. The vast, and thriving, indigenous forests east and north of the town are home to the last known forest elephant, who is basically never seen. (Until not long ago, there were three.) Most conservationists want more elephants released into the forest, but an acrimonious debate has blown up with some claiming the newcomers would not be true forest elephants and thus not appropriate. One of the best ways of getting into the forest is to do part of the **Outeniqua Hiking Trail** which runs from George to Knysna (see below). It is a tough 108-km hike but there are shorter options.

If you can get to it, the Norman-style church at **Belvidere**, on the sea side of the lagoon, is worth visiting. There is a halt there, but once again you need to tell the conductor. The beach at **Brenton-on-Sea** is an eight-kilometre (five-mile) stretch of beauty but tough to get to without a car.

Tourist information 0445 825510.
Rail information 044 8018208.

STOPPING TRAINS
Trains are big, heavy things. A Class 24 locomotive alone weighs nearly 80 tons, so it takes time for the driver to stop a train, without slamming on the emergency brakes and terrifying passengers. To request a train to stop at an unmanned halt, stand where the driver can see you, but well back from the platform edge, and make a stiff-armed chopping motion from the shoulder down. It is important to do this when the train is still a few hundred metres away. It is no use waving at the engine from beside the line as it steams into the station as this will only scare the driver, if he sees you at all, and you will probably lose your arm as well. Be careful!

Accommodation

Loads of freshly done-up B&Bs, backpackers' places and hotels. Take your pick.

Luxury

St James Club of Knysna On the Knysna lagoon, tel: 0445 826 750. St James Club has swimming pools, tennis, an aviary and a decorative koi pond. Doubles R400–R1,100pp for luxury suites. Single people pay 80% of double price.

Fancourt Hotel Montagu Street, tel: 044 870 8282. Has every activity imaginable, including two 18-hole golf courses, a golf school, tennis and squash courts, an indoor and outdoor pool, and bowling. Rooms from R1,050. No discount for singles. Play as much golf as you can in one day for R275pp.

Mid-price

Shamrock Guest House Kus Road, Glentana, 20km from George (10km from the airport), tel: 044 879 1392. Small intimate bed and breakfast. Sea views from all the rooms – eat breakfast with the whales from June to October. From R200pp.

Fish Eagle Lodge off Welbedacht Lane, Knysna, tel: 0445 82 5431. The lodge overlooks Knysna lagoon and mountains. Apartments (self-catering) are R165–R185. Rooms in the main lodge are R165. Singles pay R40 extra.

Budget

Peregrin Backpackers 37 Queen Street, Knysna, tel: 0445 23747. Has a jacuzzi and pool table. Mountain bike hire and other activities organised. Free pick-up from station. Dorms R45 for first night, R40 for second and R35 for third. Doubles R55pp first night with R5 reduction for second and third nights.

The Caboose Gray St, tel: 0445 82 5850. B&B-style accommodation with an apparent train theme, though the staff know little about trains. It is near the station, however. R70 per person per night.

Hikers Home 17 Tide St, tel: 0445 24632. Centrally located, groovy backpackers' hostel. Dorm bed R28, doubles R36 per person, camping R20 per person.

Eating and drinking

Lots of little restaurants and coffee shops. There is a new waterfront complex near the station with a few bars and restaurants and the usual spread of take-aways. One of the better options is the Tapas Bar on Thesens Island. It is a bit of a walk but the food and locally brewed beer are great.

Outeniqua Trail

The Outeniqua hiking trail used to be regarded as a killer – literally. The trail has been shortened and the stiff climb out of George has been dropped. Make no mistake, though, it is not a walk in the park, which is why you should do it in the first place. Think 108km of forest and mountainside walking. The day's walking averages 16km, between 5 and 7 hours time-wise. There are rivers to cross, many with only a cable to support yourself against the torrent. Warning notices are posted in the overnight huts when river levels are too high.

The vegetation is Cape fynbos and many, many acres of indigenous forest where the ancient (tree) giants stay. You need a permit, though; call 0445 82 5466. At R15 per person a day, it is the trail bargain of the century. The start is at Beervlei Hut, 18km from Wilderness. Fairy Knowe Backpackers would be a good base from which to do the trail.

CAPE TOWN TO NAMAQUALAND

Every year after the rains, the semi-desert of Namaqualand is transformed into a country of flowers. Carpets of wild blooms fill the valleys and spread across the mountain sides. It is almost always impressive but just how splendid this remarkable sight is depends a lot on how good the rains are and whether any hot winds blow during the brief season from mid-August to mid-September.

There is just one train to Namaqualand but it is a tougher train journey than most others in the country. The branch line north from Cape Town to this semi-desert was built to exploit some of the copper traffic then being generated by the Cape Copper Company which was mining the area, as well as to serve the interests of the farmers in the grain basket of the Swartland.

The copper deposits were first discovered by the Nama Hottentot people who used the metal to make weapons and ornaments and bartered these with other tribes. The first European on the scene was Simon van der Stel, the governor of the Cape himself, in 1685 while he was leading an expedition. He found enough copper in the shadow of Koperberg (Copper Mountain) seriously to impress his masters in the Dutch East India Company, but the distance to the Cape made exploitation impossible. Only in the middle of the 19th century did mining begin there in earnest. The copper was dragged by ox-wagon to the Orange River and then floated down to the Atlantic on barges. A harbour was later established at Port Nolloth, on the west coast.

On January 1 1876 the Cape Copper Company opened its private 2ft 6in (76cm) gauge railway line from Port Nolloth to Okiep in the heart of the copper area, and the metal moved over this line until well into the 20th century. In the early 1940s the company started sending its copper by truck to the SAR railhead at Bitterfontein and the narrow gauge railway gradually fell into disrepair. The last remnant was a short stretch from the port to a water supply at Five Mile Halt. A train would amble up the branch every few days to collect water for the town. The line finally closed in 1945, and with it one of the country's most romantic chapters of railway history.

South African-born writer and traveller Lawrence Greene remembered the railway and the people connected so closely with it.

> 'Port Nolloth and the copper mines were outposts of Cornwall for many years, and they [the Cornish miners] left many Cornish names along the line. Sailing ships from Swansea came up to the jetty at Port Nolloth and discharged coal which was railed to Okiep.
> 'The trains brought the copper ore to the port, and that went back to Swansea. Most of the work was done by Cornish miners, St Helena craftsmen and Hottentot labourers. To this day [1960-ish], old Hottentots still speak English with Cornish phrases and accent.'

The 3ft 6in (107cm) gauge railway line from Cape Town reached Bitterfontein in the 1930s. The copper traffic has dissipated, along with the mines, and traffic on the branch is scanty. However, the southern part is thriving as an agricultural carrier, especially at the end of the winter when the Swartland wheat harvest begins.

The countryside is arid semi-desert in the north around Port Nolloth until that annual miraculous transformation in the spring when the rains transform the desert overnight into a wonderland of flowers. There is only one passenger train left on the Bitterfontein branch. Once called the *Klawer Mail*, it used to run all the way to Bitterfontein. Now it goes only as far as Klawer but it is a good way of getting into Namaqualand for a weekend to see the flowers.

Once a crack train, serving the bustling copper towns of the north, the *Mail* is now reduced to a weekly sleeper service on weekends, leaving Cape Town on a Friday night and returning from Klawer on Sunday evening. All classes are available but there is no dining car. The only downside is the 03.00 arrival in Klawer on Saturday morning.

The Klawer Mail

Distance: 332km.
Frequency: Weekly.
Classes: First, second, economy.

Cape Town–Klawer 940812 Northbound (Friday)			Klawer–Cape Town 940812 Southbound (Sunday)	
dep	18.00	Cape Town	arr	06.20
dep	18.30	Bellville	dep	05.56
dep	18.50	Kraaifontein	dep	05.40
dep	20.15	Malmesbury	dep	04.30
dep	20.55	Rust	dep	03.22
dep	21.21	Moorreesburg	dep	02.56
dep	21.47	Koringberg	dep	02.28
dep	22.06	Moravia	dep	02.06
dep	22.38	De Hoek	dep	01.48
dep	22.49	Piketburg	dep	01.25
dep	23.41	Eendekuil	dep	00.31
dep	23.56	Drury's Kloof	dep	00.15
dep	00.13	Het Kruis	dep	23.58
dep	00.33	Paleisheuwel	dep	23.37
dep	01.09	Sandberg	dep	23.02
dep	01.46	Graafwater	dep	22.38
arr	02.57	Klawer	dep	21.15

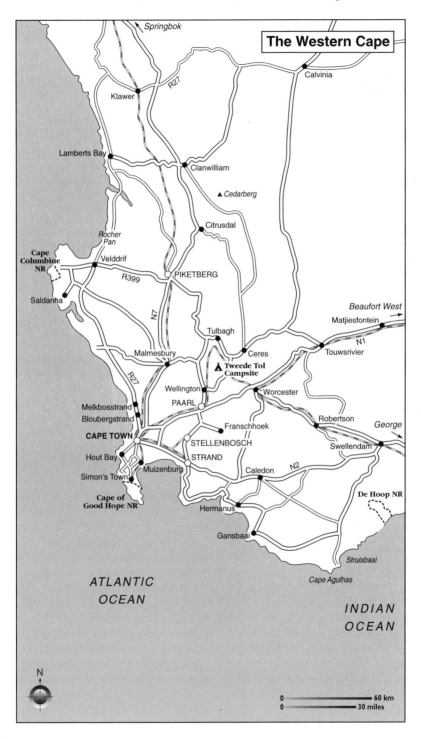

The Western Cape

Springbok

Calvinia

R27

Klawer

Lamberts Bay

Clanwilliam

▲ Cedarberg

Citrusdal

Rocher
Pan

Cape
Columbine
NR

Velddrif

PIKETBERG

R399

Saldanha

N7

Beaufort West

Matjiesfontein

Tulbagh

N1

Malmesbury

Ceres

Touwsrivier

R27

▲ Tweede Tol
Campsite

Wellington

Worcester

PAARL

Melkbosstrand

Robertson

George

Bloubergstrand

Franschhoek

CAPE TOWN

STELLENBOSCH

Swellendam

Hout Bay

STRAND

Simon's Town

Muizenburg

Caledon

N2

De Hoop NR

Cape of
Good Hope NR

Hermanus

Gansbaai

Struisbaai

ATLANTIC
OCEAN

Cape Agulhas

INDIAN
OCEAN

N

0 _____ 60 km
0 _____ 30 miles

Fares

Single fares, per person:

First   R73
Second   R53
Economy   R29

The timing allows a brief foray by bike into the surrounding area. It is, however, really a trip for the independent traveller who does not mind a little discomfort. The towns along the way between Cape Town and Klawer are mostly small, often conservative, farming communities. There is little to do here unless you are a farmer and I would recommend saving your energies for something else.

Klawer

Klawer has a nice enough atmosphere for a railway town but you are unlikely to want to spend more than a weekend here. This is really a trip for travellers with bicycles – riding out into the fields of daisies on wide, sparsely-trafficked tarred roads is an experience not to be missed. Public transport in the region is almost non-existent.

The reasonable Klawer Hotel is right next to the station which can help with the early morning arrival. Book a room in advance, though, and be careful leaving the station.

Klawer Hotel Tel: 02724 61032. Singles R95, doubles R80pp, chalets R100 for one person, R150 for two, R200 for three. If you are coming by train you *must* call in advance to arrange for someone to let you in.

CAPE TOWN TO EAST LONDON

This is the only train linking Cape Town and East London, mostly aimed at workers travelling home at the end of the month. Initially there was only economy class accommodation but there are now some first and second class coaches attached.

If you do not choose to travel in first or second you can expect the ride on this nameless service to be rough. Sleeper accommodation is limited and anyway it is a moot point whether the sleepers are preferable to riding in the bolt-upright seater coaches.

If you are a tourist, your fellow passengers will be amazed at your willingness to slum it with them and the experience – and stories – will be gripping. Watch out for *skollies* (bad people) and keep a close eye on your stuff.

Timetable

Distance: 1,534km.
Frequency: Weekly.
Classes: First, second, economy.

Cape Town–East London 14255 Eastbound (Sunday)		Station	East London–Cape Town 41256 Westbound (Tuesday)	
dep	10.25	Cape Town	arr	17.20
dep	10.55	Bellville	dep	16.56
dep	11.37	Huguenot	dep	16.09
dep	11.53	Wellington	dep	15.54
dep	13.49	Worcester	dep	14.20
dep	15.03	Touwsrivier	dep	12.29
dep	16.17	Laingsburg	dep	11.13
dep	19.29	Beaufort West	dep	08.04
dep	21.16	Hutchinson	dep	05.50
dep	23.28	De Aar	dep	04.00
dep	01.25	Noupoort	dep	02.15
dep	02.45	Colesberg	dep	00.46
dep	04.35	Springfontein	dep	23.10
dep	05.27	Bethulie	dep	22.04
dep	07.05	Burgersdorp	dep	20.40
dep	08.03	Molteno	dep	19.33
dep	08.47	Sterkstroom	dep	18.45
dep	10.00	Queenstown	dep	17.43
dep	11.15	Cathcart	dep	16.05
dep	11.49	Thomas River	dep	15.28
dep	12.28	Stutterheim	dep	14.55
dep	12.51	Amabele	dep	14.32
dep	13.42	Berlin	dep	13.48
dep	14.03	Mount Ruth	dep	13.27
arr	14.30	East London	dep	13.00

Fares

Single fares:

First	R311
Second	R222
Economy	R127

For information on **East London**, see Chapter 6, page 71.

TRAVELLING TO NAMIBIA

There is no longer any through passenger train service connecting the main South African passenger system to Namibia. There is, however, a Namibian service that runs twice-weekly from Upington in the Northern Cape via Keetmanshoop to Windhoek. This is described in Chapter 16, pages 234–7. To connect with this service the traveller dependent on public transport will have to get to Upington by bus or minibus taxi. Northbound trains depart from Upington at 05.00 on Thursdays and Sundays only.

Upington

Upington is a sprawling, affluent town on the banks of the Orange River. Large-scale irrigation has pushed back the desert and turned the town into a thriving agricultural settlement – there are even vineyards.

Accommodation

Chateau Guest House 9 Coetzee St, tel: 054 332 6504. Friendly B&B in the centre of the town. Book in advance, if possible, and arrange a pick-up from the station if you need one. Singles R82–R150, doubles R140–R200.

Getting there and away

Intercape operates the only scheduled luxury bus service connecting Upington with Johannesburg or Cape Town.

IRON HORSE AND BULLETS

The railway to Upington leaves the Cape Main Line at De Aar junction and heads off north-west into the Kalahari Desert. There isn't much out here except for sunbaked hills and saltpans. Few people other than the hardy Bushmen and, latterly, tough sheep farmers have made this their home. This was the territory then, that the railway crossed, heading for the town of Upington, an oasis along the banks of the wide, sluggish Orange River.

There was plenty of game though. Herds of springbok and gemsbok (oryx) roamed at will, and all the drivers on the Upington line carried rifles in the cab. They would single out an animal, shoot it from the moving train and stop and have a barbecue. It was as much for the passengers' benefit as anyone else's – these were the days before dining cars ran on all trains. Those long desert train journeys parched people's throats and they would drink the train dry long before the trip was over. This did not go unnoticed and watering holes began springing up along the tracks. It was the most profitable catering business anyone connected with the railways had ever seen. Then came the dining cars and track improvements and the trains got faster, and the watering holes faded into the dust of the Kalahari.

Cape Town–Upington
dep Cape Town   19.00 (Sundays, Mondays, Wednesdays, Fridays)
arr   Upington   05.00 (the next day)

Upington–Cape Town
dep Upington   20.00 (Tuesdays, Thursdays, Fridays, Saturdays)
arr   Cape Town   06.00

Single fare   R165

Upington–Johannesburg
dep Upington   05.30 (Mondays, Tuesdays, Thursdays, Saturdays)
arr   Johannesburg 15.00

Johannesburg–Upington
dep Johannesburg   10.00 (Tuesdays, Thursdays, Fridays, Sundays)
arr   Upington   19.30

Single fare   R180

As well as these bus services there are also the usual minibus taxis. The minibus pick-up point in Upington is right outside the station and the usual fare to Kimberley for example is about R60. Use your discretion in choosing your ride. If the taxi is overloaded or looks unsafe, find another one. The day I took one to Kimberley, there were 19 people and all their voluminous bags crammed inside – six people were jammed in the front seat. It can be quite an expedition.

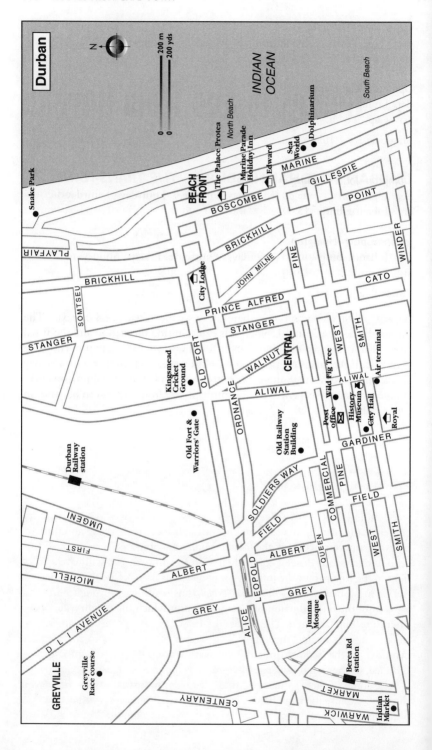

Routes to and from Durban

DURBAN TO JOHANNESBURG – *THE TRANS-NATAL*

The *Trans-Natal* is one of the best-patronised trains in the country, offering a quick overnight service between the Reef and the holiday city and harbour of Durban. It runs daily between the two cities, via Pietermaritzburg, the capital of Natal in colonial days.

Durban is traditionally a holiday town for people from 'up-country' and getting a berth during school holidays can be difficult. If you are told there is no room, ask whether any special trains have been laid on to cope with the overflow. This is normally the case these days as Spoornet responds more readily to its customers.

The *Trans-Natal*'s timings are such that it allows business-people to travel to and from meetings in either city without having to worry about the carnage of the inter-city freeway, or fork out for an expensive domestic flight. There were plans to turn the train into a business centre, complete with telephones, fax machines and work stations, but this remains an unfulfilled dream for many. All three classes of accommodation are offered and there is a full dining-car service. Once again, it is a sleeping train and, unless you are a total insomniac with brilliant night vision, sightseeing opportunities from the train are quite limited. However, the route takes you through one of the country's most historically rich regions, featuring famous battlefields from both the Zulu War and Anglo–Boer War.

Leaving Durban, the train runs briefly south before swinging into the hills surrounding the city, twisting through tunnels, over bridges and scarily sharp curves in the haul up the escarpment, through Pietermaritzburg and then up into the rich farmland of the Natal Midlands, home of Jersey cows, fine schools and a good dose of colonial fervour. In summer, you will have a bit of light in the first part of the journey, in winter, it is dark before the train leaves.

Leaving Johannesburg, the *Trans-Natal* runs south-east through industrial areas until the busy junction of Germiston after which the countryside opens up into rolling farmland. The route crosses South Africa's second largest coal mining district during the night. The names of the towns in the area are evocative of the Scottish miners who were among the first to mine here – Dundee, Glencoe and Ballengeich, as well as the more English Newcastle.

Like some of their namesakes, these are ugly, industrial towns, but if you intend to explore the battlefields or other historical sights, you will need to get off at one of them. Both up and down trains pass through the area in the small hours, so book your accommodation in advance and arrange for someone to pick you up from the station. Remember also to tell the conductor to wake you at least ten minutes before you are due to get off – the stops are brief.

Timetable
Frequency: Daily.
Distance: 722km.
Classes: First, second, economy.

Jo'burg–Durban Trans-Natal 76009 Southbound			Durban–Jo'burg Trans-Natal 67010 Northbound		
dep	18.30	Johannesburg	arr	07.44
dep	19.01	Germiston	dep	07.23
dep	19.47	Heidelberg	dep	06.30
dep	20.16	Balfour North	dep	06.04
dep	21.23	Sanderton	dep	05.06
dep	22.44	Volksrust	dep	03.46
dep	23.55	Newcastle	dep	02.34
dep	00.59	Glencoe	dep	01.26
dep	02.17	Ladysmith	dep	00.20
dep	03.22	Estcourt	dep	23.08
dep	03.58	Mooirivier	dep	22.36
dep	05.51	Pietermaritzburg	dep	20.51
arr	08.00	Durban	dep	18.30

Fares
Single fares per person:

First	R164
Second	R108
Economy	R67

Durban
Once South Africa's busiest port, Durban is still its third city, an industrial and holiday town, built around a superbly sheltered bay and mile after mile (four, in fact) of exquisite beach front. It looks a lot like Miami – it even has a Golden Mile of high-rise hotels on the front – but there are fewer Art Deco buildings. The bay is the outstanding feature, a vast sweep of water, protected by the Bluff, a low wooded headland.

Durban was the traditional playground for 'Vaalies', a derogatory name for someone from the former Transvaal province (now carved up into four smaller provinces). The Easter, July and Christmas holidays would see what looked like the entire Transvaal descend on the city's beautiful golden coast, jam its roads and fill its hotels. The locals hated them and loved them at the same time.

Durban is still a holiday town, although it is definitely a lot shabbier these days. The town council tries hard and the Vaalies still flock down here in the holiday season, but the whole occasion seems a lot more muted now.

The city is the centre of the country's Indian community, most of whom are descendants of indentured labourers brought over from India to work on the sugar estates in the 19th century. When their contracts were up, they were given the choice of returning to India or staying on to farm here. Most stayed. It is really the only place in South Africa where you can get a genuine curry on the street – this will be hotly debated – in the form of a *bunny chow*, a loaf of bread sliced in half, the middle scooped out and mutton, chicken, beef or veg curry poured into the crust. The Indian influence is everywhere in the city, from the colourful shops in Gray St, a little south of the central business district, to the temples, flashes of colour, and smells of spicy cooking.

The city's better hotels line the beach-front, almost from the channel where the bay opens into the sea, right the way up to Blue Lagoon. The area around the channel is the less salubrious end of Point Rd, full of massage parlours, escort agencies and dodgy bars, all doing brisk business with visiting sailors. The business district straddles two one-way roads, Smith St and West St, which both end just short of the Marine Parade on the sea front. To the south, the Victoria Embankment curves round the bay in a luscious sweep, fronted by luxury apartment blocks, the Durban Club, shipping offices and the two yacht clubs.

The city sprawl continues north up the coast, across the Umgeni River, to the resort town of Umhlanga Rocks, and inland to the Berea Heights, a range of hills which overlook everything.

Things to do

Durban definitely has an English seaside town feel about it, too. Think Hastings and you will not be disappointed. The **Marine Parade**, formerly a road, is now a largely pedestrianised area with long stretches of parking lot near the main beaches. The idea was to get rid of the traffic but the cars are still there in their thousands. Ignore the crazy-paving and milling skate boarders and go to **Sea World** which houses the Aquarium and Dolphinarium – both are excellent. There are dolphin shows every day and shark-feeding three times a week. Then go for a swim in the lovely warm water at **North Beach**, also a major surfing spot. If you are here in July, watch out for the Gunston 500, an annual professional surfing tournament. If you are not interested in surfing, it is still worth going to watch the antics of the Beautiful People.

The Marine Parade is the last refuge of Durban's remaining rickshaws, once a vibrant, human-powered transport fleet numbering almost a thousand, highly decorated by their Zulu drivers with beadwork, streamers and paint. Fewer than 20 are left, pulling tourists around the Golden Mile. But the drivers have the serenity and dignity of proud Zulus, so feel good about riding with one.

The **beaches**, all protected by shark nets, are superb. The warm, south-flowing Mozambique Current means the water is always around 20°C, while the sub-tropical climate ensures the mildest of winters, although it can get dangerously hot and humid in summer.

Durban has a rash of **museums** and cultural sites, including the Natural Science Museum in the ornate city hall, the Local History Museum, Port Natal Maritime Museum and the Durban Art Museum. The **Playhouse Complex** in Smith St contains five theatre venues and there is always something going on.

To get back into nature, there are beautiful **Botanical Gardens** in Lower Berea and a stretch of pristine mangrove swamp at the Beachwood Mangroves Nature Reserve just north of Durban.

The **Umgeni Bird Park** on the north side of the Umgeni River, is one of the world's finest bird sanctuaries, with about 300 exotic species enjoying the excellent weather.

Getting around

Getting around is simple once you are in the city centre, with most of the attractions situated within walking distance of each other. Durban probably has one of the best bus services using smaller buses known as Mynahs. Yes, look for the picture of the bird, get on and tell the driver where you are going. Mynahs are frequent and reliable although, like everywhere else in this country, the service vanishes at night.

Safety

Durban's population is expanding rapidly, especially since the 1994 elections. The Group Areas Act kept the masses out but now, as the overworked peasant farms just over the hills are no longer able to support the people, the army of urbanites is growing. One inevitable effect of this has been increased crime, some of it targeted at tourists who are easy pickings.

Do not wander aimlessly on the front at night, especially on the beach itself where there are no lights. Most of the muggings and stabbings seem to happen in this part of the city. Wherever you are in the city, walk with purpose and try not to be an obvious tourist – this includes not openly wearing a money-belt nor having a camera slung casually around your neck.

Lone women should avoid the Point Rd area and everyone should be careful there after dark.

The nearby townships, Umlazi and KwaMashu, are not the most welcoming places. If you must see them, go with a friend or someone you can trust who knows the area, can speak the language and will keep you out of trouble.

Practical details
Information

The tourist office is at 160 Pine St, tel: 031 304 4934. There is a branch office next to Sea World on Marine Parade and another in the domestic arrivals hall at the airport.

Airport
Some international airlines, as well as numerous domestic services, fly direct to Durban. The airport is 15km (9 miles) south of the city centre. Magic Bus runs a regular bus service into town, tel: 0800 222220.

Accommodation
Luxury
The Hotel Edward 149 Marine Parade tel: 031 337 3681. Awesome sea-front gem. Expensive, but hey... R565 single, R680 double.

The Royal 267 Smith Street, tel: 031 304 0331. Set in the city centre, it has won the Fedhasa award for 'South Africa's Best City Hotel', five times in a row. Luxury and well placed, but you pay for it. Singles from R900, doubles from R1,100.

Quaters Set in four restored Victorian houses, it has charm and character and is close to centre, tel: 031 303 5246. From R600 for a double and R450 in a single.

Mid-price
Essenwood House Essenwood Road, Berea, tel: 031 207 4547. A beautiful Edwardian house set in a large garden with swimming pool. Five rooms – four have sea views. All are air-conditioned. Double R250pp, single R350. Breakfast included.

Budget
Travellers Rest 743 Currie Road, Morningside, tel: 031 303 1064. Recommended as a safe attractive area to stay in. Dorms R45pp, doubles R55 pp. Free pick-up from airport and bus station.

Banana Backpackers 61 Pine St tel: 031 368 4062. Easy access from station. Near the beach-front, central and reasonable, but it is an area known for frequent muggings. Dorm R35pp, double is R60pp, R90 for a single.

Pietermaritzburg
The old capital of Natal, Pietermaritzburg still retains a definite last outpost feel. Many people wish it still was – you will know them by their bumper stickers with the little Union Jack on one side and the wording 'Natal – the Last Outpost'. Some people rave about 'Maritzburg, preferring its slow pace and quiet streets to life in the bigger cities; others cannot wait to leave.

One city guide says it has 'the vigour and strength of Africa in tandem with the elegance and architectural refinement of the British Empire'; whatever that means. The city is embraced by wooded hills. It was founded by Voortrekkers in 1838 – they laid out its neat grid of streets – in a valley the Zulus called *Umgungundhlovu*, 'the place of the elephants'.

The British took over in 1843 and turned the town into a garrison. The occupation brought some exquisite architecture, including the ornate town hall built in 1900, the wide avenues and streets of Victorian houses. Many of the buildings have been listed by the Historical Monuments Council, including the beautiful **Victorian railway station** which has been well-preserved despite the constant rail traffic. All this adds colour to the town's distinctly unhurried pace.

The University of Natal has a campus here (the other campus is in Durban) and the place can get quite vibrant during term time. During vacations though, man, does it get quiet. Unlike Grahamstown in the Eastern Cape, the town does not revolve around the university, though, which may be good or bad, depending on your point of view. Apart from its buildings, the city is also known for the Duzi Canoe marathon, an annual three-days of paddling and porterage to Durban. In June thousands of crazy, fit people run the Comrades Marathon between Pietermaritzburg and Durban, 90km (56 miles) of pure self-test.

The best way to see the city is to take one of the self-guided walking trails. It is not a big place and you do not want to be sitting in a car here in summer. Temperatures in the high 30s C are common.

Buildings worth seeing include the city hall, the Parliament Buildings, and the Church of the Vow, built by the Voortrekkers in 1841 to commemorate their victory over the Zulus at the Battle of Blood River in 1838. The church is now the Voortrekker Museum.

Other **museums** are the Natal Museum in Loop St, a collection of natural history, ethnology, Bushman paintings and its own section on Mohandas Gandhi, and Macrorie House which is a monument to early settler life. There's even a museum for the Comrades Marathon, at Comrades Marathon House. If you are thinking of doing it, look at the scale model of the course and check out those gradients first. Then decide.

MOHANDAS GANDHI

In 1893, a young lawyer called Mohandas Gandhi, newly arrived from India to settle a lawsuit in the Transvaal, was kicked off a train at Pietermaritzburg after being denied entry into a first class railway carriage. It was his first experience of racial discrimination and alerted him to the plight of Natal's Indians. Gandhi had not even been particularly interested in politics until that moment.

The Indians in Natal, having been released from their contracts as indentured labourers on the sugar plantations, had almost no rights as citizens and Gandhi's reputation as a highly influential lobbyist and leader grew.

During the Anglo–Boer War, he served as a stretcher bearer – he himself was at the bloody battle of Spioenkop, sparking his convictions as a pacifist.

He set up an *ashram* near Durban in 1904, while his political career took off through his membership of the Natal Indian Congress. He was arrested in 1913 after leading a march of working class Indians from Newcastle and over the Transvaal, setting off a strike of Indian workers in the south. There was a tremendous uproar in India and he was released, returning home almost immediately. By then they were already calling him the great soul, the *Mahatma*.

Tourist information
Commercial Rd/Longmarket St, next to the City Hall, tel: 0331 45 1348.

Accommodation
City Royal Hotel 301 Burger St, tel: 0331 94 7072. Singles R230, doubles R250.
Debbies Bed & Breakfast 17 Mills Circle, Hayfields, tel: 0331 61 719. Free lift
offered from Publicity House, but no late night pick-up. Singles, doubles and dorms
all R35 per person.
Sunduzj Backpackers 140 Berg St, tel: 0331 94 0072. Owners will organise trips to
Drakensberg mountains. R25 dorm room, R15 for camping.

The Battlefields Route
The centenary of the Anglo–Boer War in 1999 will be celebrated by many of
the towns around which the conflict centred. As it is, this turbulent part of
South Africa's history is well-preserved and documented and it resonates
throughout the region. If you like battlefields then this is the place to visit
them.

Because the vital, newly-built railway lines were the focus of much of the
war, many of the battlefields are on the line of rail. The railway linking the
coast and the Reef was completed in October 1895, spurred by the discovery
of gold on the Witwatersrand a few years earlier. The railway naturally became
the centre of much fighting during the Anglo-Boer War.

Ladysmith was a strategic town along the railway to the north and by
besieging and cutting the line, the Boers almost brought the Empire to its
knees. The town was cut off for 118 days before being relieved.

On November 15 1899, an armoured train was dispatched from
Pietermaritzburg and headed up the line towards Colenso, a few miles south
of Ladysmith. Young war correspondent Winston Churchill, who had just
arrived in the country to report for the London *Morning Post*, was among the
personnel aboard.

Churchill was a former cavalry officer and had seen active service in Cuba,
India and the Sudan. He was aware of how good at soldiering the Boers were,
commenting that 'the individual Boer, mounted, in suitable country, is worth
four or five regular soldiers'.

The train was ambushed just outside Colenso and derailed during a frantic
dash for the safety of Estcourt 80km away. Churchill was taken prisoner and
interned in Pretoria. He made frantic attempts to escape, finally succeeding on
his third try. It was impossible for him to make his way through Boer lines to
rejoin the British forces in the south so he headed east for the neutral territory
of Portuguese East Africa. In doing so, he made excellent use of Kruger's
railway to Delagoa Bay, clinging to the underside of a freight wagon and
evading the Boers, who were by now very interested in finding him. One of
the Boer leaders was not very impressed by the young adventurer, however.
When he was first captured, General Joubert said of Churchill that he was
nothing more than 'a bit of a newspaperman'.

Ladysmith

If you can cope with the early morning arrival or departure, Ladysmith is worth spending a day in. Attractions include the excellent **Siege Museum** on Murchison St which houses artefacts, uniforms, photographs and documents from the siege, and the **Emnambithi Cultural Centre**, 25 Keate St, for a fresh perspective on some of the other forces that shaped South African culture and history. The centre houses the Ladysmith Black Mambazo Hall which has an outstanding display relating to this superb Zulu vocal group, brought to fame by Paul Simon who recorded and toured with them in the 1980s. Both museums are open from 09.00–16.00 on weekdays, 09.00–13.00 on Saturday.

The **Soofi Mosque**, built in 1969 and now a national monument, is regarded as one of the most beautiful mosques in the southern hemisphere. The mosque stands on the site of the original mosque built by Hazrah Soofi Saheb. It is open to visitors from 13.00–14.00 and 17.00–21.00.

One of the town's little quirks is its unique collection of electrical sub-stations, built in 14 different styles ranging from Cape Dutch to Art Deco. The Tourism **Information Office** (tel: 0361 22992) has a self-guide brochure.

The town is surrounded by at least four major battlefields, including those of Spioenkop and Colenso. The battle for the hill at Spioenkop, which was of little strategic value, was one of the most futile of the war – over 2,000 men were killed or wounded, often in bitter hand to hand fighting before the British retired. The other site at Colenso, or Tugela Heights, was the scene of one of the biggest battles ever to take place in the southern hemisphere. The town is full of registered (and unofficial) tour guides who can take you around. Ask at the information office.

The *Trans-Oranje* express between Durban and Cape Town (see later in this chapter) also passes through Ladysmith once a week in each direction, from Cape Town at 01.01 on Tuesdays, from Durban at 23.12 on Wednesdays.

Accommodation

Royal Hotel 140 Murchison St, tel: 0361 22176. Friendly and just two blocks from the station. Singles R242, doubles R323.

Zulu War battlefields

The history of KwaZulu-Natal is a bloody one, with three major conflicts having spread across it since the middle of the nineteenth century. The first clashes were between Boer and Zulu as the Voortrekkers rolled into Natal in late 1837, looking for land to farm and graze their cattle.

By that time, the Zulu nation was an immense force in the region, having overcome the weaker tribes during the time known as the *mfecane* which in Zulu means 'the crushing' or 'forced migration', as some would call it. Dingiswayo, chief of the Mthethwa had begun the process but it was King Shaka, a member of the then small Zulu tribe, who created one of the most powerful empires yet seen in Africa. Shaka was a brilliant military commander. He revamped his soldiers' tactics and equipment and forged a supremely tough and effective army, leading by example and fear, and began conquering the region.

Shaka was murdered by his half-brother Dingane in 1828. Dingane tried to establish trading relations with the British, who by now had a small settlement at Port Natal. The British left the Zulu alone at first, but when King Cetshwayo, successor to Dingane, began building up Zulu fighting strength, the colonists down at Port Natal started getting nervous. The causes of the Zulu War are not totally clear but what is obvious is that a warlike king with many of Shaka's personality traits was a threat to British aspirations.

On December 11 1878, the British issued an ultimatum to Cetshwayo demanding that the Zulus abandon their traditional military structure and allow missionaries into the region. The Zulus rejected the demands. In early 1879, therefore, a British column under the command of Lord Chelmsford crossed the Tugela River into Zululand. Chelmsford camped in the shadow of the hill at Isandhlwana and then split his forces, leaving half in the unprotected camp while taking the rest off to search for the elusive Zulu *impis* (regiments) he suspected were nearby. On January 22 1879, while he was out searching, the 25,000-strong Zulu army fell on the British camp and overran it in less than two hours, killing 1,300 soldiers of the invading force.

The few survivors fled across the Buffalo River, some heading for the mission station at Rorke's Drift where a detachment of engineers and Welsh regulars was based. Defences were hastily put together before 4,000 Zulus attacked the mission after dark. The 100 defenders repelled wave after wave of Zulu fighters, until at dawn, the Zulus retired. Eleven Victoria Crosses were handed out after this engagement, boosting morale in the army. The British soon reorganised their forces to recover from the disaster at Isandhlwana. The Zulu could not hold out and their kingdom was crushed in a battle at Ulundi, Cetshwayo's capital, on July 4 the same year.

The battlefields are spooky but fascinating to visit. Gunner's Rest Battlefields Tours (tel: 0341 2 4560, or fax: 0341 2 4562) offers superb tours. Knowledgeable guides take you around the battlefield, and describe the events almost in real time. They cost R300 per car if you use your own transport, R500 if you use theirs. They cover the Isandhlwana and Rorke's Drift battlefields and last all day.

If you want to see the battlefields get off the train at Glencoe. It will be in the small hours in either direction but Gunner's Rest will send a pick-up; you must arrange this in advance, however.

Information
KwaZulu-Natal Tourism Board Dundee, tel: 0341 2 2121, or fax: 0341 2 3856.

Accommodation
Gunner's Rest tel: 0341 24560. R100 bed and breakfast for double or single.

SOUTH FROM DURBAN
Commuter services

The coastlines north and south of Durban are known, unsurprisingly, as the North and South Coasts. A railway line runs south, mostly along the sea front, to Port Shepstone, 110km (69 miles) away. There used to be a commuter train service all the way but trains now run regularly only as far as Park Rynie, 50km (31 miles) from Durban. Most of the other commuter trains running from Durban head to the outlying townships. For Durban area **MetroRail enquiries** call 031 361 8123.

One service though runs down a part of the lush South Coast, skirting the edge of the Indian Ocean, rushing over still lagoons flanked by fields of sugar-cane and what's left of the area's natural vegetation (the South Coast has been heavily developed in the past three decades and ugly resort complexes spill back from the beach-front in most of the formerly quaint seaside towns.)

Trains run regularly through the day, starting in the early morning with the last train leaving Kelso around 22.00. Single fares are R10.00 in first, R5.00 in third.

Scottburgh, the fourth station before Kelso, is probably the best place to get off. The station is right on the beach and there are a couple of reasonable places to eat. The sea is warm and the beach is protected by shark nets.

Occasional special trains organised by the Railway Society of South Africa (RSSA) are operated to Port Shepstone, usually to connect with the private narrow gauge railway there; contact the Umgeni Steam Railway, tel: 031 309 1817.

The Alfred County Railway

South Africa once had a few narrow gauge railways, mostly built in the early part of the century to serve isolated farming communities and connect them to railheads on the 'broad' gauge. These rural lines were two foot (61cm) gauge, largely because they were cheaper to build in the frequently rugged country which they traversed. A few were converted to 3ft 6in (107cm) when traffic or money allowed but, by the late 1980s, there were just five left. One, on which the famous *Apple Express* still runs (see page 77), is in the Eastern Cape Province. The remaining four were in the hilly province of Natal. All but one have been closed and the track lifted.

When the end also loomed for the Port Shepstone–Harding line in 1986, there was an outcry from local enthusiasts. Shouting was not enough and it took a hard-nosed business decision by two men, Charlie Lewis and Allen Jorgensson, to buy the railway from the government and try and win back the traffic which had been allowed to dribble away to road transport over the years. The idea was to maintain the line as a steam-operated railway, using the diminutive but advanced Garratt locomotives. Reality bit, however, and the management of the new Alfred County Railway (ACR) realised it would be far more economical to hire diesel locomotives from Spoornet for most workings, an arrangement which still continues today.

However, a large steam fleet is maintained and the railway has carried out some astounding development work on these locomotives to make them highly efficient. Some engines and a fair number of rails have even been sold to the Welsh Highland Railway in the UK. The railway's principal freight is timber.

The ACR runs two *Banana Express* steam trains every week. On Thursdays the train runs as far as Izotsha, 45 minutes out of Port Shepstone, departing at 11.00 and returning around 12.30. Return (round-trip) fares are R36 in first and R24 in tourist class. Children aged 3–12 travel at half-fare. On Wednesdays a train runs to Paddock and back in a six-hour round trip, departing Port Shepstone at 10.00 and returning at 16.00. The return fare is R80.

Paddock is close to the spectacular **Oribi Gorge**, a proclaimed nature reserve. The gorge is 24km long, 5km wide (15 miles by 3 miles) and 400m (1,300ft) deep. The 1,809-hectare (4,460-acre) reserve is made up largely of sandstone cliff and forests hiding bushbuck, vervet and samango monkeys, the occasional leopard and masses of birds. The park is controlled by the KwaZulu/Natal Parks Board who run the hutted camp in the reserve. For information, contact the Parks Board in Pietermaritzburg, tel: 0331 47 1981, or fax: 0331 47 1980.

The ACR offers day tours to Oribi Gorge in conjunction with Nongonzolo Tours – a minibus meets the train at Paddock and takes passengers to the gorge. The cost is R130, including the train ticket and bus ride back to Port Shepstone.

The ACR can also organise a ride on a freight train all the way to Harding and back. The line north of Paddock is dramatic, clawing its way across steep mountainsides before plunging into thick tracts of pine forest on the long approach to Harding. At R2,000, it is quite expensive, but then you do get your own passenger coach, with attendant, at the back of the train. The ACR also requires a minimum of 10 people to do this so at least you can spread the cost. Two day-steam safaris (30–40 people required) are also offered as are occasional steam train trips from Durban, using standard gauge locomotives belonging to the Umgeni Steam Railway (see Chapter 9).

Banana Express bookings and **information**: 039 682 4821/5003.

NORTH TO SWAZILAND AND MOZAMBIQUE

Until 1998 the rails north of Durban had not seen regular, long distance passenger trains for decades. However, since the 1994 elections and the subsequent free movement across the country's borders, Durban has become an important business centre for traders from Swaziland and, especially, Mozambique. In April 1998 MLPS accordingly began running its first ever Durban–Maputo direct passenger train. Before then, rail travellers would have to take the train to Johannesburg and stop over for a day before getting the night train on to the Mozambique border. The new train, known as the *Trans-Lubombo*, has halved the journey time to 20 hours. Accommodation is second class sleeper throughout. The route offers a number of possibilities for people wishing to visit the stunning game parks in northern Natal and Swaziland, as well as opening up a circular route linking Johannesburg, Natal and Mozambique.

The Trans-Lubombo

The train runs twice-weekly in each direction, from Durban on Tuesdays and Thursdays, and from Maputo on Thursdays and Sundays. The (one-class) **fare** is R152 one way in second class sleeper. Golela is on the South Africa/Swaziland border and Goba on the Mozambique/Swaziland border.

Trans-Lubombo 69033 Northbound Tuesday, Friday		Trans-Lubombo 96044 Southbound Friday, Monday	
dep	19.35	Durban	arr	07.35
dep	00.47	Empangeni	dep	03.35
dep	08.00	Golela	dep	21.15
dep	12.15	Mpaka	dep	17.00
dep	15.45	Goba	dep	13.00
arr	18.15	Maputo	dep	09.30
Wednesday, Friday		Thursday, Sunday	

Leaving Durban, the train runs through undulating, sugar-cane covered hills. Most of the little towns on the way are connected either with sugar farming or forestry. After crossing the wide sweep of the Tugela River, South Africa's second biggest, you are in Zululand proper. Not surprisingly, the Zulu tribal group dominates the region, which is rich with their culture and customs. It is beautiful country of forests and traditional villages of beehive huts spreading over green hills.

Game parks

The region's finest assets, as far as most tourists are concerned, are the astounding game parks, huge tracts of protected land, awash with game. There is a vast complex of over 60 parks, nature reserves and wilderness trails. All kinds of accommodation options are available to suit all budgets. For rail travellers, probably the most accessible reserves are the massive Hluhluwe-Umfolozi Park and Mkuzi Game Reserve.

Hluhluwe-Umfolozi

This park, once a hunting ground for Zulu kings, has been a protected area since 1895. Malarial mosquitoes and tsetse flies have saved the area from being invaded by farmers. The 96,453-hectare (372 square miles) park is home to the world's largest concentration of rhino, boasting 1,600 white rhino and 350 black rhino, as well as lion, leopard, buffalo, elephant, wild dog, cheetah, giraffe and scores of antelope species. Bird life is literally prolific.

The park can be explored by vehicle or from one of the four self-guided walks. Guided walks, with armed rangers, are also available along with night drives. There are also five-day guided wilderness trails, but these must be booked in advance. Accommodation is in bush lodges or the cheaper self-catering hutted camps. **Bookings and information** from the Reservations Officer, Natal Parks Board, PO Box 1750, Pietermaritzburg 3200, tel: 0331 47 1981, or fax: 0331 47 1980.

Mkuzi Game Reserve
This is a smaller reserve about 35km (22 miles) north of Hluhluwe. The reserve's wildlife includes both black and white rhino, elephant, cheetah, hyena, wildebeest, zebra, impala and other antelope. Accommodation ranges from camping sites to bush lodges. For **bookings**, tel: 035 573 0003, or fax 035 573 0080, or contact the Natal Parks Board office in Pietermaritzburg as above.

Visiting the parks
Unfortunately, there is a significant catch to planning a trip here if you are coming by rail. While the railway line passes through the towns of Mkuze and Hluhluwe, the trains do not stop. The most convenient place to get off is at the town of Golela, which is reached at 06.30 northbound and 19.00 southbound, and then catch local transport back to either of the reserves. Golela is a border town with the usual collection of unsavoury characters one finds in such places, so do not hang around. In this regard, it would be better to plan a trip to the reserves using the northbound train as the southbound train will invariably arrive after dark and I cannot really recommend that. Spoornet is looking at the possibility of including one or both towns on the train's schedule.

Golela is also a jumping off point for the St Lucia Wetland Park.

St Lucia Wetland Park
This park is a 260,000-hectare (1,000 square mile) reserve of rivers, lakes, swamps, open savannah and sand dunes. The park is bordered by the Indian Ocean and includes a long stretch of the shoreline and its coral reefs. The park is known for its huge population of hippo and many crocodiles, along with both rhino species, elephant, buffalo and heaving herds of antelope.

St Lucia's size means that it is divided into various sections. Accommodation and facilities vary in each, as do the ways of getting in and seeing the reserve. Most people drive in, and it can be unpleasantly overcrowded over Christmas, Easter and school holidays. Getting around on foot is fairly practical, and certainly one of the best ways of seeing the park is to take one of the hiking trails which traverse the Cape Vidal section. For **bookings and information** contact the Natal Parks Board in Pietermaritzburg as above.

INTO SWAZILAND
The mountain kingdom of Swaziland has the shortest railway system of any country in southern Africa, except for Lesotho, which has only a few kilometres of track. This tiny nation, bordered on three sides by South Africa and to the east by Mozambique, is a country of mountains and high plateaux.

A member of the Commonwealth, the country is governed by a strong hereditary monarch.

The climate is pleasant and temperate. Its ecological zones range from rainforest and mountainous high veld in the west to open savannah in the east. Temperatures rise and rainfall declines as the land falls off to the east. The rugged Lebombo Mountains form the border with Mozambique. The country's western border with South Africa is formed by the Mlembe Mountains. High rainfall, at least 1000mm (39in) a year, and the rivers which flow from the range, make the slopes of the Mlembe beautifully green and cool.

Swaziland was settled in about 1750 by members of the Nguni people who were making their way southward along the coastal belt. One group settled in the valley of the uSuthu River, the country's main watercourse, while others tried to move south into Zululand, only to run into the Zulus. Calling themselves Swazis after one of their chiefs, the clan thrived in the valley in spite of regular raids by the Zulu. The current Dlamini monarchy stretches back to the mid-18th century to King Ngwane III.

The first large-scale influx of Europeans followed the discovery of gold in the Piggs Peak area in the 1890s. The gold-bearing reef turned out to be a scanty one and the enthusiasm that followed the strike was short-lived. Meanwhile, the area had come under the control of the Zuid Afrikaansche Republiek, and later the British, when the Anglo–Boer War was over. Limited self-government was granted to King Sobhuza II in 1964 and independence followed in 1968. More recently there has been internal pressure to reform the monarchy and move towards multi-party democracy. Constitutional reform in 1993 introduced direct elections to the house of assembly.

Notes for travellers

Most visitors do not require a **visa** although exceptions include Austrian, French, German and Swiss citizens. Visas, however, are available free at the borders or the airport.

The unit of **currency** is the lilangeni – emalangeni in the plural – which is tied to the South African rand, which is also accepted more or less everywhere in the country. The cost of living is similar to that in South Africa.

Barclays Bank has branches in all the major towns. Hours are 08.30–14.30 on weekdays, and 08.30–11.00 on Saturdays.

The main tourist **information** office is in Mbabane, the capital (tel: 0194 42531). Mbabane, is unfortunately not served by train.

The country code for **phone** calls to Swaziland is 268. From South Africa dial 09268 before any of the Swazi numbers given in this section.

Game reserves

Possibly the finest attraction in the country, Swaziland's game parks are extremely good value compared to similar operations elsewhere in Southern Africa. The railway line runs close to four of the country's six game reserves – it in fact divides the two biggest parks – but like the parks to the south, the train does not as yet stop at the most convenient stations. You will have to get off at Mpaka and cover the remaining 40km (25 miles) on local transport (bus or minibus). You cannot get off at the Mozambique/Swaziland border as the railway crosses at a different place to the road.

The first park is the privately run 6,200-hectare (24 square mile) **Mkhaya Game Reserve** near the little village of Phuzumoya (one day you will be able to get off the Durban–Maputo train there). This reserve is known for its black rhino population. Three game drives during the day and night, walks, accommodation and all meals cost R480 per person per day in safari tents. Good value for what you get. You must arrange in advance to be picked up at Phuzumoya. For bookings, tel: 4 4541, or fax: 4 0957.

Farther north are the two national parks, **Hlane Royal National Park** – formerly a royal hunting ground – and **Mlawula Nature Reserve**, neatly divided by the railway line. Hlane, to which lion and elephant have recently been re-introduced, offers guided walking trails or self-guided game drives, for which you need your own vehicle, of course. Accommodation is in self-catering lodges and cottages, or you can camp. For bookings, tel: 6 1591/2/3.

Mlawula, which is set in 16,500 hectares (63 square miles) of bush, offers walking trails into the Lebombo Mountains. Accommodation is limited to one thatched cottage which sleeps six people in two bedrooms but it is a bargain at R180 per night (for the whole house) over the weekend, R130 per night during the week. There is also a tented camp – which has only one two-person, walk-in tent at the moment – at R60 per night. You can bring your own tent, however. For bookings, tel: 09268 3 8885, or email <k.roques@iafrica.sz>. There is a station right in the reserve but trains do not stop there. Yet.

The **Mbuluzi Game Reserve** is a private reserve on 23,000 hectares (89 square miles) just north of Hlane, lying between the Lebombo Mountains to the east and the Mbuluzi River to the west. The reserve is well-stocked with all the indigenous antelope species, along with giraffe, hippos and plenty of crocodiles. Walking trails are its main attraction along with guided game drives.

Warning These parks are all in malarial areas – take the precautions described in Chapter 2, page 10–11.

Accommodation

There are three lodges, each with 3–4 double bedrooms, sleeping 6–8 people at R600 per lodge per night. For **bookings**, phone 3 8861. It is a fully-equipped self-catering affair so bring your own food and booze. Pick-up from the Mpaka station is possible but must be arranged in advance by calling the reserve.

INTO MOZAMBIQUE

The train crosses the border at Siweni and runs down to the little Mozambican town of Goba. The line has recently been refurbished, having been partially destroyed during Mozambique's civil war. The going is still slow, however.

The wrecks of derailed and blown-up trains still litter the bush, silent reminders of decades of terror. The countryside is also still quite unpopulated – most people fled to the towns during the war and many have not returned.

Around Boane, the vegetation becomes more lush and tropical as the railway levels out on Mozambique's coastal plateau. The slow roll into Maputo is through the waving grass and reeds of the plain, and hundreds of cheering, screaming children run out of their trackside *shambas*, excited, as children are everywhere in Africa, by the miraculous passage of the train. Enjoy.

For more information on **Mozambique**, see Chapter 17, pages 257–71.

DURBAN TO CAPE TOWN – *THE TRANS-ORANJE*

The weekly *Trans-Oranje* express could be one of the world's classic train journeys, a 2,010-km (1250-mile) coast-to-coast traverse of southern Africa, crossing two mountain ranges, the green pastures in Natal, sweeps of maize belt in the Free State, and the awesome, compelling wastes of the desert country of the Karoo. It is such a pity that most of the journey is done at night.

At 37 hours, it is South Africa's longest train ride, two nights and one day. If the timings were changed so that passengers had two days and one night on the train, all the cool scenery would be seen in daylight, including the long haul up to Pietermaritzburg from Durban, the crossing of the Drakensberg, between Ladysmith and Harrismith, the winelands of the Hex River valley and the crossing of the Hex River mountains. Right now, passengers have the somewhat drab maize lands of the Free State and parts of the Karoo between Kimberley and De Aar to fill their daylight hours.

Scenery worries aside, it is still a very soothing way to travel between Cape Town and Durban. The train has all three classes of accommodation and a full dining car with a well-stocked bar.

Distance: 2,024km.
Frequency: Weekly.
Classes: First, second, economy.

Cape Town–Durban *Trans-Oranje* 16003 Eastbound			Durban–Cape Town *Trans-Oranje* 61006 Westbound	
dep	18.50 Mon	Cape Town	arr	06.05* Fri
dep	19.20	Bellville	dep	05.41*
dep	20.01	Huguenot	dep	04.56*
dep	20.14	Wellington	dep	04.42*
dep	21.15	Wolseley	dep	03.40*
dep	22.05	Worcester	dep	03.06*
dep	22.37	De Doorns	dep	02.21*
dep	23.22	Touwsrivier	dep	01.35*
dep	00.35	Laingsburg	dep	00.11*
dep	01.48	Prince Albert Road	dep	22.43
dep	04.00	Beaufort West	dep	21.05

dep	05.54	Hutchinson	dep	18.44
dep	07.56	De Aar	dep	17.00
dep	09.26	Oranjerivier	dep	15.09
dep	10.34	Modderrivier	dep	13.54
dep	11.53	Kimberley	dep	13.15
dep	12.41	Perdeberg	dep	11.48
dep	13.15	Petrusburg	dep	11.12
dep	13.49	De Brug	dep	10.37
dep	15.10	Bloemfontein	dep	09.45
dep	15.55	Brandfort	dep	08.33
dep	16.30	Theunissen	dep	07.55
dep	16.50	Virginia	dep	07.22
dep	17.22	Hennenman	dep	06.59
dep	18.30	Kroonstad	dep	06.15
dep	19.55	Arlington	dep	04.30
dep	21.15	Bethlehem	dep	03.35
dep	22.59	Harrismith	dep	01.46
dep	23.45	Van Reenen	dep	00.40
dep	01.22*	Ladysmith	dep	23.20
dep	01.49*	Colenso	dep	22.47
dep	02.35*	Estcourt	dep	22.08
dep	03.16*	Mooirivier	dep	21.36
dep	05.05*	Pietermaritzburg	dep	19.51
arr	07.15* Wed	Durban	dep	17.30 Wed

★ Denotes 2 days later than original departure date.

Fares

Single fares:

First	R425
Second	R286
Economy	R179

Of these stops, **Durban**, **Pietermaritzburg** and **Ladysmith** are described earlier in this chapter. **Kimberley** and **Cape Town** are discussed in Chapters 6 and 7 respectively.

Harrismith

At the foothills of the northern part of the Drakensberg, Harrismith is better known as a halfway point on the main road between Johannesburg and Durban. It is a pleasant enough town, named after the colourful Cape governor Sir Harry Smith. The town boomed during the Kimberley diamond rush in the early 1870s, becoming a staging point on the transport route. Now its coffers are partly filled by the hordes of motorists who pass through during school holidays on their way to the coast and back.

Most of the town's attractions somehow centre on the flat-topped mountain which dominates it. The Harrismith **Wildflower Gardens**, containing about

1,000 species of plants found in the Drakensberg, are at the foot of the mountain, about 5km out of town.

The nearby **Mount Everest Game Reserve** covers about 1,000 hectares of mountainside, stocking among other species, a couple of rhino. Horses or 4x4 vehicles are available for hire.

Tourist information 05861 2 3525.

Rail information There are no passenger staff at Harrismith station. Buy your ticket from the conductor if you are getting on here.

Accommodation

Not a lot. There are a couple of motels dotted around but these tend to be out of town.

Harrismith Inn tel: 0586 622 2151. Singles R169, doubles R199.

Bethlehem

The town was founded in 1864 and is one of the nicest towns in the Free State, with willow trees lining the banks of the Jordaan River (named by Voortrekkers as their 'Jordan') and wide, quiet streets. Life ticks over here and there is not a lot to do except relax. It is a good base from which to explore the eastern part of the Free State. The scenery – sandstone outcrops and buttresses – is dramatic and the area's caves are covered in **Bushman paintings**. It is easily one of the most beautiful parts of the country, especially in the green of mid-summer. It gets bloody cold in winter, though.

The **buildings** made from sandstone are lovely, including the Magistrate's Office on Louw St and the Nederlands Gereformeerde Moederkerk around which the town was built.

Bethlehem is also the headquarters of the **Sandstone Steam Railroad**, a private initiative to take over freight and passenger trains on the secondary main line to Bloemfontein. See Chapter 9 for further details.

Tourist information tel: 058 303 5732.

Accommodation

Royal Hotel 9 Boshoff St, tel: 058 303 5448. Another Royal Hotel – every town has one but it is not a chain. Singles R100, doubles R150.

Bloemfontein

Both the provincial capital as well as the country's judicial capital, Bloemfontein, 'spring of flowers', was founded around 1854 when the Orange Free State was first proclaimed as a republic. Then it was just a handful of houses, apparently named after 'Bloem', a local farmer's favourite cow which jumped a fence and got eaten by a lion.

Hobbit creator J.R.R. Tolkien was born here in 1892 and the jaded will tell you there is no better place to nurture a fertile imagination.

Bloemfontein is literally in the middle of the country, quite hot and quite mellow. Its natural beauty lies in its tree-lined streets and the bulk of Naval

Hill which dominates the town. For Afrikaners, it is an important city, a cultural, historical and soulful place.

Buildings worth seeing include the Old Residency (where the republic's presidents used to live) on President Brand St, the Old Raadsaal (government assembly) with its thatched roof and dung floors, the Greek/Renaissance inspired Fourth Raadsaal and the Herbert Baker-built Anglican cathedral on St George's St.

There is an Anglo–Boer **War Museum** on Monument Rd, near the fairly sobering **National Women's Memorial** which remembers the 27,000 Boer women and children who died in concentration camps during the war. The 36m (120ft) high sandstone obelisk towers over statues of two women, one holding a dying baby, the other looking out over the plains of the Free State. The ashes of British activist Emily Hobhouse, who alerted the outside world to the existence of the camps, are buried at the foot of the monument.

On a lighter note, there is a 'liger', a cross between a lion and a tiger, which lives at the **zoo**, perhaps in line with the Tolkien theme.

Four passenger trains pass through Bloemfontein – the daily *Algoa* and *Amatola*, the *Diamond Express*, which starts its journey here (see below), and the *Trans-Oranje*, so it is easy to spend a day or three here and then move on at will. The *Diamond Express* runs daily to Kimberley, giving you a connection to the *Trans-Karoo* if you want to head for Cape Town.

Tourist information Hoffman Square, between Maitland St and St Andrew's St, tel: 051 405 8489.
Rail information tel 051 408 2407/2941.

Accommodation
City Lodge Voortrekker/Parfitt Av, tel: 051 477 9888. They say no frills and mean it, but it is clean and safe. Singles R239, doubles R278. Breakfast is an extra R29 per person.
Taffy's Backpackers 18 Louis Botha St, tel: 051 31 4533. Bikes for hire so you can get around this very flat town at will. Double R40 per person, R30 dorm room, R15 for camping.

BLOEMFONTEIN TO PRETORIA – *THE DIAMOND EXPRESS*
Distance: 737km.
Frequency: Daily, except Saturday.
Classes: First, second, economy.

Pretoria–Bloemfontein *Diamond Express* 85036 Southbound			Bloemfontein–Pretoria *Diamond Express* 58035 Northbound	
dep	18.35	Pretoria	arr	07.45
dep	19.07	Kaalfontein	dep	07.16
dep	19.18	Kempton Park	dep	07.06
dep	19.40	Germiston	dep	06.48

dep	20.40	Johannesburg	dep	06.25
dep	21.21	Krugersdorp	dep	05.17
dep	21.38	Randfontein	dep	05.00
dep	22.19	Oberholzer	dep	04.05
dep	23.15	Potchefstroom	dep	03.00
dep	00.09	Klerksdorp	dep	01.45
dep	01.33	Makwassie	dep	00.11
dep	02.23	Bloemhof	dep	23.23
dep	03.13	Christiana	dep	22.24
dep	04.37	Warrenton	dep	21.39
dep	06.20	Kimberley	dep	20.20
dep	07.09	Perdeberg	dep	19.00
dep	07.44	Petrusburg	dep	18.26
dep	08.19	De Brug	dep	17.51
arr	09.10	Bloemfontein	dep	17.00

Fares

Single fares:

First	R113
Second	R77
Economy	R45

The original *Diamond Express* was designed as a semi-luxury train, aimed at enticing business travellers off the airlines and into the trains. The service was timed to allow people to leave Pretoria or Johannesburg at night, arrive refreshed in Kimberley or Bloemfontein, do a day's work and get back on the return train in the evening.

It was, and still is, a great idea, if only South Africa's business travellers could be persuaded to use the train. It may yet happen.

Meanwhile the train continues to run, although there is nothing to distinguish it from South Africa's other passenger trains. It is the only passenger train running between the Reef and Bloemfontein and Kimberley and as such it is a useful train for people wanting to visit both cities. It is also a useful train if you want to get from Bloemfontein to Cape Town and have missed the weekly *Trans-Oranje*, as there is a connection with the *Trans-Karoo* at Kimberley. (The reverse direction is not as good as the northbound *Trans-Karoo* passes through Kimberley at 20.51 while the eastbound *Diamond Express* only arrives at 06.00 the following morning. That's a long night on an empty platform.)

Railways for the Enthusiast

South Africa was the last large-scale user of steam locomotives in Africa, boasting a fleet of over 2,500 engines at the start of the 1980s. Today there are a mere handful left in normal service, but a reasonably progressive outlook on the part of the railway museums means that the working steam that is left is high on quality.

STEAM SERVICES
The *Outeniqua Tjoe-Choo*
Officially, there is one fully steam railway left in the country, running between George and Knysna on the Garden Route (see page 106). The choice of location was inspired – the line runs through incredible forests and over wide, still *vleis* (lakes). At the heart of the Garden Route, it is a railway whose trains, theoretically, should be packed with tourists. Two mixed passenger/freight trains run along the line each day.

OTHER STEAM
The *Union Limited*
The *Union Limited* is a restored passenger train whose facilities echo the steam-hauled days of the first *Blue Train*. The train is based in the Western Cape, from where it runs on nine-day trips up to Oudtshoorn in the Little Karoo. The train is steam-hauled throughout, using locomotives from a large and varied stud of preserved engines.

Fuller details are given in Chapter 10.

Transnet Heritage Foundation
The Transnet Museum uses its own locomotives to haul the *Union Limited*. But these are also used on regular special trains out of Cape Town and around the province. Day trips often run up into the apple orchards of the Ceres valley or along a rickety branch line to Franschoek in the winelands. These are often poorly advertised, check with the Museum **information** office, tel: 021 449 4931, or email: <steamsa@transnet.co.za>.

The museum locomotives are kept at Dal Josafat near Paarl, a quick trip by local train from Cape Town. Phone in advance if you want to make a visit, tel: 021 449 4931.

Steamnet 2000

Steamnet 2000 is run by a hard-core group of enthusiasts dedicated to keeping at least some steam running on the Steel Kyalami between De Aar and Kimberley. Named after the Formula One race track in Johannesburg, the Steel Kyalami was the last running ground of the massive 25NC 4–8–4 behemoths, among the last steam locomotives built for South African Railways between 1950 and 1955.

Other than in China and India, the line was one of the last places on earth where enthusiasts could see superpower steam hustling real freight and passenger trains at high speed on a real main line. Every other main line was electric or diesel but the romance lived on here. At the little lineside hotel at Witput, gricers from all over the world would gather – especially in winter when the desert light was exquisite – and spend the day on the terrace, swapping loco stories, guzzling beers and rushing out to the trackside whenever an NC and train came pounding by.

The whole place was a maverick magnet. Some of the drivers gave up their lives in Europe and moved to South Africa to drive steam locomotives, among them legendary figures like John Gilberthorpe, Richard Niven and Tony 'Ashcat' Marsden. Some of them are still here, driving diesels now, but still getting the odd chance to crack open the throttle of an NC on a charter freight.

The end came quickly in 1992, Salmon Nel moved his hotel elsewhere and not many people stop over at Witput anymore. The hotel is still there but, somehow, it is not so much fun to lie in bed and listen to diesels thunder past – they shake the walls and seem to pass a little too close now.

Kimberley depot, however, still has quite a large dump of NCs, some of which have been leased by Steamnet 2000. The Steamnet crew organises regular chartered freights to De Aar and back.

Information tel: 0531 33339, or 082 8562277 (mobile).

The Sandstone Steam Railway

This is a new operation on the beautiful Bethlehem line through the sandstone outcrops and farmland of the eastern Free State. The railway's owners plan to operate steam-hauled freight and passenger trains using massive 25NC Class locomotives bought or leased from Spoornet. Passenger trains will be hauled by the steam giants. Special trains will also be operated over public holidays and festival times like the Cherry Festival which happens not far south at Ficksburg. **Contact** 011 463 4071.

Alfred County Railway

The Alfred County Railway is a private 2ft gauge line from Port Shepstone to Harding in KwaZulu-Natal. Diesel freights run to and from Harding and steam-hauled passenger trains to Paddock and Izotsha on Wednesdays and Thursdays respectively. (See page 128 for a fuller description.)

South African National Railway Steam Museum

This museum, also known by the acronym Sanrasm, is the preservation arm of the Railway Society of Southern Africa. Various locomotives are kept at an industrial site near Krugersdorp, west of Johannesburg, and steam-hauled trains occasionally run to Magaliesburg from Johannesburg.

For **information**, tel: 011 888 1154, or fax: 011 888 5934.

Friends of the Rail

This Pretoria-based group maintains and operates a couple of Museum locomotives, running trips out to Cullinan and Hartebeespoort Dam. For **information**, tel: 012 46 5988.

Umgeni Steam Railway and Natal Railway Museum

This well-developed preservation group is based in Durban. They run regular trips behind steam, in a set of classic coaching stock, on the Old Main Line which twists its way out of Durban up into the hills.

For **information**, tel: 031 309 1817, or 031 305 6764.

Natal Railway Museum

This museum is based at the little station of Hilton, just north of Pietermaritzburg. Monthly steam trips go to nearby Cedara – basically a siding with an agricultural college and not much else – and to the little town of Howick on the second Sunday of every month.

For **information**, tel: 0331 43 1857.

Inchanga Nursery Railway

This narrow gauge railway operates at Inchanga Nurseries near Durban. The nursery belongs to the railway and provides all its plants.

For **information**, tel: 031 764 2567.

Apple Express Society

This organisation operates the famous *Apple Express* steam train up the narrow gauge railway out of Port Elizabeth into the Langkloof (see page 77). There are regular monthly trips. If you are feeling strong you can race the train in the annual Great Train Race in September. The runners invariably win.

For **information**, tel: 0426 40 0619.

Oosterlyn Express

The *Oosterlyn Express* is a Sundays-only steam-hauled train which runs down the Escarpment from the uninviting railway town of Waterval Boven to Waterval Onder and back. The operators have acquired three Class 15F 4–8–2 steam locomotives and painted them up nicely. The round trip takes about two hours. Before the trip, you can wander around the rail yard and watch the crew prepare the locomotive.

For bookings and **information** call (013262) and ask for 14, during business hours.

Reefsteamers

A group of steam nutters based in the old steam locomotive shed at Germiston junction, east of Johannesburg. The group has access to a few hefty steam locomotives including the country's last operable Class 12AR 4–8–2, a truly massive engine, and a Class 25NC 4–8–4. Work parties meet on weekends to do restoration work on other deserving locomotives. Regular special trains are run down to Potchefstroom Dam. For **information**, call 011 650 9899.

Other steam services

Other preservation groups connected with steam are the **Epping Railway Operating Group** in Cape Town, for information, tel: 021 591 5708; and the **Border Steam Society**, which runs occasional steam trips out of East London, for information, tel: 0431 41 1986.

The **Railway Society of Southern Africa** (RSSA) is an umbrella body for regional preservation and rail enthusiast groups with branches in all the major cities. *SA Rail & Harbours*, the society's quarterly magazine, is about the most useful regular intelligence on what is happening inside the Southern African rail scene. A subscription costs around R80 per year. For more information, contact editor Terry Hutson at 031 466 1683.

INDUSTRIAL STEAM AND VINTAGE ELECTRICS

Until a few years ago, the gold and coal mines were avid users of steam locomotives, and the industrial fleet was as varied as it gets. However, as Spoornet closed more lines and yet bought more locomotives, there was soon a surplus of cheap diesels available for hire and many mine railways snapped them up. There are no steam locos now in use at gold mines, which is progress for you. The **Sappi Saiccor** pulp and paper plant, at Umkomaas just south of Durban, is the last general industrial user of steam.

The **Libanon** and **Venterspost** gold mines, south-west of Johannesburg, use ancient steeple cab electric locomotives, bought decades ago second-hand from the diamond mine railways of the then South West Africa. Some of the locos have been rebuilt into modern, antiseptic boxes, but a number have kept their original 1902-vintage outline. You will need a car to get there.

The mines are naturally highly security conscious and arrangements must be made in advance through the Kloof Gold Mining Company, the owner of both mines, by calling Goldfields of South Africa's public relations department on 011 639 2092. They will make sure someone is available to give you a tour.

Security

The areas around the mines are not particularly safe. There are large migrant worker populations as well as sporadic outbursts of faction fighting and general labour unrest. If there is a problem, the mine managements are unlikely to let you in. If you do go, take the usual precautions, especially in the surrounding countryside. A number of enthusiasts have been relieved of both gear and cars at gunpoint when stopping in lonely places to photograph trains.

10

Luxury and Special Trains

Steam may have gone from South African metals, along with damask tablecloths in the dining cars, and wood-panelled sleepers may have been replaced with Formica. Well, not totally. These things can still be experienced thanks to the stubborn efforts of a few individuals who are determined not to let the heritage go. It will cost you of course, but then again the woes of South Africa's rand go a long way to easing the pain if you are paying in hard currency.

These are not trains that necessarily go from one point to another either. They are ambling trains, where you can sit in a lounge car with an attentive drinks waiter hovering nearby, enjoying the book in your lap or the awesome smells drifting down from the kitchen car, or simply taking in the view and fantasising about Africa. The people who run these trains are very good at selling dreams.

THE *PRIDE OF AFRICA*

It is hard to beat this train on the luxury and romance scale. Owner-creator Rohan Vos claims it is the most luxurious train in the world and he is probably right. The trains are indeed the dream of entrepreneur Vos who had the idea of buying and fixing up an old railway coach to attach to the back of freight trains when he wanted to take his family away on holiday. The railways were going to charge him a little too much for the privilege, but he realised in his musings that there was a place for a special kind of train. So he bought three unused steam locomotives from Spoornet, refurbished them and began scouring the country's junk yards for suitable carriages which were also restored at some cost.

The idea was to provide the ultimate African railway experience by running luxury steam-hauled trains to uniquely African locations like the bushveld, Victoria Falls, Maputo in Mozambique, and Cape Town. Using steam became a problem as most of the vital servicing facilities have long since been removed by Spoornet – these days Rovos Rail's steam locomotives are used only for departures from Pretoria and shorter charter trains.

There are three train sets in service. The original Edwardian train is a rake of beautifully restored wooden coaches, some with balcony ends, a refurbished dining car and an observation car with a glassed-in end. The Edwardian was the sole set in use until the mid-1990s when the company realised that it would have to get newer coaches, capable of faster speeds and of being converted to air-conditioning, a crucial amenity for the luxury traveller in the sapping heat of a lowveld summer.

The new sets are former main-line steel coaches, gutted and redone completely. Like the original train, the new coaches each have at most three immense wood-panelled bedrooms, each with private bathroom facilities. The attention to detail is almost painful, from writing desks to a well-stocked bar and beds crisply made and turned down at night. The food is superb, backed by an outstanding cellar.

No more than 72 passengers are carried (48 on the Edwardian train) in 32 De Luxe suites and four Royal suites. The only real difference between the two is the size – there are just two Royal suites per coach so the bedrooms are enormous. The fare includes all meals and drinks and excursions off the train to places like the Kimberley diamond museum or to wine farms for tasting, just in case you did not get enough on the train.

After quite a bit of experimenting, the *Pride of Africa* has settled down to serve a few key routes: Pretoria to Cape Town and then up the Garden Route to Knysna and back; Pretoria to Victoria Falls; and Pretoria to Komatipoort, next to the Kruger National Park and some of the best game country in the world. Once a year, the *Pride of Africa* makes an epic journey from Cape Town to Dar es Salaam and back, a 17-day mission as far north as trains can currently go on 3ft 6in track. This little indulgence costs US$7,200–$8,800, depending on type of accommodation, and it is probably worth it. If you want to travel the same route but have less money, there is always the Tazara Railway's *Kilimanjaro Express* at around US$60, first class. In 1998, the *Pride of Africa* ran to Swakopmund in Namibia for the first time, a trip which is scheduled to become a regular fixture.

There is nothing like going to Africa on a train like this, despite the disturbing colonial echoes. The newer trains have large, open balconies on the lounge car where you can sit and watch the country slip past. But even the shorter trips come at a price of course.

Sample fares

Pretoria–Cape Town	De Luxe R4,795	Royal R6,595.
Pretoria–Victoria Falls	De Luxe R5,595	Royal R7,595.

On the Cape route, passengers spend two nights and two days aboard the train so there is plenty of time to over-indulge.

Bookings
Tel: 012 323 6052, or fax 012 323 0843. You can also visit the Rovos website: <http://www.rovos.co.za>, or email <reservations@rovos.co.za>.

THE *BLUE TRAIN*

Everyone has seen the picture, surely? The thin blue line with a bright white roof, rushing past the rich green of the De Doorns vineyards. A legendary name among the world's luxury trains, the *Blue Train* is an institution on South African metals. The railway's own luxury train, its ancestry lies in the *Union Limited* (see below) but the train has been running as the *Blue Train* since the 1940s. The train has just undergone a R70 million refit – President Nelson Mandela rode on its inaugural run to Cape Town in 1997. Remarkably, it was the first time he had travelled long-distance on a train.

In 1972 the old clerestory-roofed stock was replaced by sleek, totally sealed carriages which form the basis of today's trainsets. From its origins the train was designed to be a showcase for South Africa. In the dark days of apartheid, though, it often ran nearly empty, despite being 'fully booked' as far as government propaganda was concerned, and staff morale had plummeted. It was a costly service to run, and the railways have not been known for their willingness to suffer loss-making passenger trains. Hiking fares naturally did not help the train's case either.

The tourist boom of the 1990s and a general resurgence of interest in train travel (in the affluent West, at least), gave Spoornet new hope. The train was pulled apart, new staff recruited and the whole thing was handed over to a dedicated division within the Spoornet company.

In the quest for revenue, the *Blue Train*'s operators have been forced to look further than the traditional Pretoria–Cape Town route. The train now also runs to Victoria Falls and back six times a year. On the Cape route passengers spend one night aboard, and two nights on the Victoria Falls run.

The accommodation is not as lavish as the competition, but it is pampering enough. The food is excellent and varied. The train is air-conditioned throughout, so all doors and windows are sealed, which takes away a lot of the magic of travelling by train in Africa. Fares are quite high and I have heard more than a few locals say, with some accurate cynicism, that South Africans cannot afford to travel like this in their own land.

Sample fares
Cape Town–Pretoria	Luxury R4,500	De Luxe R4,200
Cape Town–Victoria Falls	Luxury R5,400	De Luxe R5,100

Times
The trains (there are two sets in service) run between Pretoria and Cape Town on selected days of the month, departing in each direction on Mondays, Wednesdays and Fridays, arriving the following day. The journey takes about 26 hours.

Bookings
Blue Train Reservations, PO Box 2671, Joubert Park 2044; or tel: 011 773 7631, or fax: 011 773 7643. There is also a website <http://www.bluetrain.co.za>.

THE *UNION LIMITED*

The original *Blue Train*, the *Union Limited* was, and still is, brown. At least that is the way it should be, as any enthusiast with a feeling for detail will tell you. The fact that the *Union Limited*'s operators have painted some of the coaches blue may rankle with purists but the train does look smart.

The *Union Limited* and *Union Express* were the crack mail trains of the 1920s and 1930s, rushing between the gold fields and Cape Town, meeting the mail ships right on the quayside in Cape Town harbour. The coaches had 'brown varnish' wooden bodies, leather interiors and clerestory roofs. They were well-built and many survive, which is key to the train's restoration.

The train's accommodation is comfortable, but it makes no pretence at being a pure luxury train. Rather it is aimed at enthusiasts who want to recapture an era of train travel when you got soot in your eyes and in your food, and nights were spent being rocked to sleep in crisp railway sheets with the sound of an engine working hard drifting back past your windows.

The *Union Limited* is now run by the Transnet Heritage Foundation, a semi-autonomous body within Spoornet which also looks after and operates the company's preserved steam and diesel locomotives, and maintains historic rolling stock. The project is largely the work of a supremely dedicated couple, Ian and Jenny Pretorius, known to all local steam freaks. The *Union Limited* tours are the only real steam safaris currently run. The train, a refurbished rake of 1930s and 1950s stock, is used on regular six-day journeys from Cape Town up to Knysna and back, as well as on longer, specialist trips, aimed at enthusiasts, on which steam power is used during the day and diesels at night.

The six-day *Golden Thread* tours are leisurely. The train ambles around the Western Cape, stopping for barbecues, wine-tasting and to visit ostrich farms. At some places the train is staged overnight. A unique spin on the usual runs are the *Golden Thread* Skycoach tours where you travel partly by train and the rest of the time in restored Douglas DC-3 or DC-4 Skymaster piston-engined airliners belonging to South African Airways' Historic Flight. On some journeys the old airliner will do a low flypast over the train.

The specialist safaris use as much varied steam locomotive power, and on different branch lines, as they can get their hands on.

Once a year, the train travels up to Victoria Falls, a total immersion in railway nostalgia for those who can afford it.

Accommodation is either in four berth compartments (but for two people only) or two-berth coupés (for one). The train also has three deluxe suites 'for elegant travel'.

Fares

Fares are a lot cheaper than the more luxurious alternatives detailed earlier in this chapter but still quite a lot of money.

Golden Thread tours
Vintage First class	R3,000	all in, except for drinks.
De Luxe suites	R12,000	per couple.

Specialist rail safaris
From   R4,000   per person
Rising to   R9,500   for a 13 day tour of Namibia.

Bookings
Phone 021 405 4391, or fax 021 405 4395.

BUSHVELD TRAIN SAFARIS
With the cost of most leisure (as opposed to scheduled) rail travel out of
financial reach for many people, it was only a matter of time before someone
like 'Boon' Boonzaaier, a former teacher, came along with cut-price rail-based
holidays. Boonzaaier hires coaches, locomotives and essential crew from
Spoornet and runs tours to scenic parts of the country. All tours start in
Pretoria and head off to various destinations, including the Escarpment
country near Tzaneen in Mpumulanga, to the Mkhaya Game Reserve in
Swaziland, Port Shepstone on KwaZulu-Natal's South Coast, and
occasionally, to the Garden Route town of Knysna. The tours are a good way
to see the country, especially those parts which other passenger trains do not
reach, and you will meet some interesting people.
    By cutting out extra train crew – there are no dining cars and no bedding
stewards – Boonzaaier is able to keep costs down. Passengers bring their own
bedding, while food is prepared by the local communities and church groups
at pre-arranged wayside sidings and stations. The food will more than likely be
traditional Afrikaner fare like *potjiekos* (stew cooked slowly in a cast-iron pot
over an open fire) and home-baked bread.
    Six different tours are offered, running regularly throughout the year. The
Bushveld Safari (goes from Pretoria to the western edge of the Kruger
National Park), the Graskop Safari, KwaZulu-Natal Safari, Swaziland Safari,
Knysna Safari and the Hantam Safari. The last of these runs three or four
times in late August and early September, taking people up to Namaqualand
from Cape Town to see the annual riot of wild flowers bloom in the desert
after the first rains. The Swaziland Safari goes to Mkhaya Game Reserve in
Swaziland, offering those who cannot afford the staggering prices charged at
some game lodges in South Africa, a crack at seeing some of the 'Big Five',
including the endangered black rhino.
    Accommodation is in standard Spoornet four-berth compartments and
two-berth coupés.

Fares
These are shown per person and vary according to how many people
(indicated in brackets) share a compartment.

Bushveld, Graskop, KwaZulu-Natal Safaris

Compartments	R700 (2)	R650 (3)	R550 (4)
Coupés	R700 (1)	R650 (2)	

The *Knysna Safari* costs R2,400 per person.

Bookings
Tel/fax: 014 736 3025, or 082 920 7576 (mobile).

SHAMWARI RAIL SAFARIS
One of the first special train operators was African Rail Safaris who attach two dedicated, clients-only, coaches to the back of the *Algoa* passenger train between Johannesburg and Port Elizabeth. Guests are met at the station and taken to the 14,000-hectare (35,000-acre) reserve which has lion, elephant, buffalo, rhino, giraffe, hippo and at least 18 species of antelope.

Accommodation in the reserve is luxurious, and fairly pricey, starting at R1,250 per person per day sharing.

The African Rail Safari **prices** are R950 per adult, R475 per child, both one-way and irrespective of where you get on or off the train. The price includes afternoon tea, dinner, bed and breakfast. The coaches are scheduled on the Thursday *Algoa* from Johannesburg and the Friday *Algoa* from Port Elizabeth.

Bookings
African Rail Safaris, tel: 011 773 8920, or 011 774 2082.
Shamwari Game Reserve, tel: 042 203 1111.

THE *SHONGOLOLO*
South Africa's *Shongololo* is a different rail travel concept, a kind of rail-drive cruise. The *Shongololo* (named after a common millipede) ambles around the country, dragging a few minibuses in specially adapted wagons. Passengers spend the days touring in the minibuses and overnight on the moving train. You can cover a hell of a lot of country this way!

Various tours are offered. Call 011 453 3821 for **information** and bookings.

Zimbabwe:
Background Information

11

FACTS AND FIGURES
Location

Zimbabwe is situated on the southern end of the great African plateau, and is bordered by South Africa, Botswana, Zambia and Mozambique. The nearest coast is 500km (310 miles) away to the west. The upland centre is cut by rivers which flow into Lake Kariba, a gigantic man-made inland sea to the north, and the Zambezi River which marks the country's northern border. Rudyard Kipling's famous 'great grey-green, greasy Limpopo River' is the southern border with South Africa. The country's most phenomenal natural attraction, the Victoria Falls, are in the north-west corner on the Zambezi River.

Size

Zimbabwe covers an area of 390,580km^2 (150,800 square miles).

Geography

Zimbabwe is basically a plateau on top of a larger plateau, framed by mighty rivers to the north and south and flanked to the east by a ridge of mountains which lie along its border with Mozambique. Much of the country is 600m (1,960ft) above sea level while its highveld region, a 650-km (400-mile) long plateau lies at 1,500m (4,900ft). The larger proportion of the country's agriculture – maize, tobacco, cattle ranching and dairy farming – and most of the heavy engineering and industry takes place on the highveld. The lowveld spreads away from the central plateau, gradually becoming bush country and rolling into the enfolding arms of the river valleys. After plunging over Victoria Falls and squeezing through the Batoka Gorge, the Zambezi River widens out into the largely man-made 282-km (174-mile) long Lake Kariba, the creation of which by the Kariba Dam generates 40% of the country's electricity through hydroelectric power.

The Eastern Highlands form the border with Mozambique and incorporate the Nyanga, Bvumba and Chimanimani national parks. The area is cut with trout streams, forests, coffee and tea plantations, creating a bizarre mix of the Scottish Highlands and Indian hill country.

The whole country is dotted with rock outcrops and piles of boulders which hide thousands of Bushmen paintings; the boulders and rock outcrops (known as Gommos) are the prevalent feature of the landscape west of Bulawayo.

Capital

Harare is Zimbabwe's pleasant, high-lying capital city. The city was called Salisbury until independence in 1980.

Population

The population of Zimbabwe is around 13 million. There are relatively few large towns and the ratio of urban to rural dwellers is low. There are two main ethnic groups: the Ndebele (or Matabele) and the Shona, also known as the Mashona. The Matabele, outnumbered four to one by the Mashona, traditionally live in the south-west part of the country. There has been – and probably always will be – significant tension between the two.

Government

The Mashona are the ruling class in the state. About 80% of MPs are elected and serve five-year terms. Every six years parliament elects a president, who is both head of government and head of state and is eligible for re-election. Robert Mugabe has remained president since independence in 1980, despite widespread and apparently growing unhappiness with his leadership style.

The leading party ZANU-PF is a coalition, formed at independence, between Mugabe's Zimbabwe African National Union and Joshua Nkomo's Zimbabwe African Patriotic Front. The coalition split for a time in the 1980s when ZANU became more powerful. PF members returned to the bush to fight until 1987 when a unity agreement was signed with Nkomo, who had fled to safety in Britain.

With the major opposition force brought on-side, Mugabe tried to make the country formally into a one-party socialist state but this move failed. Other opposition parties have since emerged but repression continues and, until quite recently, most people were afraid to speak out against the government.

Major towns

Harare, the capital, is by far the largest town in the country with a population of around 2.5 million people. Bulawayo and Mutare are Zimbabwe's second and third cities respectively. After that, towns are mostly tiny.

Economy

After South Africa Zimbabwe has the most diversified economy in southern Africa, based on a modern infrastructure. Mining and agriculture are the leading activities, but there are also relatively strong light industrial and engineering sectors. Mineral resources include gold, coal, asbestos, nickel, copper, silver and titanium. The country is also famous for its emeralds.

Per capita GNP is estimated at US$509. There is still a great imbalance in the distribution of wealth between white and black.

The economy took a severe beating from a prolonged drought in the late 1980s, which only broke in 1993. There are also large balance of payments and budget deficits, aggravated by certain government policies. After independence the government wanted to even out the inequalities between black and white incomes, but changed course in 1991 when it realised it would have to encourage economic growth first. A bitter structural adjustment programme followed, moving the economy towards a more market-oriented system. As in many similar situations, the bitterness came with the resultant job losses and higher inflation and cuts in welfare spending.

At the end of 1997, the Zimbabwe dollar slumped heavily on world money markets, great for tourists but causing further hardship to the already stretched locals. Riots broke out early in 1998 when the government slapped further taxes on food staples such as maize flour – the key ingredient in just about every main meal for the poor – and people took to the streets in Harare to protest at the government's mismanagement of the economy. Unemployment is currently around 35%. Mugabe's presidency is embattled but he is holding on for now.

Languages
The three official languages are Shona, mother-tongue to about 70% of Zimbabweans, Ndebele and English. Ndebele, which derives from Zulu, one of the most widely spoken languages in South Africa, is first language of the Matabele people and is most widely spoken in Bulawayo and in Matabeleland in the country's south-west. In practice English is the language of government and everyday communication, making Zimbabwe very simple for readers of this book to get around in and be understood. Most people in the towns speak English fairly fluently, although you may have a problem being understood in the more remote rural areas.

Currency
The unit of currency is the Zimbabwe dollar, which is divided into 100 cents. Zimbabwe's dollar has not held its value terribly well in recent months so travelling on hard currency is quite pleasing. The rate of exchange in mid-1998 was roughly £1 = Z$30 and US$1 = Z$18. The South African rand is quite strong here by comparison with its value against other currencies, but dollar or sterling travellers' cheques are the best way to carry money.

Banks and foreign exchange
Travellers' cheques and foreign currency notes of all major currencies can be exchanged at any commercial bank or foreign exchange bureau, and most of the better hotels have exchange facilities for guests, although staff will often refuse to serve non-residents. New rates are posted daily. Banking hours are 08.00–15.00 on Mondays, Tuesdays, Thursdays and Fridays. Banks close at 13.00 on Wednesdays and 11.30 on Saturdays. Harare's Airport Bank is open outside normal banking hours, usually to coincide with international arrivals.The main banks are Barclays, Standard Chartered and Zimbank with branches in most of the larger towns.

With the currency fluctuating as it does, you may want to shop around for the best rate. Major railway stations all have exchange bureaux and I have found that these generally give much better rates than those in the towns.

Credit cards

You can avoid the general 15% sales tax levied on most goods and services if you pay by credit card since the tax does not apply to transactions settled in foreign currency. Visa and Mastercard are the standards, Diners Club and American Express almost unheard of in many places. Keep a cash stash for those no-credit card days.

Budgeting

Travellers have scored well since the Zimbabwe dollar began plunging in 1997 and, although the country is more expensive than it used to be, most things are still a bargain, with the possible exception of hotel rooms – especially in Victoria Falls.

There are basically two economies in Zimbabwe. The first exists for travellers carrying hard currency, the other is based on the Zimbabwean dollar. This means that tourists are charged a much higher rate, usually payable in US dollars or sterling, for things like hotel rooms, plane tickets and safaris. Hotels and game lodges are supposed to charge customers in hard currency to help the government build up its forex reserves. Not all places do, though, and certainly if you are a low budget traveller, the dual economy is unlikely to affect you.

Staying in backpackers' lodges, cooking for yourself and using local transport could keep living costs to around US$20 per day. At the other extreme, if you want to stay in the admittedly magnificent Victoria Falls Hotel, a single room is around US$300 per night. Train tickets, eating out and accommodation are generally excellent value and visiting game parks like Hwange is incredible value for what you get.

Climate

Zimbabwe has one of the best climates on the planet, its altitude making it relatively temperate for a country in the tropics. Summer really starts in November with the arrival of the rainy season when it gets genuinely hot in the lowveld and the cities in the afternoons. The build-up to afternoon thunderstorms in the early summer is often intense and the relief when they break is tremendous. The winter months from May to August are dry and sunny, but it often gets very cold at night.

Average summer temperatures range from 20°C to 25°C (68°F–77°F) on the plateau and 35°C (95°F) and higher in the lowveld and Zambezi valley, where the heat can be bludgeoning. Always use plenty of high-factor sun-cream, wear a wide-brimmed hat and drink lots of water.

Peak holiday periods are normally December–January and at Easter. Trains, buses, hotels and game parks get very full at these periods. Visiting South Africans, who take their holidays at the same time, add to the pressure.

HISTORY

The people known as the San – nomadic hunters – were the first to roam Zimbabwe and are now immortalised in their rock paintings which decorate an estimated 30,000 sites. The paintings depict hunting and daily life as well as more spiritual matters, reflecting a people who lived in total harmony with the animals and plants.

Zimbabwe has good land and it was a natural step for some of the San to settle and begin keeping livestock and growing crops. By about AD 300 the ancestors of the Shona had begun slowly drifting into the region also. They were cattle herders and farmers and controlled a trade system based on gold and ivory. They established a series of powerful regional dynasties, the southern axis of Africa's Sudanic civilisations.

A large stone-walled town now known as Great Zimbabwe was built around Masvingo in the south of the country near the end of the 11th century AD. It marked a radical change from villages of mud huts as the stone walls went up on the hill. Great Zimbabwe remained a centre of power, trading with the Swahili people on the east coast, until about 1450 when its influence began to decline, probably because too many cattle and too much farming exhausted the lands nearby.

The Mutapa state stepped into the resulting power vacuum and would last until the 20th century. The Mwene-Mutapa were the first people to encounter Europeans, after the Portuguese arrived on the east coast, and initially maintained friendly trading relations with them. The Portuguese, however, had heard the legend of fabulous gold in the interior and gradually moved inland, setting up trading posts and introducing crops from the New World, such as oranges and maize, now the staple food of southern Africa. Trade in slaves and land was brisk until 1663 when the ruling king was assassinated and the new ruler ended Portugal's dominance.

Meanwhile, another nation, the Torwa, was rising in the south-west. The Torwa also had well-developed building skills and were responsible for many of the fine stone ruins in the area around Bulawayo. The Torwa were wealthy and their ruling classes wore fine cotton clothes, and copper and gold jewellery, bought with taxes levied on the farmers and traders. A drop in gold exports marked their end and their power crumbled, helped by the warlike Rozvi, an offshoot of the Shona, who invaded from the north.

The Rozvi were immensely powerful, ruling with the help of an efficient army which was able to plunder whatever the dynasty did not get in trade. The Rozvi hammered the Mutapa as well and were only unseated when invaded by the Nguni people, who were fleeing the terrors of the expanding Zulu kingdom in the south. Two Nguni leaders fled north: Mzilikazi and his Khumalo clan (later to become the Ndebele), and Shoshangane who invaded and subjugated the Ndau people in southern Mozambique, and formed the Gaza state. The Gaza state ruled by fear but crumbled because of internal power struggles, finally being conquered by the Portuguese in 1895. The Shangaan language is one of the only reminders of the Gazas.

Mzilikazi fared better. Having survived the terrors of Shaka's *mfecane* or 'forced migration', Mzilikazi was driven out of his first sanctuary in the Magaliesburg mountains by the Boer Voortrekkers, and moved farther north to set up his capital at Bulawayo in the 1840s. The Ndebele enjoyed a brief period of prosperity, herding cattle but never quite managing to conquer the Shona.

The coming of the Empire

In 1870 ivory hunter Frederick Courtney Selous – a name embedded in the history of this land – wandered into Zimbabwe, looking for gold. He was not the first European here. Apart from the Portuguese, a Scottish missionary named Robert Moffat arrived in 1854, followed shortly afterwards by his son-in-law Dr David Livingstone, the first white man to look into the chasm at Victoria Falls. However, Selous found primitive gold mines in the north-east and stories of abundant gold wealth in the area soon filtered back to South Africa and Britain. In fact there was never much gold in Zimbabwe (although there are still a few productive mines today), but by the time this was discovered, another outpost of the British Empire was well established.

Cecil Rhodes

Once described as 'a Colossus', Rhodes' incredible ambition built a nation and shaped the history of several more. Rhodes had made a fortune in the Kimberley diamond fields, quickly assuming control of the bulk of the workings, but he largely missed out on the gold rush to the Witwatersrand in South Africa. His dream was to create a British sphere of influence from the Cape to Cairo, in which a railway line would be the golden thread binding all together.

A highly skilled political operator, Rhodes managed to get the British government into the Bechuanaland Protectorate (Botswana) and then arranged a Royal Charter for his British South Africa Company (BSAC) to govern the country north of it. In 1890 he sent a column of policemen and settlers into the Shona territories north and east of Matabeleland and settled them on the hill where Harare stands today.

The gold strike the settlers were hoping for never happened and they turned to farming instead, occupying more and more land for their cattle and crops. The Ndebele king, Lobengula, was keen to co-operate and Rhodes, initially, did not want to tangle with this powerful nation. Lobengula kept his regiments on a short leash, knowing that his kingdom was no match for the settlers' superior firepower. Rhodes presented Lobengula with a treaty which prevented him from making any agreements with anyone but the British. Lobengula refused to sign, but the Portuguese and Germans who also coveted the region did not know that. The king was then compelled to agree to the Rudd Concession which allowed miners into Matabeleland. The British invasion had begun.

In 1893 Lobengula sent a raiding party down to Masvingo to deal with some Shona who had cut the telegraph wire. The local BSAC commander, Leander Starr Jameson – who later wrecked his master's political career by his Jameson Raid in the Transvaal – used the incident as an excuse to invade Matabeleland, supported by a British infantry battalion. Lobengula tried desperately to avoid war. He sent peace emissaries to Cape Town, but they were intercepted and killed. The invasion was brief. Lobengula's regiments were machine-gunned and Bulawayo razed. The king fled into the wilderness where he died a year later.

By 1895 the country was known as Rhodesia, with its capital at Salisbury. The Shona and Ndebele initially resisted, rising up against the settlers in the First *Chimurenga* (war of liberation) but were quickly put down.

However, the BSAC was disappointed that the promised mineral riches never materialised, and by the 1920s, the company wanted to be rid of Rhodesia. A referendum offering the whites a new constitution was held in 1923 and the self-governing state of Southern Rhodesia was created. (Zambia was then known as Northern Rhodesia.)

Following the 1930 Land Apportionment Act, which effectively set half the country aside for whites including most of the fertile land, the Shona and Ndebele were gradually dispossessed. Their communal lifestyle disintegrated as they were compelled to join the white-run labour market, working in the mines and the growing industrial sector. In 1951 the government passed the Land Husbandry Act, further eroding black farmland in favour of white ownership. The evicted farmers were banished to reserves where they were settled on small-holdings and allowed to keep no more than six head of cattle apiece.

In 1957 Joshua Nkomo formed the Southern Rhodesian African National Congress, on the back of growing resentment among blacks. In 1963 the movement split into the Zimbabwe African National Union (ZANU) and the Zimbabwe African People's Union (ZAPU). By this time, white Rhodesians, led by Ian Smith, were clamouring for full independence from Britain, but Britain would not grant independence unless certain conditions, mainly concerning the absent rights of black people, were met. On November 11 1965 Smith unilaterally declared independence. The United Nations immediately imposed sanctions, while ZANU and ZAPU took to the bush to start the long and vicious fight for freedom. The first battle took place in April 1966 at the little town of Chinhoyi, 115km (71 miles) north of Harare, where ZANU guerrillas were cornered by security forces and killed in a seven-hour running battle. (The well-known Zimbabwean band the Bhundu Boys had a hit song about this incident on their album 'Pamberi'.)

For a while the Rhodesian Army had the upper hand. The army was well-trained and well-equipped, supported by aircraft and helicopters. The guerrillas kept up a violent terror campaign against farms, mission stations and vehicles on lonely roads. But when ZANU's military commander, Josiah Tongogara, returned from military training in China, he brought with him a battle plan of Maoist strategies, mobilising support from the people, developing a network of intelligence gatherers and food providers in the villages. The rural people were caught in the middle, harassed by security forces during the day, and guerrillas at night. To counter the guerrillas' growing support net, the government forced over a million black farmers into Protected Villages.

By 1975 the guerrillas were operating from bases in Mozambique which had gained independence from Portugal the same year and whose government was sympathetic to the liberation struggle. The Rhodesian Army launched attacks on guerrilla bases in Mozambique but, by 1978, half the country was controlled by the guerrillas and white Rhodesians were living under siege conditions. Smith eventually relented and agreed to attend the Lancaster House talks in London in 1979. Earlier peace negotiations, such as the South African- and Zambian-brokered talks in a railway carriage on Victoria Falls bridge in 1976, had all broken down, mainly over the issue of majority rule. Smith's attempt to ward off the inevitable by bringing moderate black politicians, such as Bishop Abel Muzorewa, into a coalition government also failed.

Now, in London, the future was unstoppable. An agreement was signed on December 21 1979, and free elections followed in February 1980. ZANU took 57 of the 80 seats (20 seats were reserved for whites at that time) and Robert Mugabe became president, a post he has held ever since.

Post independence

With most of the country's leaders now Marxist, the new government tried to implement a command economy, nationalising heavy industries and buying up businesses. Government soon employed 25% of the work-force. The change was rapid and wrecked the economy. Red tape and inefficiency choked the country. Whites who had not fled before independence began drifting away, many seeking refuge in what was still white-ruled South Africa.

Meanwhile in Matabeleland, still a ZAPU stronghold, dissidents began returning to the bush, saying that the war was not over. An arms cache was found on Nkomo's farm and he was expelled from the cabinet. Attacks on farmers began mounting and Mugabe acted swiftly, sending the brutal, Korean-trained Fifth Brigade to quell the disturbance. It was a secret campaign of genocide, with an estimated 20,000 people murdered over a few years. In 1987 the two parties merged again, Nkomo was reinstated and, by 1988, the rebellion was over.

The government held on to its original economic policies for as long as it could but, by the late 1980s, the economy was in disarray, with strikes called by the powerful trade unions making the situation worse. An election was held in 1990 but the only credible opposition, Edgar Tekere's Zimbabwe Unity Movement, won only two seats. However, half the registered voters failed to turn up at the polls, reflecting the deep satisfaction in the country at large.

The issues are still not resolved, despite (and in some respects because of) intervention from the IMF. The economy has been liberalised under a five-year structural adjustment programme, but this has still to deliver the promised jobs and economic stability.

One of the biggest issues is the land question. Under the terms of the Lancaster House agreement, the government was to be given funds from outside to buy land from white farmers and resettle thousands of families. By 1997 the process was far from complete. In November that year, Mugabe, responding to growing discontent, announced the wholesale seizure of 1,400 farms, including some coffee and tobacco plantations. There was a vehement protest from white farmers and the international community, forcing Mugabe to recant. At the time of writing, the matter is still not settled.

PRACTICAL INFORMATION
Embassies
All foreign embassies and consulates are in Harare.

Australia Karigamombe Centre, 4th Floor, 53 Samora Machel Av; tel: 4 75774-7.
Canada 45 Baines Av; tel: 4 733881.
France Ranelagh Rd, Highlands; tel: 4 498096.
Germany 14 Samora Machel Av; tel: 4 731955-8.
Malawi Malawi House, 42 Harare St; tel: 4 705611.
Mozambique 152 Herbert Chitepo Av; tel: 4 790837.
Namibia 31A Lincoln Rd, Avondale; tel: 4 47930.
New Zealand Batanai Gardens, 57 Jason Moyo Av, Harare; tel: 4 728681.
South Africa High Commission Baker Av/Angwa St; tel: 4 753147-9, or fax: 4 757908.
Tanzania 23 Baines Av; tel: 4 721870.
UK Corner House, 7th Floor, Leopold Takawira Av; tel: 4 793781.
USA 172 Herbert Chitepo Av; tel: 4 794521.
Zambia Zambia House, Union Av; tel: 4 790851.

Zimbabwean high commissions abroad
Zimbabwe has 36 high commissions around the world including in the UK, USA, Australia, Germany, France, South Africa, Italy, Japan, India and Kenya.

Tourist offices overseas
South Africa Upper Shopping Level, Carlton Centre, Johannesburg; tel: 011 331 3137.
UK 429 The Strand, London WC2; tel: 0171 836 7755; or fax: 0171 379 1167.
USA Rockefeller Centre, Suite 1905, 1270 Av of the Americas, New York, NY 10020; tel: 212 332 1090; or fax: 212 332 1093.

GETTING THERE
By air
At least 30 airlines fly to Zimbabwe, either to Harare, or to the ever-popular Victoria Falls, which is served by direct charter flights from the UK. If you are coming from the UK, shop around for a good deal as there are many to be had. If you are in London pick up a copy of *TNT*, the Australasian free weekly, at just about any tube station, and hunt through the travel section for the best fare.

The Europe–Zimbabwe/South Africa route has become highly competitive in recent years as more and more carriers begin tapping into the southern African tourist boom. Tickets from London to Harare start as low as £450 return. British Airways flies three times a week from Gatwick to Harare, Air Zimbabwe four times a week. The official return fare is £960 in high season, £750 in low season, although there are usually substantial discounts on these. Lufthansa, Air France, and KLM each have two flights a week from Frankfurt, Paris and Amsterdam respectively, and Air Portugal flies once a week from Lisbon. Tickets on these carriers usually cost around £500.

There are no direct flights from North America to Zimbabwe – the best bet is to fly to South Africa from either New York or Miami and catch a connecting flight. Or better still, make the connection by train. The round trip Apex fare costs about US$1,334 in low season, US$1,596 in high season from either city to Johannesburg. If you are coming from Canada, you will have to fly to London to make a direct connection, or to New York or Miami for the SAA flights.

From Australia, only Qantas – A$2,630 high season round trip, A$1910 low, three times a week – and Malaysian Airlines, twice a week, offer direct flights. Gulf Air flies three times a week from the Gulf States, while EgyptAir flies three times a week from Sydney to Harare, via Singapore and Cairo. From New Zealand, South African Airways and Air New Zealand fly direct to Johannesburg, NZ$2,900 in high season, NZ$2,660 in low season, or go to Australia to connect with Qantas or Air Malaysia.

Overland
From Botswana
There are four border crossings from Botswana, but most travellers come through Kazungula (where Botswana, Namibia, Zimbabwe and Zambia meet), Kasane west of Victoria Falls, or at Plumtree in the south-west. Mpandamatenga border post is far off the beaten track. If you are on the train – either the daily *Botswana Blue* (see page 240) or the weekly *Bulawayo* train from Johannesburg (page 84), customs and immigration formalities are handled on the train. Delays because of over-zealous officialdom are frequent.

From Mozambique
There are three border crossings on this frontier, too, although that at Mavue in the south-east is infrequently used because of a complete absence of public transport. Nyamapanda is the border point for travellers coming from Malawi or Tete city in Mozambique, while people coming from Beira will cross at Mutare in the Eastern Highlands. The train from Beira does not actually cross the border; rather passengers have to detrain and continue on foot to the border post.

From Namibia
The crossing point is at Kazungula. Note that there is scant transport to or from this location. There are, however, weekly minibus services between Windhoek and Victoria Falls. (See Victoria Falls, pages 189–93)

From South Africa

Beitbridge on the Limpopo River is the only crossing point. Despite the amount of traffic going through, it is not open 24 hours a day and a late arrival here is to be discouraged. Few frontier towns are nice, but the area on either side of the border here is particularly insalubrious.

There are no longer any through trains from either Bulawayo or Harare via this border point. The weekly *Bulawayo* train between Bulawayo and Pretoria now goes via Gabarone in Botswana (see page 84). However, the daily *Doily* train (page 80) between Johannesburg and Zimbabwe actually crosses the river and turns around at Beitbridge station itself. This is a convenient option if you have arrived at Beitbridge by bus from somewhere else in Zimbabwe, or if you are heading north. Zimbabwe customs are cleared at the station, while South African officials board the train on the other side. This means you do not have to schlep on foot through the road-users' customs and immigration point, very welcome if you happen to be travelling with a large wooden giraffe.

There is plenty of transport to and from Beitbridge railway station – just make sure the bus/taxi driver understands what you want. Note that the station is about 5km (3 miles) from the Beitbridge town itself.

Another train option with which to reach this crossing is the daily *Bosvelder* train (see page 80) between Johannesburg and Messina, the frontier-boom town 30km (18 miles) south of the border. The *Bosvelder* arrives from the south at 10.16 and leaves again for Pretoria at 13.45. There are plenty of minibus taxis running between the Messina railway station parking lot and the border post – pay no more than R10 and be selective about who drives and which taxi you go in. Remember, if the tyres are bald, it is a warning you should heed.

From Zambia

The main crossing point is at Victoria Falls, by way of the gorgeous iron Victoria Falls bridge. There is supposed to be a daily shuttle train between Livingstone in Zambia and Victoria Falls, but this depends on whether Zambia Railways can spare a locomotive to run the service at the required time. The alternative is to take a relatively cheap taxi ride each way. Note that the two immigration posts are about 1.5km (1 mile) apart, separated by the Batoka Gorge, so when you arrive at the first post, the taxi driver will normally wait while you clear immigration before driving you over the bridge to the opposing post. It costs around Z$20 for a taxi from Victoria Falls town to the border.

There is also a road crossing at Chirundu, on the Zambezi River below Lake Kariba. This bridge is one of only three bridges over the Zambezi between Kariba and the sea capable of carrying the weight of a vehicle – the other two are in Mozambique.

Red tape
Visas
Visas are not required for citizens of the USA and most EU or British Commonwealth nations, with the bizarre exception of South Africa. Citizens of about 40 other countries do need visas, including citizens of Israel, Portugal, Greece, India and all countries in Eastern Europe. South Africans can get their visas free at the point of entry; nationals of other countries must get their visas from a Zimbabwean High Commission before travelling to Zimbabwe. Over-the-counter visa applications take 7–14 days to process. All visas are single-entry and valid for three months. Multiple-entry visas, valid for six months, are available only in Harare.

Entry requirements
Officially you will have to have a return ticket and proof of sufficient funds before you will be let into the country. Although the rule seems to be ignored, it is best to be prepared – you may meet the new immigration official eager to make his mark by throwing the book at you. A yellow fever inoculation is required if you have come from an infected area. Your passport must also be valid for at least six months from the date of entry.

Immigration and customs
If crossing independently into or out of the country, be aware that none of the border posts is open 24 hours a day. Beitbridge – the only crossing point into South Africa – is open between 05.30 and 22.30, Victoria Falls is open 06.00–20.00, while the remaining posts are open 06.00–18.00. You may not import or export more than Z$500 per person – remember this when they ask you at customs. All foreigners pay a US$20 departure tax if leaving on an international flight. If you want to work in Zimbabwe, you will need permission from the Chief Immigration Officer.

Bribery
Corruption is endemic in Africa and everyone here seems to have a favourite story of greed. That said, I have never once been encouraged to bribe anyone, anywhere. At a time when ordinary people are all too well aware of the excesses of their government, resorting to bribery might be taken as a deep insult. Bribing a policeman could generate the kind of travel experience one would rather not have.

Bureaucracy
A somewhat bloated civil service means that things can happen exceedingly slowly in government departments. There is not much you can do about it except smile and be accepting – throwing a tantrum in public is considered bad form and will not get you half as far as an ingratiating smile. On the other hand, you may find no bureaucracy at all where you would expect there to be plenty. To get a photographic permit to ride on one of Bulawayo's last working steam locomotives in daily revenue service took no more than a trip up to the

17th floor of railway headquarters and the signing of one form – total elapsed time, 15 minutes.

Safety

Zimbabwe is generally a safe country. There is street crime directed against tourists, but it tends to be exceptional rather than rampant. There is a visible and pretty efficient police force, and most people have a healthy respect for authority here. The basic rules of travel apply. There are places in all the towns which are unsafe for tourists, and you should not venture into any of the townships except in a group and with someone you can trust who can show you around and deal with any unwelcome attention.

Unsafe places in Harare include some of the nightclubs and hotel bars. Some hotels are nothing but brothels and the clientele will be fairly rough – women on their own should stay away from any bar/club where there are few female customers. Even a woman with a male companion may be pestered in some of the bars in Harare. In Bulawayo, the more remote parts of the Centenary and Central parks are unsafe, even during the day.

Women travelling alone are likely to get a fair amount of attention, although much of it will be genuine, harmless curiosity, or pity that you are not married and do not have family to travel with. Police travel on most trains and the conductors and train crew will go out of their way to make sure you are OK. While there are no taboos against women travelling alone, this is a chauvinist country, despite the considerable contribution women made during the freedom struggle. You will at times get unwelcome attention even in public but Zimbabweans as a rule do not tolerate harassment of anyone. Use common sense – do not hitchhike alone and never wander into obviously unsafe places such as working men's beer halls, which you will hear long before you see.

The usual con artists and pickpockets one finds all over the world hang out at all train and bus stations; police and fellow passengers will be voluble in their warnings. If it is dark when you arrive, heed the warnings and spend money on a cab.

Changing money on the street is probably one of the biggest sources of trouble. For starters, it is illegal and many of the changers are either plain-clothes policemen or moonlighting police informers. The rest will very quickly and efficiently rob you and there is no legal remedy. Challenging them can result in nasty incidents as we found out in Victoria Falls, which probably has the highest concentration of money changers per foot of pavement of anywhere in southern Africa.

Tourist information

There are tourist information bureaux in all the bigger centres but their usefulness tends to vary from place to place and day to day. Some are friendly and helpful, others patently not so.

Bulawayo Opposite the City Hall which fills the entire block between Leopold Takawira and 8th Av; tel: 9 60867; or fax: 9 60868.

Harare Unity Square, Second St/Jason Moyo Av; tel: 4 705085/7.
Mutare Robert Mugabe/Herbert Chitepo; tel: 20 64711.
Victoria Falls Parkway/Livingstone Way; tel: 13 4202.

When to visit

There is never really a bad time to visit Zimbabwe, but winter from May–September offers the best combination of game viewing and pleasant daytime temperatures. Animals tend to concentrate around the water holes in winter, but disperse after the summer rains and hide in the thick bush. The incidence of malaria is also significantly lower in winter. The winters are dry and warm although nights in the bushveld and the Highlands can be bitterly cold. Summers in the lowveld are very hot with temperatures often well over 35°C (95°F) during the day and it can get up to 40°C (104°F) or more in the Zambezi Valley. The rainy season begins in November and lasts until January. At this time the Victoria Falls is dry over about two-thirds of its width. By April, however, the Zambezi will have been swollen by the summer rainfall in Angola and western Zambia and the Falls will be the mass of spray and thunder that most tourists prefer to see.

Public holidays

Apparently emulating its southern neighbour, Zimbabwe is overrun with public holidays. The 13 days off include Christmas Day and Boxing Day (December 25, 26), New Year's Day, Good Friday and Easter Monday, Independence Day (April 18), Workers' Day (May 1 or 2), Africa Day (May 25), and Heroes Defence Forces Day (August 11/12). Schools run a three-term calendar with month-long holidays over Easter, Christmas and August–September.

What to take

The advice given under Practical Information for South Africa in Chapter 3 (page 29) applies equally to Zimbabwe. In short, travel light, wear cotton and bring something reasonably presentable to wear to government offices when you need that visa extension or in case someone asks you out to dinner. If you do not have it, you will need it.

Like South Africa, the country is largely westernised as far as clothing goes. Adult men will often be giggled at for wearing shorts – the overall tone is one of fairly tidy dressing. Travellers in six-week-old T-shirts are not welcomed with open arms. There seems to be a streak of conservatism running, like the north–south mountain range through eastern and southern Africa, and grungy, crusty types are generally regarded with distaste.

Odds and ends

Although much is imported from the south, you can find more or less anything you are likely to need quite cheaply in Zimbabwe. All the larger towns have supermarkets and pharmacies and prices for things like insect repellent are fairly low. If you need specialised camping gear, it is best to get this either in South Africa (if you are coming from there) or before you leave home.

GETTING AROUND

Zimbabwe is so simple to get to and travel around. Few people can afford cars so the government has made sure the public transport is good. You have the coolest trains and buses to pick from and the general lack of traffic means the roads are in pretty good nick.

As described in the following chapters, trains will get you to, or at least relatively near, most of Zimbabwe's attractions. Use them – they are clean, safer than road transport, cheap and efficient, a free room for the night or a magic carpet depending on your sensibilities. Go by train if you can. However, there will be times when you are forced to go by bus or plane.

By bus

Internal bus services vary from the truly sublime to the classic overloaded nightmare with bald tyres. There are two kinds of service: luxury, long-distance coaches, connecting the main cities, and the ubiquitous, smoky local buses which go everywhere else. Bulawayo to Harare by fast coach costs around Z$280.

The local buses are loads more fun and a whole lot cheaper. You will meet the smiling face of Zimbabwe this way, and windows that open mean you will see, hear, taste and smell more of the country. Not all of them are slow either – our trip from Bulawayo to Beitbridge was done at high speed in a bus belonging to the groovily named Shu-Shine Bus Services (a legendary name in Zimbabwe bus travel) which rattled, shook and roared its way to the border in just over four hours, and cost a bargain Z$60, less than US$5. Do yourself a favour, though – check the bus itself before you hand over any cash, and if the driver has the aura of a frustrated cowboy, find another bus.

By taxi

There are two kinds of taxi: normal passenger cars and minibuses. The former are confined to the towns and are reasonably cheap. Agree on the fare before you get in. Taxis do not normally cruise around but are hailed at dedicated taxi ranks outside stations, airports and hotels.

Minibus taxis offer a faster (but often more dangerous alternative) to the buses over long distance. Like the buses, quality of services varies enormously. Some taxis are in superb condition, are well-driven and no overloading is allowed; many others are the stuff of travellers' nightmares. Be sensible about this – if the vehicle, driver or loading looks dodgy, move swiftly along.

By car

An easy option, and necessary if you want to do extensive self-guided touring of game parks like Hwange. Cars can be rented in all the major towns but are quite expensive. Budget on spending about US$60 a day for a hire car.

The country's road system is extensive and under-trafficked, and fuel is reasonably cheap.

Most major attractions, including Hwange, the Matopos Range, Victoria Falls and the Eastern Highlands, are accessible on good tar roads, but you will need a 4x4 if you are heading for Matusadona, Mana Pools, Chizarira and Gonarezhou. You will need an international driver's licence and may need to take out Zimbabwean third party insurance. Check with one of the motoring organisations at home before you go. Zimbabwe drives on the left.

Zimbabwe has some of the loveliest roads on the continent – well-kept, empty and traversing beautiful scenery. Most Zimbabweans cannot afford their own cars which means traffic is minimal, saving on road repairs and making long journeys to those places trains do not reach a satisfying experience. The downside of all this is that humans and domestic animals spill out onto the road instead – be sharp, especially at night. In bushveld areas, watch out for wild animals on the road – they get transfixed by the headlights and often fail to move out of your way.

By bike

This is some of the best cycling country in the world, on tarred but relatively empty roads and under clear skies 80% of the year. Combining a bike trip with train travel will basically open up the whole of Zimbabwe to the independent traveller, bar the game parks. Bicycles are common transport here although they tend to be the big, heavy solid kind with no gears, thick tyres and pedal-operated, back-wheel brakes.

The people will welcome you with joy, especially out in the rural districts. There is great mountain biking in the Eastern Highlands especially in the Bvumba district (see pages 204–05). Biking will put you out in the countryside, and moving at the same somnambulent pace as the country you really will meet Zimbabwe this way. With some judicious planning, you will be able to catch night trains elsewhere when it is time to move on farther.

Bring specialist spares with you if your bike is fairly high-tech as only basic items – tubes, chains, pedals – are readily available. Also remember that distances here are vast and you will spend a lot of time in apparently deserted countryside. The heat can be punishing, so take along plenty of water with you and rest up in the heat of the day.

A word of warning; keep a good look out for bad driving, especially on the part of hectically overloaded buses. 'Might is right' is the founding principle of road law in Africa and sensible cyclists stay out of the way.

Bicycle hire

Bikes can be hired in some places. In Harare try Bush Trackers at the Bronte Hotel (tel: 4 303025), and at Victoria Falls there is a large bike hire service next to the tourism office on the main street where you can rent a bike for around Z$70 a day. If you want to be assured of getting a problem-free machine, bring your own (see Chapter 1 for advice on this).

By air

Air Zimbabwe Express pretty much has a monopoly on domestic flights, but it is a good service and the airline has high operational standards, using Boeing 737 and Fokker 50 aircraft. There are daily flights between all the main tourist and business centres. Fares are not low and there are no bucket-shop deals – for example, Victoria Falls to Harare costs around US$220, the same price as a ticket from Harare to Dar es Salaam in Tanzania. Air Zimbabwe has offices everywhere, otherwise drop in to a travel agent. Other airlines flying internally are Zimbabwe Express Airlines and United Air Company, which is linked to Air Zimbabwe.

ACCOMMODATION
Camping

There are sites in all the wilderness areas and holiday areas; many of them are in caravan parks. Prices are low but vary according to facilities and location. Most sites have showers and toilets and there will often be a cooking area nearby. Expect to pay around US$3–US$5 per night.

Budget

Backpacking is relatively new to Zimbabwe but the number of hostels is growing rapidly. In places like Victoria Falls backpacker accommodation is the only real alternative to the town's overpriced hotels. Hostels tend to be converted, rambling, and sometimes very old, houses. Dorm beds start around Z$30–Z$40 a night on average, doubles start at about Z$60. They are good places to meet like-minded travellers, and the information gleaned is often priceless. Many places will send someone to pick you up from the station or airport but phone ahead to check.

The *BUG* book (sold in all good backpacker places) is a pretty comprehensive guide to just about every bit of budget accommodation in Zimbabwe, as well as South Africa, Mozambique, Namibia, Botswana, Swaziland and Lesotho. Its content is updated regularly – ask at travel agencies for new information.

Moderate and up

Hotels are graded on a one- to five-star system and are mostly adequate by international standards. The leading chain is Zimbabwe Sun Hotels, which has establishments located in just about every tourist destination and all major towns. Hotels tend to be quite expensive because of the two-tier pricing system for tourists and locals.

Safari lodges

These are usually found in or near game reserves. Prices are usually quite high, but the standard of accommodation tends to be excellent. Staying at a safari lodge normally includes activities such as guided game drives and walks in the bush. There are a number of tour and safari operators who run lodges across the country. Try **Shearwater Adventures** (4 757831), **Safari Par**

Excellence (4 720527) or **Safari Consultants** (4 720527). In the Eastern Highlands, the safari lodges give way to country-style retreats and hotels where the emphasis is still on enjoying the outdoors.

Game and nature reserves

All the government-run national parks offer some kind of self-catering accommodation in chalets, *rondavels* and cottages. All are sparsely furnished but include fridges, cooking utensils, blankets and linen. Such accommodation is generally a bargain and very popular, especially during school holidays, so you need to book well in advance. Facilities are spotless but basic and you will often have to share ablution blocks. There is sometimes a restaurant attached to the camp but most of the places are strictly self-catering. Prices start at around US$15 per night for a double-bedded chalet.

EATING AND DRINKING

There are two staple foods in Zimbabwe, meat and *sadza* (stiff, slow-cooked maize porridge) and the two are normally served together. The meat can be anything from beef to wiry country goat. *Sadza* with relish is actually really tasty and it can be bought just about anywhere, from bus stations to city restaurants. Like the rest of southern Africa, Zimbabwe is very meat-oriented and it can be tough for vegetarians to find good, square meals aside from *sadza* and beans. Excellent food, however, can be bought from street hawkers who sell all kinds of fruit and vegetables, peanuts and delicious corn on the cob which is roasted over a brazier.

The barbecue or *braai* is a firm southern African tradition, certainly among whites. At many *braais* you will be served only meat and little else except for beer to wash it all down. Fish is somewhat rare in this landlocked country although you can find superb trout up in the Eastern Highlands and bream at Lake Kariba. Many people subsist on *kapenta*, tiny dried fish from Kariba. *Kapenta* is an acquired taste like whisky, but not as satisfying.

Hotel and restaurant food echoes the country's meat-and-two-veg colonial past, but at least you know what you are getting, even if it is bland. Most hotels serve traditional English breakfasts and follow up with immense buffets at lunch time. There are alternatives, such as a few Greek, Portuguese, Italian and Chinese restaurants in Harare and Bulawayo, but these are quite thin on the ground. Most towns and cities have been overrun with fast-food culture so junk-food lovers will not go hungry.

Beer-lovers will not be disappointed – drinking revolves around beer and the choice is enormous. Most local beers are lagers or pilseners, always served ice-cold, or the traditionally brewed *chibuku*, another acquired taste but one worth getting right. The leading beer is the green-bottled Zambezi Lager – the label is a picture of Victoria Falls. South African beers such as Castle, Lion and Black Label have a devoted following. *Chibuku* has the consistency of porridge and is not found in most bars, being more of a peasant drink. Try it if you have the opportunity.

Zimbabwe's wine industry is also on the up, although the opening of the borders following democratic elections in South Africa has brought stiff competition from Cape wines. Quality does vary and this is definitely a case of getting what you pay for, so splash out.

Various kinds of bottled spring water are available, all taken from sources in the Eastern Highlands. Also look out for Mazoe orange squash, one of the best of its kind in the world.

SHOPPING

Apart from curios, fabrics and possibly emeralds and semi-precious stones, there is not a lot to spend money on. Some of the curios are superb although there is an amazing amount of awful kitsch hippo, elephant and buffalo carving in stone and wood. Curio markets cluster around every tourist centre and you will have to bargain fiercely to avoid being ripped off. Look out for quieter markets away from the jostling artefact hunters, or wait until you are in a smaller town.

The Shona people are internationally known for their stone carvings and you can buy works from leading galleries in Harare or from the shops attached to them. Other stuff worth looking for is copper-ware, jewellery and pottery, or locally made clothes and fabrics, products of Zimbabwe's own cotton industry. The fabrics are usually covered with striking, bold patterns and designs and make great wall hangings, sarongs and emergency blankets. You can visit crafts-people at their homes; ask in the National Gallery shops or at tourist information centres for details.

The wood carvings come with an emotional and ecological price. The demand for carvings has resulted in the decimation of vast chunks of hardwood and softwood forest. It is difficult to justify tree conservation to people whose only income is from carvings, but at some stage the trees will become seriously threatened. It is a very tough choice – you will have to decide what feels right.

General shopping is centred around department stores and supermarkets. Trading hours for most shops are 08.30–17.00 Monday to Friday, and 08.30–13.00 on Saturday. Supermarkets and flea markets are usually open on Sunday mornings, too.

Photography

Zimbabwe's natural beauty is astounding. Bring a camera. Most international film brands are available along with the full range of processing services from one-hour or same-day labs. However, photographic equipment is absurdly expensive and fast film is almost impossible to find outside Harare, so bring along a few rolls from home. X-ray machines at all airports are film-safe.

Southern Africa's light is harsh and bright and shooting in the middle of the day is not recommended as the pounding sunlight tends to flatten even the most striking subjects. The best time for photography is in the early morning and late afternoon when the light softens and becomes gold. After that the biggest challenge will be to keep your film cool and your camera gear away from dust. Carry your cameras and lenses in a plastic bag inside your camera bag to prevent dust from getting in, and stash the film in the middle of your bag or backpack. Wrapping the film containers in a damp towel will help keep them cool.

Media and communications

Although most of the newspapers are government-owned, local media is vibrant and becoming more controversial, probably in line with the mood of the people. There are a number of daily and Sunday papers and plenty of magazines. The *Herald* is one of the most popular dailies. The two state-owned television channels, ZTV1 and ZTV2 broadcast 15.00–23.00 daily. Aside from party news broadcasts, much of the programming is imported from the US and there is little local content. There are a couple of radio stations where you can get to grips with Zimbabwe's vibrant music scene.

Post

Postal services are reliable and pretty cheap. Do not expect any great speed though – postcards sent to the US, for example, can take months to reach their destination. Post offices are open 08.30–16.00 on weekdays and 08.30–11.00 on Saturdays. Courier services are available if you have rush mail – call DHL on 4 792881.

Telephone

Zimbabwe has a fully automated dialling system and making internal calls at least is fairly straightforward. The international dialling code is 263 for dialling in, 110 and then the appropriate country code for dialling out. All Zimbabwe numbers given in this and the following chapters include the relevant national area code which should be omitted in the usual way when making a local call.

There are public phone boxes in all the main centres, with rows of phones outside post offices. Trying to dial overseas from a call box is an immensely frustrating experience. Expect to queue at a working public telephone and have plenty of Z$1 coins handy. A better idea is to buy a phone card – the Z$200 is the best if you are calling overseas – as card phones are now widespread. Better still, go to a special phone centre and book a call. It will be more expensive but at least the connection will be made. Ask at the post office or at tourist information for the nearest phone centre.

If you are planning to use the phone a lot around the country, buy a phone card. The card-operated phones are usually in better order than coin phones. The Z$200 card is good value for money and you will not have to keep running back to the post office to buy another one.

Emergency telephone numbers

To contact the emergency services dial 999 and tell the operator whether you need fire police or ambulance.

Zimbabwe's Railway Network

12

When you go to Zimbabwe you will probably see an ad for pep pills with the slogan 'Mmmm, it works' all over the country, and fortunately for the traveller so does NRZ, the National Railways of Zimbabwe. Although significantly smaller than its South African counterpart, NRZ is considered by many to be the second-best system on the continent.

THE NRZ SYSTEM

The 2,745-km (1,706-mile) network is based on the pleasant, slow-moving town of Bulawayo, the country's second city. Lines radiate north to Victoria Falls, south to connect with Botswana Railways at Plumtree, and eastwards, via Somabhula junction, to Harare. The line from Beitbridge on the South African border also joins the Bulawayo–Harare line here.

There are a few branch lines, most of which run out of Harare, but only the route to Chiredzi on the Beitbridge–Somabhula line has any passenger service. Eastwards from Harare, the railway loops down to the edge of the escarpment to the hill station of Mutare on the border of Mozambique and the heart of the Highlands, the country's coffee- and tea-growing region.

History

The history of Zimbabwe's railway system is inextricably linked with Cecil Rhodes, the pioneering entrepreneur whose vision of a railway linking Cairo to Cape Town was central to his grasping political and business ambitions on the continent. In his excellent *Railways of Southern Africa*, O.S. Nock calls Rhodes 'that colossus of Imperial development'. Having made his fortune in the diamond fields around Kimberley, Rhodes wanted to expand into the potentially rich country north of the Limpopo River.

With Rhodesia soon in the firm grip of his British South Africa Company, the way was clear for Rhodes to push ahead with his Cape-to-Cairo dream. The uncertainty over the future of the Bechuanaland Protectorate (now Botswana) nearly derailed his ambitions, however. While the local chiefs appreciated the benefits of British protection, they were not eager to have a railway line cut through their territory.

Rhodes decided it would be easier to build a railway from the east coast instead. The Anglo–Portuguese treaty of 1891 kicked off construction of a line from the port of Beira to the boundary of Britain's sphere of influence at

THE VICTORIA FALLS BRIDGE

The gorge carved out of rock by the thundering Zambezi River after its dramatic plunge over the falls was one of the most challenging obstacles confronting Rhodes and his railway builders. Rhodes himself never saw Victoria Falls, but he was the ultimate marketing man. He stipulated that the line should cross the Zambezi close enough to allow passengers to see the falls from the train and for the spray to fall on the coaches. The graceful bridge that resulted from his orders is still the centrepiece of the view from the verandah of the gardens and terrace of the Victoria Falls Hotel, itself a lasting monument to the colonial vision of Africa.

The designer was George Andrew Hobson, who by all accounts was pure engineer and no romantic. The spray which Rhodes wanted so dearly must have made working conditions utterly miserable during the rainy season – the columns of mist rise 900m (3,000ft) when the river is in full force. Hobson was heard to mutter that at least it was no worse than the rain in Scotland.

From an engineering point of view, the actual spot chosen for the bridge could not have been better, combining the minimum distance to be spanned – 200m/650ft – with a solid foothold on the rock. The bridge builders wanted to spend as little as possible on excavation and the forward planning was so well done that, while the project lasted 14 months, only nine months of that was actual building. So accurate was the building that the cantilever arms extending from each side of the gorge linked perfectly on April 1 1905.

Getting the necessary 750 tonnes of steel across to the other side was another problem. The nearest point where small boats could navigate the Zambezi was four miles upstream but the girders would have to be hauled through the bush to the lip of the gorge. The Zambezi is also infested with crocodiles and hippos, making the prospect of boat-work quite unpalatable. Instead, a massive cable was slung across the gorge on which ran an electric carrier, dubbed 'Blondin' by the workers. 'Blondin' ferried steel for the bridge and also enough rails and sleepers for the line to the north to be pushed ahead at the rate of one mile a day.

The bridge is a two hinged, spandrel-braced arch, 150m (500ft) long. Over 1,860 tonnes of steel were used, giving a total bridge weight of 3,320 tonnes. The contract to build it was won by the Cleveland Bridge and Engineering Company of Darlington which undercut even George Pauling's tender for the job. Sadly, Rhodes never saw his dream fulfilled – he died in 1902 before the contract was awarded. The first train, bearing the legend 'We've got a long way to go' steamed over the new bridge on 12 September 1905, driven by Mrs Pauling. But the first living creature to cross the £72,000 structure, was a full grown leopard.

Umtali (now Mutare). Legendary engineer George Pauling was awarded the contract to build the 2ft gauge (61cm) railway which was apparently intended from the start to be an independent entity from the rash of 3ft 6in gauge (107cm) lines spreading elsewhere across Africa.

Construction of the railway was an engineer's nightmare. Finding enough willing labour was difficult in a region which was underpopulated for good reason. The harsh tropical climate, disease and wild animals decimated the track gangs – in the two year period 1892–93, over 60% of the staff died on the job. Rhodes, concerned about these difficulties on the Umtali line, meanwhile revived the original plan to link Bulawayo by a line from the south through Bechuanaland which he also wanted to bring under the control of his British South Africa Company.

The Matabele Rebellion was the start of a tumultuous time in the region. BSAC staff were murdered and the trouble in Matabeleland spilled over into Mashonaland. It marked the end of Lobengula's kingdom as BSAC forces turned on him. Despite an early victory for the Ndebele when they massacred an imperial force on the banks of the Shangani River, the king realised it was an unequal contest, fled north and shortly afterwards killed himself. Morale plunged among the Matabele and the rebellion faltered.

In October 1894 Rhodes threw a dinner party at which George Pauling was invited to extend the Cape Government Railway north from its then terminus at Vryburg to Mafeking. It proved to be an opportune moment. In 1895 tribal warfare brought chaos to Matabeleland and Mashonaland, while a rinderpest epidemic had wiped out thousands of cattle. Until the epidemic, oxen had been the primary transport in the region, hauling loaded wagons at walking pace at best; now no-one dared use them. Soon after Rhodes was forced to resign as premier of the Cape Colony following the humiliating failure of the Jameson Raid and he was therefore able to throw himself into the task of getting rails to Salisbury (Harare) from the east and to Bulawayo from the south.

Pauling undertook to build the 640km (400 miles) of line which separated Bulawayo from the northernmost rail-head in South Africa in 400 days. The slender line of communication pushed rapidly out into the desert, but with only a single track with widely spaced passing loops and the sleepers laid on the unballasted earth. The rails reached Bulawayo in October 1897, and the Beira line also reached Umtali in February 1898 despite all its problems.

Bulawayo's citizens were delighted. The coming of the railway turned the city's fortunes around, saving it from the impending obscurity of a colonial backwater. No less than four special trains, carrying hundreds of VIPs – many of whom had travelled from Britain especially – came from the south for the opening ceremony, performed by Sir Alfred Milner, Governor of the Cape Colony. He called it a 'great day in the history of South Africa and of the Empire'. A banner displayed at Bulawayo railway station was emblazoned with the words 'Our two roads to progress; railroads and Cecil Rhodes'. Nevertheless, the haste with which the line had been built was immediately apparent – the third and fourth special trains, one of which was carrying journalists from Britain to cover the event, were so delayed by a derailment that they arrived long after the opening ceremony was over.

Nonetheless railways spread rapidly across the country after that. Salisbury and Bulawayo were linked by October 1902 despite construction delays caused by the outbreak of the Anglo–Boer War in South Africa. A 3ft 6in gauge line from Salisbury to Umtali was opened in May 1899. The 2ft gauge line from Umtali to the sea suddenly made little sense, and by August 1900 the whole railway had been converted to 3ft 6in.

The Cape-to-Cairo dream was still alive and Rhodes forged ahead with a line north from Bulawayo to Victoria Falls, reached in May 1904. The deep Zambezi River gorge proved to be less of an obstacle than expected and the railway was soon pushing deep into what is now Zambia, reaching the Belgian Congo (Zaire) border in 1909.

Rhodesia's entire network was operated by the Mashonaland Railway Company until 1927 when Rhodesia Railways became the working company. By 1936, Rhodesia Railways owned and operated all the lines in Southern and Northern Rhodesia (Zambia), as well as the Vryburg–Bulawayo section from South Africa through Bechuanaland. In 1947, when Southern and Northern Rhodesia, and Nyasaland (Malawi) were grouped into the Federation of Rhodesia and Nyasaland, the Rhodesian government took over all the federation's railway assets. Railway building continued in Southern Rhodesia itself, with lines spreading out from Salisbury into the nearby rich farming country. After the federation was dissolved in 1963, and Southern Rhodesia became simply Rhodesia, Rhodesia Railways remained as the national rail authority.

While Rhodesia always had a common border with South Africa, the line from Somabhula – a junction on the Bulawayo–Harare line – to Beitbridge on the Limpopo River was only opened in 1974. This route effectively made obsolete the long haul to the south via Botswana.

Rhodesia Railways became the National Railways of Zimbabwe following independence in 1980, painted its diesels yellow and began sending its mighty fleet of Garratt steam locomotives to the scrapyards.

PASSENGER TRAINS

What Zimbabwe lacks in sheer number of passenger trains is well compensated by their class and style. Trains are still operated according to a tradition which includes sit-down service in the dining cars attached to all trains and the chance to travel in clerestory-roofed sleeping cars with wood panels and leather seats.

From the hub and railway headquarters of Bulawayo services run daily to Victoria Falls and Harare, while a mixed train runs to Chiredzi down in the south-east. A daily train also links the capital, Harare, with Mutare on the border with Mozambique. Each train has an opposite partner, making eight trains in total.

The system is also served by two long-distance international trains, one each originating from South Africa and Botswana. The South African service, known as the *Bulawayo*, links Bulawayo with Johannesburg, with one train per week in each direction (see page 84). Until recently, the South African train ran via Beitbridge, on the Zimbabwe–South Africa border. However, the high trackage charges levied by NRZ, on top of chronic delays, have resulted in this train now being re-routed via Mafikeng and Gabarone, restoring the old through service via Botswana. It is also possible to cross into Zimbabwe from South Africa using the daily *Doily* train from Johannesburg to Beitbridge (see page 80), but this does not connect with any onward rail service. The train from Botswana, known as the *Botswana Blue* (see page 240) is one of Africa's cleanest passenger trains, but should not be confused with South Africa's *Blue Train* which is something else entirely. The *Botswana Blue* runs daily between Bulawayo and Lobatse, south of Gabarone.

Northward, there is a once-weekly shuttle which ambles over the bridge between Zimbabwe and Zambia. This takes the form of a Zambia Railways economy class coach tacked on to the back of the transfer freight train and is the only regular passenger link between the two countries.

There are no through services as yet between Zimbabwe and Mozambique but these are likely to start up as soon as new coaches are put in service on the existing routes, freeing up some of the older stock for use on the Mozambique lines.

Accommodation

NRZ has a straightforward first, second and economy class system. The difference between first and second is muted, with four people in a first class sleeper compared with six in second. There are also a few first and second class two- or three-berth coupés on all trains but these tend to be snapped up way in advance.

In both higher classes, there is a chance of riding in one of the older, wood-panelled sleepers (although not much longer as they are being phased out). This is an event in itself. Try it and let some railway romance wash over you. Passengers are assigned to sleepers at random, but you can always ask. The normal response will be, 'We don't know what cars this train will consist of', but even so there is a good chance that you will find yourself in the wooden car. Failing that, try working on the conductor as soon as the train is on its way. If he can find someone willing to swap, he will do it.

Economy class is really only for the hardy or seriously cash-strapped. Most economy class coaches are of the sit-bolt-upright-on-hard-plastic-seat type, although there are also what can only be described as hard sleepers. Since local people use the trains to move vast amounts of personal effects or goods bound for market, a trip in economy is likely to be the definitive African railway experience. Coaches are densely packed with humanity and goods, and there is the risk of having your valuables stolen in unguarded moments. If you want to sleep, upgrade.

Men and women are segregated in sleeper accommodation but couples can travel together if they reserve the entire compartment. In first class coupés this is simple since there are only two berths. In second class coupés, however, there are three berths, which would mean buying up the extra berth. In a six-berth compartment, this approach starts getting a little expensive and is not likely to endear you to the people left behind because the train was full.

Change is coming to NRZ, however, with a shake-up of passenger services due by the end of 1998. The wooden sleeping cars – a maintenance nightmare for the overworked carriage and wagon examiners – are being retired and will be replaced with new steel coaches, undoubtedly with the same dreary Formica panels so beloved by progressive railways everywhere.

NRZ has spent about US$22 million on new coaches to replace the ailing 1950s' stock currently in use. The new coaches will be able to travel at higher speeds and will be insulated against heat, noise and vibration. This means that travellers will no longer have the simple joy of pushing the window down and leaning out into the fresh African night, but then there will be videos, canned music and radio channels instead. The coaches have been designed with disabled passengers in mind, which is something of a first for African railways, and shows that NRZ has learned something from its overseas counterparts and started taking notice of the disabled community. Classes in the new coaches embrace economy which seats 96 people, standard with 66 passengers and sleeper class which can accommodate 26 passengers. The seats in standard class are the airline body-contoured, reclining type. There is a reading light above every seat. Vending machines are available in both standard and economy class coaches.

The new trainsets were due to be in service by June 1999. However, rail projects on the continent have a way of taking much longer than anticipated and the wooden sleepers could still be in service past the end of 1999.

Fares

Fares are absurdly cheap by world standards and anyone used to travelling on one of the British railway companies or Amtrak will be in constant ecstasy over how far the Zimbabwe dollar will take them, literally. Passenger trains are regarded as a national asset here, so are heavily subsidised by the government. Fares are worked out on a zone basis, with each zone 40km (25 miles) long.

Prices are not expected to change dramatically as long as the Zimbabwe dollar remains relatively stable. At the time we went to press, fares on the four NRZ-run trains were as below (all prices in Zimbabwe dollars).

Bulawayo–Victoria Falls
Bulawayo–Harare

First class	Z$132.00
Second class	Z$105.00
Economy class	Z$54.60

Harare–Mutare

First class	Z$82.25
Second class	Z$67.50
Economy class	Z$31.85

Bulawayo–Chiredzi

First class	Z$141.75
Second class	Z$112.50
Economy class	Z$59.15

Booking

Booking train tickets in Zimbabwe is a mostly pleasurable, hassle-free experience. Tickets can be booked at all stations for any journey. Credit card bookings can also be made (from abroad if you wish) by calling the Bulawayo office on (+263) 9 322 410/310. However, using the phones in Zimbabwe can be frustrating and, until the promised cellular network is in place, a journey to the nearest station is your best option. Early booking is advised on popular trains such as the *Victoria Falls Mail*, especially over weekends and school holidays, as the trains tend to get packed out very quickly at these times.

Concessions

More than any other rail operator in the region, NRZ offers various discounts to pensioners, the disabled, school children and travellers in groups. However, there are no rail passes or multi-trip tickets available.

Ten or more people travelling first or second class get a 10% discount on single journeys and 25% on return journeys. Elderly people get 25% off on both single and return journeys in both classes except on Fridays, Saturdays and Sundays and in the period 10 days before the beginning of any public holiday. Disabled travellers are eligible for a 25% reduction on all journeys and all classes. Children under three years travel at half price in all classes.

Be warned, however, that granting of concessions is subject to availability of berths during peak periods.

Surcharges

In a vain attempt to stop everyone from travelling at once over public holidays, NRZ has implemented a 20% levy on all tickets issued for travel at these times. While extra trains are usually laid on at times when demand threatens to swamp the railway network, NRZ urges would-be passengers to 'travel earlier to avoid the congestion and the levy.'

Train facilities
Eating and drinking

Dining cars are attached to all but the Bulawayo–Chiredzi trains. In keeping with the inconvenient turn-of-the-century railway tradition, diners eat off china plates with real knives and forks, while white-jacketed waiters sway up and down the coach, balancing plates with unruffled ease. The food is fairly basic, sometimes greasy, but always edible and filling. Here, as on other railways in the region, the national staples are beef stew or chicken, served with rice or *sadza*. If you are a vegetarian, remember that Zimbabwe, like all the other countries in the region, is a meat-oriented society. You will get the same vegetables with a fried egg balancing on top.

By all means take additional food such as fruit and snacks. The water on the trains is safe to drink, but if you prefer mineral water, take your own.

The bar in the buffet coach, always next to the dining car, serves both local and 'imported' (that is, South African) beers. Zambezi Lager, identifiable by the picture of Victoria Falls on the label, is the best local beer. No Zimbabwe train experience would be complete without a few Zambezis to grease the wheels.

Bedding

Bedding which consists of a bedroll of crisp-ish linen, blankets and pillows is supplied free to all full-fare first and second class travellers. Use it gratefully – it makes a freshly laundered change from a sleeping bag and it is generally cooler, too.

Baggage

Excess or very bulky luggage will be carried in the baggage van on the same train as you. First class passengers are allowed 50kg/110lb free, second class 35kg/77lb, and economy class 25kg/55lb. It may occur to many foreigners watching Africa on the move that the allowances need reversing since the economy class passengers are usually the ones who travel heaviest. Enjoy travelling weightless.

Bicycles

Bicycles will normally be carried free of charge in the baggage van on your train. However, if your bike weighs more than your baggage allowance, it becomes a parcel which must be paid for.

Motorcycles and cars

These can be sent by train but the cost, in the case of cars, makes it uneconomical. Motorcycles are treated as parcels and are usually sent on the same train.

Parcels

The parcels service is guaranteed overnight to all major towns. There is a parcels section at all stations.

Safety and security

Zimbabwe has not escaped the global scourge of theft on trains and travellers are warned to be vigilant. That said, the trains here are probably the safest in the region, possibly because of the very visible police contingent which travels on most trains.

Standard procedures apply. Close the windows at night or if leaving the compartment – people have lost their belongings to quick-witted operators who wait on station platforms at night for such golden opportunities as these. Get the conductor or other train crew to lock your compartment if you plan to leave it empty. Ideally, someone trustworthy should be in the compartment at all times. You will most likely find yourself sharing a compartment with strangers – use your own judgment. I have never once had a problem on any of my trips on NRZ, cheerfully leaving the compartment for hours on end but with my pack stowed safely out of sight on the top luggage rack. Chain your bag to the rack if you want to be extra secure. It is a good idea to keep your money and passport in a money belt and to wear this when you sleep.

Be super-alert if travelling economy class where you will usually be battling for space in an open, seater carriage. Most travellers, however, have no problems and it is a good way to meet hard-living Zimbabweans. People will usually be friendly and interested in you. Use your judgment, especially when accepting offers of food and drink.

Station services
Cloakrooms
Left luggage facilities are available at all main stations. Charges are as low as Z$6 per package for 24 hours. Consider this option before dragging your pack out into the city streets on a mid-summer's Zimbabwe day.

Bathing facilities
Bulawayo, probably because it is the headquarters of NRZ, is the only station with bathing facilities at the time of writing, although Harare should be similarly equipped by the time this book is published if present plans go ahead. Showers cost Z$6.40 per person.

Porters
Porters will help you with your bags at Bulawayo and Harare. The service is free to railway customers, but tips are very welcome.

STEAM IN ZIMBABWE
Zimbabwe has the largest active fleet of steam locomotives in daily revenue-earning service on the whole continent. Embracing three classes of Garratt articulated locomotive, they are used for shunting in the yards around Bulawayo and for short-haul workings out on the main line.

NRZ had a large fleet of Garratts in service until foreign railway consultants arrived in the early 1990s and persuaded the administration that steam was archaic and inefficient and should be abandoned. The fact that the railway's diesel fleet was in considerable disarray, with many locomotives awaiting spares or heavy repairs, was apparently of little relevance. The Garratts were duly dispensed with, although a great number were retained for shunting and reserve in times of motive power shortages. NRZ has subsequently rationalised its diesel fleet into a handful of types and as motive power availability improves, so steam's last stronghold has been weakening.

Still, on just about any morning down at Bulawayo locomotive sheds, you will find ten or more Garratts being prepared for the day's work. Although well down on the hundred or so engines which were based in the city until the early 1990s, the atmosphere of a working steam depot remains as magical. The steam sheds face east, right into the sun which, as it rises, picks details of the hissing giants out of the gloom. There is always activity, whether watering, coaling, greasing or stoking, and the shed staff scurry around urgently as they start another long day of keeping the elderly machines in working order. As the day begins so the crews start easing their locomotives away from the shed one by one, over the turntable and into the maze of Bulawayo's freight yards.

Visitors are welcome at the shed as long as they have a photographic permit, obtainable from the NRZ publicity officer who can be found on the 6th floor of NRZ headquarters in Fife St, Bulawayo, tel: 9 322410. You can also spend a day **riding on a steam locomotive**, but you will need an indemnity form, also available at the headquarters building, this time from the System Manager's office on the 17th floor.

The usual train to ride is the daily shuttle which lollops 20km (12.5 miles) up the main line to a massive cement factory. Be prepared for a long day (the crew may make as many as four return trips) and take a large bottle of water as it gets wickedly hot in the cab. If you have ever dreamed of working on a steam locomotive, the experience will either cure or inflame you.

Both permits are issued free of charge and visitors need to take full responsibility for themselves – Zimbabwe is no nanny state – but there is always someone who will be glad to show you around.

Luxury steam services

Zimbabwe has all the right ingredients for classic African railway travel – a large fleet of working steam locomotives, a luxurious train which captures the feeling and deep nostalgia of train travel before Formica, and railways that run through wild bushveld, alive with exotic animals, to romantic destinations like Victoria Falls.

Good co-operation between the railways and private operators has ensured that the steam infrastructure remains intact. Although the North Line from Bulawayo to Victoria Falls was dieselised some years ago as we have seen, NRZ has agreed to maintain it as a steam railway, complete with the necessary supporting facilities, allowing steam haulage all the way to the Falls and back.

Train de Luxe

Without a doubt the most romantic way to travel to Victoria Falls is on Rail Safaris' *Train de Luxe*, with a steam locomotive up front and wild animals bounding away from the trackside.

The *Train de Luxe* is named after the luxury trainset commissioned by Cecil Rhodes in 1900. He dreamed of a train which would take passengers off the mail ships from Britain in Cape Town and carry them in absolute luxury into the heart of Africa. Despite the disruption caused by the Anglo–Boer War, then in full swing, the train was delivered on time in 1902 and to Rhodes' specifications, boasting, among other things, the first full-service dining car on the continent. This set of seven coaches made up the first through train to run from Cape Town to Victoria Falls when the link was completed in 1903.

The new *Train de Luxe* has been running since 1986 and offers an outstanding romantic African railway adventure. Steam locomotives are used throughout and service is based on old-fashioned British Pullman standards. The owners make no claims to running an hotel. The brochure says, 'Memories will be stirred of journeys taken long ago when passenger trains carried you in a more relaxed and fine world to universities, weddings and personal great occasions.'

The 'new' train is made up of vintage rolling stock, ranging from a 1908 dining car, rebuilt in 1951, to 40-year-old sleeping saloons, recently retired from NRZ.

The emphasis of the train is on railway heritage and romance, allowing passengers to relive the past. Accommodation is in three classes – Emerald, Ivory and Heritage – reflecting the three markets the train is aimed at. Heritage class, for rail fans and steam enthusiasts looking for a bit of nostalgia, consists of twin or single compartments in traditional leather-upholstered and wood-panelled sleeping cars. The Emerald and Ivory classes are more luxurious. Emerald class is the top end, with cabins containing private lounges and en-suite bathrooms, and individually controlled air-conditioning. Ivory class cabins and suites do not have private bathrooms, although there is a basin in every compartment, nor is there air-conditioning. This is not a problem in winter but could be sharply relevant in the middle of a Zimbabwean summer.

The train runs on three routes out of Bulawayo, to Victoria Falls, Harare and Johannesburg, according to an exacting tour programme. Various itineraries and tours are offered, from overnight runs to a four-night adventure from Harare to Victoria Falls, which includes a stopover and tour in Bulawayo. The operating season begins in April and runs through to the end of the year, with the winter months between May and August being the most popular. The Victoria Falls route is understandably the busiest, but the train runs to Harare every two weeks and once a month to Johannesburg, making it very accessible to travellers who wish to transfer directly from either of these international airports.

The timings on the northbound Victoria Falls run mean that you get to see a lot more of Zimbabwe than you would slumming it on the regular *Victoria Falls Mail*. Departing just before lunch, the *Train de Luxe* ambles into Matabeleland, passing thatched *shambas* out of which hurtle shrieking, laughing children, thrilled as always by the miracle of a passing train. By late afternoon, the farmlands have given way to forests of teak and blackwood, before the slow night run down into the bushveld. At dawn, the train is entering the Zambezi National Park – early risers will see giraffe, wildebeest, zebra and all sorts of antelope. Lions are sometimes seen from the train, but they do not seem to share the same enthusiasm for passing trains as the village children.

The operators also run golfing safaris off the train, stopping over at some of the country's best golf courses. While the golfing safaris are mainly aimed at large charter groups (of up to 52 people), smaller groups are able to get on to golf tours if there is space available.

Fares

Sample fares on the *Train de Luxe* are as follows:

Bulawayo–Victoria Falls

US$610.20 per person	in an Emerald suite
US$339.00 per person	in an Ivory cabin
US$322.05 per person	in Heritage class

Harare–Bulawayo

US$392.00 per person	in Emerald
US$218.00 per person	in Ivory
US$207.10 per person	in Heritage

Prices include all table d'hote meals. Bookings can be made through Rail Safaris' office in Bulawayo, tel/fax: (+263) 9 755575/322822, or email: <railsaf@acacia.samara.co.zw>.

Victoria Falls Safari Express

Possibly the only regular way to relive Rhodes' wish that spray from the Victoria Falls should wet passing trains is on the *Victoria Falls Safari Express,* which runs daily across the bridge in the high season.

This is a relatively new operation, using one of three restored steam locomotives, coupled to a 1900-vintage first class coach and an exquisite dining car. The regular loco is the 10th Class No 156 *The Princess of Mulobezi.* At the time of writing, this engine was in the workshops for a protracted overhaul and the train was being hauled by one of two Zambian Railways 12th Class 4–8–2s.

The usual trip is a tea run across the bridge, leaving Victoria Falls at 10.00 and pausing briefly on the bridge before sauntering over to the Zambian side, returning at 12.30. The trip is billed as 'an authentic tea party in a unique location', for which experience you will pay US$90. Other possibilities are the Moonlight Dinner Party train which leaves at 18.30 for a three-hour outing in the African bush, and a late afternoon Bridge Run where guests can sip champagne and pretend to be Empire builders.

The train is available for conferences and group excursions, weddings and celebrations. Trips are also sometimes arranged on part of the old Zambezi Sawmills Railway, a legendary former logging railway in Zambia (see Chapter 17, page 247).

For bookings, tel: (+263) 13 2069 or +263 4 727366/fax 4 705852, or email: <fallsexp@mail.pci.co.zw>.

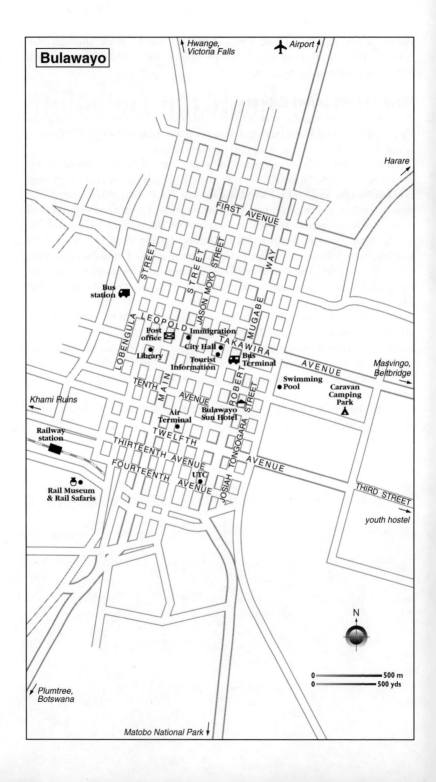

Routes in Zimbabwe

13

BULAWAYO TO VICTORIA FALLS

It is hard to beat the *Victoria Falls Mail* for a dose of African rail romance. The Bulawayo–Victoria Falls train runs overnight in each direction and has all the drama and excitement you could hope for from a long distance African train ride.

The *Mails* are still regarded by NRZ as crack expresses. They carry the post and vast numbers of people. They also run at night because most of the passengers are workers and this way their employers do not lose a day's output.

Departures are classic African theatre. The station will likely be overrun with people, many of whom are not actually travelling but have come to help friends or family get on, or others who have just come for the show. At peak holiday times and weekends, there will be crowds of people trying to buy tickets at the last minute, badgering the conductor even as he blows his whistle. If you are one of them, he may tell you to get on the train and a ticket and berth will be sorted out on the move. If there is absolutely no room in first or second, the conductor will impress this on you. Do not argue – he knows. Join the heaving scrum in economy or wait for tomorrow's train.

The *Mails* usually leave on time, although be prepared for inexplicable delays. Railways work in mysterious ways generally, and even more so in Africa.

Northbound trains leave Bulawayo at 19.00 daily, arriving at Victoria Falls at 07.00, while southbound trains leave Victoria Falls at 18.30 and arrive in Bulawayo at 07.00.

Times

(main stops only)

	Northbound Daily, all classes			Southbound Daily, all classes	
dep	19.00	Bulawayo	arr	07.00	
dep	19.13	Mpopoma	dep	06.47	
dep	21.37	Sawmills	dep	04.24	
dep	01.29	Dete	dep	00.50	
dep	03.04	Hwange	dep	22.22	
dep	04.15	Thomson Junction	dep	22.00	
arr	07.00	Victoria Falls	dep	18.30	

Fares

First class	Z$132.00
Second class	Z$105.00
Economy class	Z$54.60

Bulawayo

Bulawayo is a spacious, friendly place with tree-lined streets and a distinctly slow-moving feel. Home to almost one million people, it is the administrative capital of Matabeleland as well as the headquarters for the National Railways of Zimbabwe (NRZ). The tourist board will tell you proudly that Bulawayo is twinned with Aberdeen in Scotland. No one else seems to know, though.

The city, originally called Gu-Bulawayo 'place of the man who was killed' – apparently a reference to executions carried out by Mzilikazi at the birth of the Ndebele nation, was founded in 1872 by Lobengula, the old warrior's son. The Ndebele burned their city when the first European prospectors and fortune-seekers arrived in 1893. Dr Leander Starr Jameson laid out a new town on the site, and it grew with phenomenal speed as prospectors rushed in from the south. Though only limited amounts of gold were found in Matabeleland, there was enough to ensure a small gold mining industry, while white farmers hurried to grab and develop the surrounding fertile land.

Bulawayo was at the centre of the Matabele Rebellion in 1896 but was never attacked. Most of the fighting took place to the south in the Matopos Hills, from which the Ndebele conducted a tenacious guerrilla campaign. Cecil Rhodes managed to negotiate an end to the fighting, promising better treatment of the Ndebele, and Bulawayo began to grow once more.

The railway from Mafeking reached the city in 1897, and began heading east to Salisbury and north to coalfields around Hwange. The coming of railways to Bulawayo was key to turning the city into the communication, tourism and agricultural centre it still is.

Practical details

Airport

The airport is 22km north of town. Air Zimbabwe operates a bus between the airport and the Bulawayo Sun Hotel on Josiah Tongogara St. A taxi to the airport costs about Z$120.

Station

The railway station is off Lobengula St, on the corner of 13th Av, south-west of the city centre. Trains leave from here to Victoria Falls, Harare, Gabarone, Johannesburg and Chiredzi. There are no local services. For train enquiries, tel: 9 322411; train reservations, tel: 9 322310. However, I suggest that you go to the station personally, if you can – that way you will at least get served.

Information

The Publicity Association office is under the City Hall clock tower, Fife St. The office is open daily 08.00–16.30, tel: 9 60867.

Above Balancing rocks, Matobo
National Park, Zimbabwe (AZ)

Right Dhows at sunset, Inhambane,
Mozambique (AZ)

Below Victoria Falls, Zimbabwe (AZ)

Above Old steam trains in the South African National Railway and Steam Museum, Krugersdorp, near Johannesburg (AZ)

Right The weekly train from Xai-Xai to Manjacaze in Mozambique stops at a rural halt to load wood. (PA)

Below Maputo railway station, Mozambique (PA)

Above Consolidation No 06, an ailing survivor
and the Xai-Xai bush railway's last working
engine, Mozambique (PA)

Below Steam loco crew, Xai-Xai, Mozambique (PA)

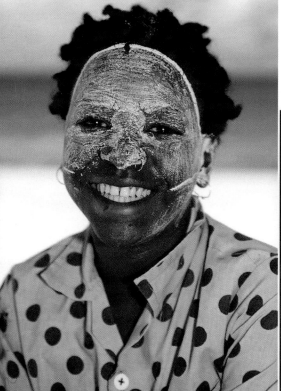

Above Curio stall showing characteristic Zimbabwean statues, Kariba Town, Zimbabwe (AZ)

Left Makua girl with painted face, Pemba, Mozambique (AZ)

Below Makishi dancer, Victoria Falls town, Zimbabwe (AZ)

Getting around
By bus
Bulawayo has two main suburban bus services. Buses for the northern, eastern and southern suburbs run from the City Hall Terminal on 8th Av, between Fife St and Robert Mugabe Way. Buses to the south-west and western suburbs go from the terminus on the corner of Lobengula St and 6th Av.

By taxi
Various taxi firms will compete for your custom, especially at the railway station. Take a taxi, rather than risk walking, if you arrive after dark. If you need a cab early in the morning or late at night, there is a phone at the Hotel Cecil from which you can make a free pick-up call to Rixi Taxi, arguably the nicest cab company in town.

While most taxis are metered, not all the meters work, and it is better to negotiate the fare before climbing in. Fares keep fluctuating along with the erratic performance of the Zimbabwe dollar – certainly pay no more than US$2 for a ride from the station to the centre of town.

By bicycle
The wide streets, slow-moving traffic and flat terrain make Bulawayo a superb place to cycle around. Bikes can be hired at Studio 6, National Art Gallery, tel: 9 72939 or Dra-Gama Tourist Services, Shamrock House, corner of 8t Av and Josiah Tongogara St, tel: 9 72739.

Sightseeing
If you want to get to grips with the country's ancient history, then the **Museum of Natural History** is the place. Realistic dioramas of all Zimbabwe's birds, animals and fish life are the main feature, along with a collection of insects, and numerous artefacts related to African cultures and the European invasion. A stuffed elephant – at 5.5 tonnes and 3.53m (11ft 7in) tall apparently the world's second largest – dominates part of the display with its 41kg (90lb) tusks. The country's pre-history is covered in detail, as is its geology, mineral wealth, weaponry and arts. The museum is situated in Centenary Park and is open every day 09.00–17.00. Entry is US$2.

The two main **parks**, Centenary and Central, are adjoining 45-hectare (110-acre) green spots, good places to find a tree and hide from the sun in. Centenary Park boasts a 2ft gauge railway, using a locomotive from the old Beira–Umtali line. The railway runs on weekends. Venturing into the more deserted areas of either park is risky, and you should avoid both at night.

With Bulawayo the country's railway centre, the city is a natural home for the **Zimbabwe National Railways Museum** which comprehensively covers the story of the country's railways. Situated just behind the railway station in the suburb of Raylton, the museum has a large collection of locomotives, railway coaches, wagons, buildings and equipment. The main office was once the corrugated iron station at Shamva before being plucked out of the bush.

Rhodes' plush private saloon, built in 1896 is among the exhibits along with other classic superbly preserved wooden coaches. The locomotives range from tiny *Jack Tar*, engine No.7, which was used on the construction of the Beira–Umtali line, to a massive 20th Class 4–8–2+2–8–4 Garratt. The museum owns all the steam locomotives still working on NRZ, and supplies locomotives to pull Rail Safaris' *Train de Luxe* (see page 179) as well as other enthusiasts' trains. The *Train de Luxe* is based at the museum, so even if you cannot afford to ride it, at least you can see it.

Entry to the museum is a paltry Z$5. The affable curator, David Puttnam, was until recently, the chief mechanical superintendent at Bulawayo steam shed. If you want stories about Zimbabwe's railways, and a cup of tea, he is the man to speak to.

To get to the museum, cross over the tracks on the iron footbridge from Platform 1 at the station, turn left into the road and walk down the road until you see the old locomotives on the right. Hours are 09.30–12.00 and 14.00–16.00 Tuesday to Friday, and 15.00–17.00 on weekends. The lunchtime closing is ignored more often than not.

Accommodation
Budget
Shaka's Spear corner of Jason Moyo St/2nd Av, no phone at time of writing. A clean, relaxed backpackers' place run by Natalie. Some doubles, otherwise airy dorm rooms. Good food available on request. Z$60 for a dorm bed, Z$80 per person in a double room.
Hotel Cecil Fife St/3rd Av, tel: 9 60295. Basic but clean doubles with air conditioning at Z$250 per room.

Mid-price
Zak's Place 129 Robert Mugabe Way, tel: 9 540129. 34 rooms with en-suite bathrooms situated downtown. Double US$38, single US$28, bed and breakfast.

Eating and drinking
Being a relatively cosmopolitan town, Bulawayo has the usual flood of take-away places and bakeries, but there are a couple of outstanding restaurants. One such is the **Matabeleland Safari Grill**, perhaps better known as the 'Cape to Cairo', on Leopold Takawira.

The courtyard behind the **Palace Gardens Hotel** is an excellent spot to unwind in and meet locals during the day, especially on Friday afternoons when live bands perform. Basic bar meals are available but most people go for the beer.

If you are doing your own cooking, a good place to buy fruit and vegetables is at the big **Makokoba market** near the Renkini bus station. Another smaller but equally good market happens every day one block east of Jason Moyo Av, between 4th Av and 5th Av. General groceries can be bought at Haddon & Sly on the corner of Fife St and 8th Av.

Safety

With its sleepy pace and apparent lack of malice, Bulawayo must rank as one of Africa's safest cities. On my last visit to Zimbabwe, there were anti-government riots going on in Harare, yet Bulawayo was utterly calm. Having said this, the usual rules apply. Do not walk in Centenary or Central Parks at night, and if you are on your own you should avoid the more remote areas by day, too.

The area around the railway station is rife with pickpockets and muggings are common. In fact on arriving in Bulawayo by train, strangers are likely to come up to you and warn you about the unsavoury types hanging about at the entrance. There are usually plenty of taxis in the car park in front of the station – if you are not sure of your bearings, take a cab.

Most trains arrive in the morning so there is not the usual frisson of a night arrival in a strange city. The Renkini Bus terminal is like any bus station in the world – keep a sharp eye on your belongings and be alert.

Around Bulawayo
Matobo National Park and the Khami Ruins

Probably Bulawayo's best asset, the Matopos Hills are a 50-mile long concentration of granite outcrops, caused by natural erosion along the central ridge which runs east to west across the country. With their weird, contorted shapes, and hundreds of caves, the hills have an extraordinary power about them. The Karanga people who originally lived in the area, believed that primeval powers lived among the rock castles and domes, and their priests worshipped there. Many of the caves contain well-preserved Bushman paintings. King Mzilikazi is buried in a cave on a granite outcrop, while Cecil Rhodes' tomb faces north off one of the domes. The graves of Leander Starr Jameson and the men of the Shangani Patrol who died pursuing King Lobengula are also here.

The British South Africa Company, adding to land already bequeathed by Rhodes to the people, created what is now the Matobo National Park, arguably one of Zimbabwe's finest parks. Herds of sable antelope, giraffe, eland, buffalo, zebra, wildebeest and kudu roam the park. There are also a few, heavily protected, white and black rhino in the western part of the reserve.

The walls and terraces of the Khami Ruins are the remains of one of the country's largest stone-walled settlements, dating back to Zimbabwe's pre-history. The site was supposedly one of the last to be inhabited before the people fled from the invading Nguni groups from the north. There is evidence that these people were trading with the Portuguese, indicated by a stone Dominican cross in the middle of one enclosure.

The only way to get to the Khami Ruins and the park is by road. A number of Bulawayo-based operators offer tours to both – ask at the tourist information centre for a list. Alternatively hire a car in Bulawayo. The Khami ruins are 23km (14 miles) from the city so hiring a bicycle and pedalling out there is a further option for the energetic.

THE VICTORIA FALLS ROUTE

After leaving Bulawayo, the line runs north-west straight through Matabeleland, a place dotted with *shambas* and subsistence farms, which gradually give way to a land of trees – mopane, acacia and teak, among others. Real bush country is only reached in the early hours of the morning. The trains amble along at a very relaxed pace so as not to arrive too early at their destinations. This is a train to sleep on – the slow rocking of the coaches will defeat even determined insomniacs.

Dinner gets under way about an hour into the journey. The dining car is a superb place to spend the evening. Little has changed since the 1920s – you are served by stewards in white jackets and eat off real china. There is a bar at the end of the coach, normally presided over by one, extremely pressured, barman. Finding a seat is normally not a problem and the staff do not object if you linger. Most people tend to finish dinner and return to their compartments, but many stay on and nurse both beers and conversation well into the night. It is a good place to meet Zimbabwe. A few Zambezis are a great leveller and you may find people opening up more than they would in casual encounters elsewhere. Closing time is around midnight.

On the northbound run, the train runs along the eastern boundary of Hwange National Park around dawn. If you want to do a bit of game spotting, get up early and look out of the left (west) side of the train. Many of the animals vanish when trains approach but you may see the odd herd of impala, kudu, or elephant who ignore the intrusion into their world.

Collisions with animals unfortunately happen regularly on this section of the railway – in fact trains are the biggest single killer of animals in the park. The train drivers on the section all have frightening tales of animal accidents – hitting an elephant at high speed will be as bad for the train as the elephant.

Hwange National Park

Hwange is Zimbabwe's greatest game park and the most accessible. Around 15,000km² (5,800 square miles) in extent, it carries a huge number and variety of animals. The park, which is mostly hot, sandy country, developed almost by accident as wild animals retreated away from the ever encroaching humans who were taming the good farmland to the east, north and west. Apart from hunting parties of San Bushmen and the odd European explorer, nobody went into the area. In 1928 the Rhodesian Government proclaimed the area as a game reserve, and camps and roads were built. Today there are just three camps in Hwange, all served by an extensive but unobtrusive road system.

The game is prolific – hundreds of elephant and herds of 1,000 or more buffalo are often seen, along with all kinds of antelope including the magnificent gemsbok (oryx) which are normally only found in much drier localities.

The main camp and Sinamatela camp are open all year round, while Robins Camp and the remainder of the reserve are open from June 1 to October 31. Accommodation in the camps consists of chalets, cottages and lodges, along with camping facilities.

Unless you have your own car, the only way to get around the park is on one of the organised tours which run through the reserve. There are quite a few operators, offering different packages from two-hour to all-day game drives, and three- or four-day safaris for backpackers. Prices start around US$11 for a two-hour trip, rising to around US$100 a day for the all-inclusive safaris. Many of the operators will also pick guests up from Dete railway station.

Dete
Dete is the official railway station for Hwange National Park but it is not a welcoming place at 01.00, roughly the time at which trains both to and from Bulawayo pass through. The station itself is a long way from the park entrance so travellers arriving here by train will have to sleep either in the station waiting room or have arranged accommodation in advance at the nearby, tatty, Game Reserve Hotel, tel: 118 366.

A better option is the **Wildside Budget Guest House** near Dete which offers accommodation at US$7.50 a night and four-hour game drives the next day for US$30. Someone from the lodge will meet the train at Dete provided the booking has been made in advance. Phone 118 446, or fax 118 395.

Hwange
Hwange is not much of an improvement on Dete. It is a coal mining town and there are few diversions. Steam enthusiasts, however, will get a kick out of visiting the colliery which uses a few, well-maintained, Garratts to drag heavy coal trains up to the NRZ exchange sidings. Probably the last 'show' of its kind in Africa, it is a guaranteed pulse-racer for steam people.

Victoria Falls
'Scenes so lovely must have been gazed upon by angels in their flight.' So wrote British missionary David Livingstone, believed to be the first white man to see the Victoria Falls, in 1855, though there is speculation that Portuguese traders coming overland from the east may have beaten him to it. Livingstone named the falls after his Queen; the local people called the cataract *Mosi-oa-Tunya* – 'the smoke that thunders'. When the Zambezi is in flood, the spray can be seen from as far as 80km away. People arriving by air will see what looks like a fire in the bushveld below.

The columns of spray rise 900m in the rainy season between March and May, blanketing the area around the falls in mist, and creating a lush, permanent rain forest full of ferns, orchids and blood lilies on the lip of the gorge, a welcome change from the hot and humid bushveld of the Zambezi River valley.

The falls, caused by cracks in the underlying sheet of lava which forms the surface of this part of the continent, are an anomaly in the path of the great Zambezi River which meanders slowly across the otherwise flat plains of Zambia. The river tore into the cracks and gouged out the trench which is now the Batoka Gorge. That took a mere 500,000 years.

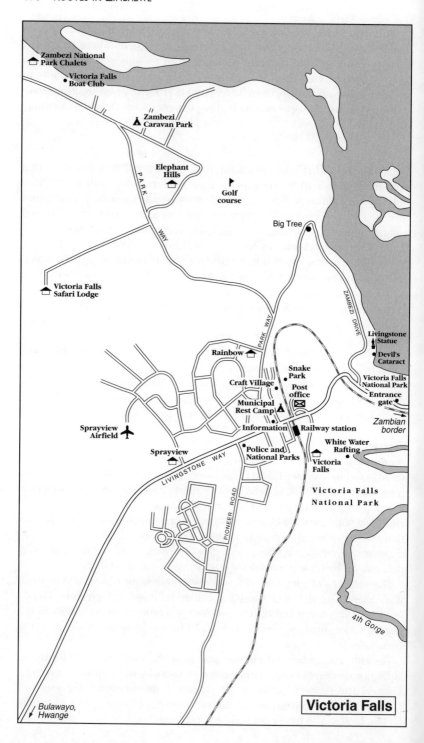

Zambezi National
Park Chalets

Victoria Falls
Boat Club

Zambezi
Caravan Park

Elephant
Hills

PARK WAY

Golf
course

Big Tree

Victoria Falls
Safari Lodge

ZAMBEZI DRIVE

Rainbow

PARK WAY

Livingstone
Statue

Devil's
Cataract

Snake
Park

Craft Village

Post
office

Victoria Falls
National Park

Entrance
gate

Municipal
Rest Camp

Information

Zambian
border

Sprayview
Airfield

Sprayview

Railway station

LIVINGSTONE WAY

Police and
National Parks

White Water
Rafting

PIONEER ROAD

Victoria
Falls

Victoria Falls
National Park

4th Gorge

Bulawayo,
Hwange

Victoria Falls

The river is almost 2km wide at the falls, with an average flow of 550 million litres (120 million Imperial gallons) of water a minute over the five cataracts – the Devil's Cataract, Main Falls, Horseshoe Falls, Rainbow Falls and the Eastern Cataract – each of which is separated from the others by islands of rock at the lip of the chasm. After peaking in April, the river drops to its lowest level in October which marks the end of the dry winter season.

There are two ways to experience the falls – from the 2,340-hectare (5,780-acre) **Victoria Falls National Park** on the Zimbabwean side, and from the Zambian, and less-touristed, side of the river. The national park surrounds the falls and stretches back 500m (550yd) from the falls and the edge of the river. A path meanders along the edge of the gorge with lookout points scattered the whole length of the chasm. There is always at least one magnificent rainbow. The falls are at their most magical in the early morning or evening when the soft light turns the mist into a pink and gold curtain.

The **Devil's Cataract**, where part of the river is squeezed into a gap a few metres wide, is the most savage section of the falls, flowing at more than 160km/h (100mph) when the river is in flood. A statue of the great explorer broods stonily over the torrent.

In the height of the dry season, as much as two thirds of the falls dry up, leaving only the Main and Devil's Cataracts on the western side still flowing. While the spectacle is reduced, the more adventurous can pick their way over the rocks of the dry river bed from the Zambian bank to **Livingstone Island** and repeat the explorer's experience. 'Creeping with awe to the verge I peered down into the large rent which had been made from bank to bank of the broad Zambezi.'

To do this, you have to clear both Zimbabwe and Zambian customs – get a one day visa at the Zambian immigration post – and then walk down from the post to the river. Watch out for snakes and be extra careful walking across the now dry river bed which consists of acres of slippery, jagged rock. The edge of the falls is also slippery and it is a long plunge to the rocks below. The sunset from the Zambian side is miraculous but, if you stay to watch, remember to take a torch for the walk back. Steer well clear also of the herd of resident elephants who come down to the Livingstone Island area at night to drink – they do not welcome intruders and it would be a bad place to be charged by elephants.

If you get bored of watching the thundering water, other diversions include flips over the falls in light aircraft, white-water rafting, boogie-boarding in the Batoka Gorge, or a 90m (300ft) bungee jump off the Victoria Falls bridge. Do not worry about how to find the operators who arrange these amusements – they will find you.

At rates which start at US$180 per person per night in a double, many budget travellers might be put off staying in the **Victoria Falls Hotel**, an African colonial classic, built in 1904 as a crucial part of Rhodes' Cape-to-Cairo dream. However, even impoverished sandal-wearing backpackers are allowed to take afternoon tea on the terrace overlooking the bridge and the Batoka Gorge, and buy, briefly, into the colonial myth. I recommend this –

endless cups of tea and a silver cake tower stacked with scones, smoked salmon sandwiches and pastries. You can pretend you are staying there and the deferential white-jacketed waiters will play along with you.

You can explore farther up the river on one of the many sundowner cruises which start a few kilometres above the falls and drift leisurely upstream for a while and return after sunset. Prices vary but the spectacle does not. Check whether all drinks are included when you compare prices.

Information

The helpful tourist information centre is opposite the shopping complex in the main street, tel: 13 4202. The friendly staff can tell you anything from where to stay to how you can hire mountain bikes for the day.

Getting there and away

Other than the **trains**, of course, there is also an international **airport**, 20km from town on the Bulawayo road, and served by a number of European airlines, as well as by Air Zimbabwe and South African Airways. Many package holidays begin or end here. Shuttle buses meet most flights.

There are also various long-distance **buses**, some luxury standard and quite expensive, as well as local buses which run shorter distances. Timetables can be found at the tourist information centre.

Travellers going on to **Namibia** will need to plan carefully. At the time of writing, the best option was the Namvic Shuttle which runs once a week from Windhoek, the Namibian capital, to Victoria Falls and back, leaving from Windhoek's main bus terminal at 04.30 on Thursdays and leaving Victoria Falls at 11.00 on Sundays, from outside the Safari Par Excellence tour offices. The trip takes almost two full days and costs R600, but this does include a sunset cruise at the overnight stop on the Kwando River in Caprivi. Seats can be booked through the Windhoek office, tel: (+264) 61 124 7297, or the various tour operators in Victoria Falls.

For travellers heading to **Botswana** who do not want to take the train from Bulawayo, one of the best options until recently was the Botswana Bus, a nine-day game tour rather than a straight bus ride. Unfortunately at the time this book was going to press reports suggested that this service was no longer running. Previously, the bus spent two days in the massive Chobe Game Reserve in northern Botswana and three days in the fabulous Okavango Delta, an oasis in what is otherwise a scrubby desert. It departed every other Friday and cost US$395 one way. It may be worthwhile asking at tourist information or at one of the hostels in Victoria Falls in case it has been revived or replaced.

Travellers heading for **Zambia** should check if the shuttle train is running. This is a much nicer way to cross the border in either direction, saving you a taxi ride or the long slog on foot to and from each of the customs posts.

The shuttle, which is a passenger coach coupled onto the back of a cross-border freight train, is supposed to run daily between Livingstone in Zambia and Victoria Falls town. At the time of writing, however, the situation was confused, with railwaymen on the Zimbabwe side claiming not to have seen it for some time. Zambian railway officials were adamant the shuttle ran, but on Fridays only, departing Livingstone at around 06.45, depending on shunting movements. It was cancelled on a recent occasion when I was supposed to ride it as there was no locomotive available to pull it. The truth may be that Zambia Railways has to foot the bill for the shuttle and staff have said that running the daily service was proving too costly. The Friday train seems to have been retained to benefit Livingstonians who want to stock up on cheaper goods over the border. For onward travel north into Zambia from Livingstone, see Chapter 17, page 245.

Safety
Victoria Falls town itself has boomed in recent years and unfortunately has not escaped unharmed, having sacrificed its quiet charm on the altar of tourism. Prices are high and visitors are pestered by street sellers and money-changers. Beware of the latter – most are unscrupulous, highly skilled conmen. Changing money on the street is illegal in Zimbabwe, so many of them moonlight as police informers. Use a bank, be happy. Muggings are also on the rise, so be careful walking around after dark. Do not walk alone between the National Park and the town at night.

Accommodation
Victoria Falls has literally cashed in on the tourist boom and is one of the most extortionate places on the continent. Budget accommodation is a relative term but there are a number of new options to help you avoid forking out at the, admittedly gorgeous, Victoria Falls Hotel.

Luxury
The Victoria Falls Hotel tel: 13 4203. If you want to pay to live well, when you arrive at the Falls, there is no other option. It's a full-on walk back into colonial times. Lunch and dinner can be served on the terrace whilst watching the mist rise from the thunderous falls over the Batoka Gorge. If you are lucky, a dare-devil may just leap off the edge of the Victoria Falls Bridge on a piece of bungee cord. All this as you sip your tea. The standard rate for a double room is US$378, a single is US$303.

Mid-price
Sprayview Hotel corner of Livingstone Way and Reynard Rd, tel:13 4344/5/6. Doubles from Z$873, singles Z$633. For Victoria Falls, this is a bargain hard to beat, if you want to stay in a hotel and not a hostel.

Budget
Moira's One of the best-kept secrets of Victoria Falls are the private homes which have been opened as guest-houses. One of the finest is at 357 Gibson Rd (no phone at present) where there are double rooms, two thatched double huts, one dormitory and a swimming pool. It is self catering, but Moira and Vic's cool quiet garden is an outstanding place to recover from the rigours of African train travel. The cost is Z$150 per person, regardless of where you sleep.

Zambezi National Park

The 56,000-hectare (216 square mile) Zambezi National Park begins 6km from Victoria Falls town and runs for 46km up the western bank of the river and 26km inland. There is a good road with pleasant picnic sites throughout. The mammals in the park include elephant, lion, cheetah, leopard, zebra, buffalo, waterbuck, kudu and the ubiquitous impala. The river is full of crocodiles and hippo – stay away from the river banks.

The best way of exploring the park is by car, which can be hired in Victoria Falls. There are two fishing camps in the park as well as a few six-bed lodges right on the river. **Bookings** can be made through the National Parks booking office in Harare, tel: 4 70 6077, or fax 4 72 6089.

HARARE TO BULAWAYO

A lot of travellers use this train, mainly as a connection with the international airport in Harare but it is not a key-to-adventure train, running as it does through Zimbabwe's industrial heart. Like all NRZ trains, it runs at night, taking a leisurely 10 hours for the 350km (220 mile) journey.

The line of settlements between the two cities grew up along the railway line, relying on mining and farming. There is not a lot to see here – the towns are pleasant enough but diversions are thin on the ground.

The biggest town is **Gweru**, a mining, industrial and railway centre with a population of about 350,000. The town's strategic importance centres around the nearby junction between the railway line from South Africa and the Harare–Bulawayo main line, as well as a diverse minerals base, including chromite, nickel, iron ore and quartz.

Chegutu, just south of Harare is a vital cattle, maize and wheat centre. Kadoma, another industrial town north of Gweru, earns its bread from textile manufacture and cotton weaving, while KweKwe is a steel and gold mining town. The train rushes past these towns in the night. Stay on it!

If you are coming from Harare and heading for Chiredzi, the closest railhead to the **Gonarezhou National Park** on the southern border is Somabhula Junction. However, while the daily return mixed from Bulawayo to Chiredzi – the only NRZ train which goes south from here – also passes through Somabhula, it does so at 00.59, more than two hours before the train from Harare comes through at 03.34. There is not a lot of diversion in Somabhula for the next 22 hours. If you want to get to Gonarezhou from Harare by train, your best bet would be to stay on the overnight train from Harare to Bulawayo and take the Chiredzi train from Bulawayo the following evening. The connection does not work in reverse either as the Bulawayo–Harare train passes through Somabhula long before the mixed from Chiredzi comes through. The Chiredzi–Bulawayo service is explained in more detail later in this chapter.

Times
(main stops only)

	Northbound Daily, all classes		Southbound Daily, all classes	
dep	21.00	Bulawayo	arr	06.40
dep	21.13	Mpopoma	dep	06.26
dep	00.01	Somabhula	dep	03.44
dep	01.15	Gweru	dep	03.00
dep	02.30	Kwekwe	dep	01.24
dep	04.00	Kadoma	dep	00.01
dep	04.40	Chegutu	dep	23.15
arr	06.50	Harare	dep	21.00

The morning arrival in Bulawayo gives you plenty of time to make the onward connections in Bulawayo with trains to Victoria Falls, Botswana and Johannesburg.

Fares
Harare–Bulawayo, one way:

First $132.00
Second $105.00
Economy $54.60

Harare
Harare is one of Africa's nicest capital cities. Situated 1,471m (4,825ft) above sea level in the middle of fertile farmland, this city of 2.5 million people is a vibrant and happening place, a mix of first world trappings and raw Africa.

The city is made by its trees and flowers which have survived the ravages of empire building and post-colonial chaos. The result is a combination of shaded streets and large parks which soften the standard high rise blocks and industrial sprawl. The wide streets are a hangover from colonial days when the pioneers needed plenty of room to manoeuvre their ox-wagons.

The Shona, who today are Zimbabwe's ruling class, were the first people to settle on the flats below a *kopje* (hillock) they called Neharare Tshikomo, the hillock of Neharare, named for one of their chiefs who is buried there. The first Europeans arrived on September 13 1890, when Cecil Rhodes' Pioneer Column planted a Union Flag on the bare but very fertile earth and started building Fort Salisbury around it. Their contracts complete, the men of the Pioneer Column then wandered off into the surrounding countryside to look for gold or to expropriate land for farming. Rhodesia was born.

Although hammered by a severe malaria epidemic, the pioneers stayed on and soon more settlers began arriving from the south, lured by dreams of gold and hunger for land. The town grew into a municipality, became the country's capital in 1923, and continued to flourish through the period of the Federation of Rhodesia and Nyasaland. Following UDI in 1965, Salisbury merely ticked over until Zimbabwe became fully independent in 1980. The new

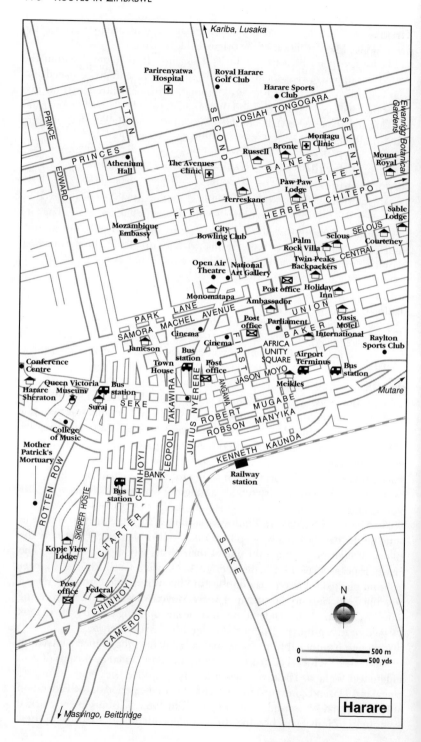

Kariba, Lusaka

Parirenyatwa
Hospital

Royal Harare
Golf Club

Harare Sports
Club

MILTON

PRINCE

EDWARD

PRINCES

Athenium
Hall

The Avenues
Clinic

SECOND

JOSIAH TONGOGARA

Russell

Bronte

Montagu
Clinic

BAINES

SEVENTH

Mount
Royal

Ewanrigg Botanical
Gardens

Paw Paw
Lodge

FIFE

HERBERT

CHITEPO

Sable
Lodge

Terreskane

FIFE

Mozambique
Embassy

City
Bowling Club

SELOUS

SELOUS

Palm
Rock Villa

Selous

Courteney

CENTRAL

Open Air
Theatre

National
Art Gallery

Twin Peaks
Backpackers

Post office

Holiday
Inn

Monomatapa

Ambassador

UNION

PARK LANE

MACHEL AVENUE

Post
office

Parliament

BAKER

Oasis
Motel

SAMORA

Cinema

International

Raylton
Sports Club

Jameson

Cinema

FIRST

AFRICA
UNITY
SQUARE

Airport
Terminus

Bus
station

Conference
Centre

Town
House

Bus
station

Post
office

JASON MOYO

Bus
station

Mutare

Queen Victoria
Harare Museum
Sheraton

Bus
station

ANGWA

Meikles

SEKE

Suraj

TAKAWIRA

JULIUS NYERERE

ROBERT MUGABE

College
of Music

ROBSON

MANYIKA

Mother
Patrick's
Mortuary

KENNETH KAUNDA

ROTTEN ROW

SKIPPER HOSTE

CHINHOYI

BANK

LEOPOLD

Bus
station

SEKE

Railway
station

CHARTER

Kopje View
Lodge

Post
office

Federal

CHINHOYI

CAMERON

N

0 _____ 500 m
0 _____ 500 yds

Harare

Masvingo, Beitbridge

government, eager to silence any colonial echoes, immediately renamed the capital Harare, a corruption of the original chief's name.

Harare is a good base from which to organise further travel within the country or to obtain visas for surrounding countries that are to be visited.

It is a relatively easy place to walk around, with the centre based on two grids, the main area of the town and that on the *kopje*. The flashy shopping and banking area is on 1st St Mall, bounded by Samora Machel Av, Julius Nyerere Way and Robert Mugabe Rd.

Practical details
Airport transfer
Harare International Airport, 15km (9 miles) south-east of the city is served by a frequent bus service which connects with departures and arrivals. The city terminus is at the corner of Speke Av and 2nd St. The fare is Z$60. A taxi from the airport to town costs around Z$100. Agree on the fare before setting off. Harare's Airport Bank is open outside normal banking hours, usually to coincide with international arrivals.

Station
The station is on the corner of Kenneth Kaunda Av and 2nd St. The bookings office is open 08.00–13.00 and 14.00–16.00 on weekdays and 08.00–11.30 on Saturday. The ticket office (where you actually buy your ticket) is open on weekdays 08.00–13.00, 14.00–16.00 and 19.00–21.30. Opening times on Saturday are 08.00–11.30 and 19.00–21.30, and 19.00–21.30 on Sundays.

While the evening opening times coincide with the departure of the daily trains to Bulawayo and Mutare, trying to get tickets just before departure time is not a recommended African travel experience, especially at peak times like school holidays. Buy them a few days before.

Information
The Harare Publicity Association office is at the south-west corner of African Unity Square, on Jason Moyo Av between 2nd St and 3rd St, tel: 4 705085/7. It is open 08.00–17.00 on weekdays and until noon on Saturdays. The usefulness of this particular office seems to wax and wane but it is worth trying. The bureau does produce *What's on in Harare*, a useful monthly guide to city happenings.

The more upbeat Zimbabwe Tourist Bureau office, open from 08.00–13.00 and 14.00–16.30, is on the corner of Jason Moyo Av and 4th St.

Post
The main post office is on Inez Terrace. Hours are 08.30–16.00 during the week and until 11.30 on Saturdays. The post restante service is available only at the main post office.

Books and maps
Kingston's has two branches, in the Parkade Centre, 1st St, and at the corner

PARTYING IN THE CITY THAT NEVER SLEEPS
Jono Waters

Even though all those free non-racial and democratised babies who arrived around the time of independence are just starting to make the legal drinking age, the sad thing is that relaxed inter-racial mixing barely goes on. The city centre venues and those in the south are fairly welcoming of all races, but the local whites tend to drink at venues in the northern suburbs where they mainly live.

Harare means 'the one that does not sleep', and its party crowd rarely goes to bed much before 04.00. The city centre and the south are where you will find the fun. Most places are relatively safe, so long as you don't have tourist stamped on your head or wrapped around your waist. You are unlikely to be hassled inside a venue although, if you are white, you may find yourself being stared at briefly as *murungus* are not a regular feature. However, the locals are very friendly and are always keen to engage in a conversation.

The best way to find out what gigs are on is to check the entertainment page in the *Herald*, Harare's daily, especially on Fridays. Rumba is the local sound and Leonard Dembo is probably the most popular artist at the moment. Veterans Oliver Mtukudzi and the Black Spirits and Thomas Mapfumo and Blacks Unlimited still have good followings and can sometimes be seen at Club Hideout 99 in Lochinvar or the Skyline Motel (19 km on the road to Beitbridge). Current flavour of the month is Andy Brown and The Storm, whose 'hybrid' form of music does seem to have a unifying influence on the multi-cultural crowds, even though he sings almost exclusively in Chishona, the local vernacular. Zairean *kwasa-kwasa* is extremely popular and visiting stars fill stadiums.

Harare's social set are a fickle bunch and the crowd that is attracted to a nightclub can change in a fortnight. The older venues include Circus Nite Club in the Strathaven Shopping Centre, Underground on Mbuya Nehanda Street, Sandro's. Sarah's on Jason Moyo Avenue, where the gay community hangs out, and Club Sahara on Rhodesville Avenue, host alternative raves on selected nights.

Going out to 'white' places is obviously a lot more expensive and more than two nights in the same one will bring home just how small the white gene pool is. It is broadly divided along two lines – the more traditionally-minded Rhodies, and the rest who don't really attract a label other than Zimbabweans. Rhodie hangouts include the Sports Café at the Chispite Shopping Centre, the Keg & Sable at the Borrowdale Shopping Centre, and Bulldogs just next to it in Sam Levy's Village. For those looking for a bit of an alternative *jol* (party), try the Bizarre Bar in Kamfinsa Shopping Centre. Xscape in Sam Levy's Village is also very popular at the moment, and is not as Rhodie as the Sports Café.

of 2nd Av and Jason Moyo Av, with the best book selection in Zimbabwe. Grass Roots, Jason Moyo Av, has books on politics, socialism, local issues and natural history, among other subjects.

Maps of Harare and Zimbabwe generally are available from the Publicity Association or the Surveyor General's office, Electra House, Samora Machel Avenue.

Safety

By day, Harare is a generally placid, easy-going place, now that policing has been improved. You must still watch out for the groups of pickpockets. At night, however, the risk increases significantly and you should not walk anywhere – use both taxis and common sense. If you are unsure whether you will be safe wherever you wish to go at night, check with hotel staff.

Sightseeing

The city's finest attractions are its parks with their shade trees and flowers. **Cecil Square** in the centre of the town is shaded by particularly beautiful trees. The **Harare Public Gardens** literally extend over the whole city via avenues of trees and there is always something flowering in the town. Many of the trees are exotic, including Mexican feather duster trees, jacarandas, Australian flame trees and a gigantic Himalayan cypress in the main gardens. Spring and early summer, September to November, are Harare's most colourful times, when many of the trees are in full blossom. From the air, the jacarandas all but hide the city in a purple haze.

Don't miss the **miniature Victoria Falls** in the gardens, a scale replica of the original, complete with mini-Zambezi River, gorge, railway bridge and real rainbows. Unlike the original, a year-round supply of water is also guaranteed.

Architecturally, Harare is a mixture of colonial musings and sixties' bureaucratic detachment. Some of the more interesting buildings include the Market Hall, built in 1893 and still a marketplace, the Italian Renaissance-inspired Town House and the Parliament building which was meant to be a hotel until the Rhodesian Army commandeered it as barracks in 1896. More colonial buildings line Robert Mugabe Av.

The city is home to some of the wildest **tobacco auctions** in the world. Tobacco is the country's single biggest source of foreign exchange. Sales – which visitors are welcome to watch – are held daily between April and October as the harvest comes in. The main auction hall is on Gleneagles Rd in Willovale, reachable on the Highfields bus from the stop on the corner of Robert Mugabe Av and 4th St.

The **Queen Victoria Museum** is worth visiting if you want to get a reasonable grip on the country's natural history. The display includes a collection of Bushman paintings, artefacts from Great Zimbabwe, wildlife habitats and fossils. The museum is in the Civic Centre between Pennefeather Av and Rotten Row and is open 09.00–17.00 daily. Entry costs Z$2.

For superb African art and sculpture, lose yourself on the first floor of the

National Gallery, situated in the Harare Gardens on the Park Lane side. The collection of African artworks of all kinds is regarded as one of the best in the world. The gallery is open 09.00–12.30 and 14.00–17.00 daily, except Mondays.

Around Harare

The city is blessed by its pleasant surroundings which include at least two national parks and some weird rock formations at Epworth Mission. Sadly, there are no local trains out of the city – the two branch railways which run north-west and east out of the city carry freight only. Hiring a car is the best way to get around, although there is plenty of local bus transport, too. Travellers with their own bicycles will be amply rewarded with some stunning rides.

Lake Chivero, 32km (20 miles) south-west of the city, is the major source of Harare's water. The dam has the usual boating and fishing facilities one would expect on a large lake. Swimming in the lake is not advisable, however, on account of crocodiles and bilharzia. The southern shore is a game reserve in which large herds of different antelope species wander at will in their natural habitat. The main attractions for most visitors, however, are the vivid Bushman paintings in the rock shelters in the surrounding hills.

Ewanrigg National Park is a beautiful 40-hectare (100-acre) garden created decades ago by an enthusiastic gardener and farmer, Basil Christian. He collected aloes and cycads from all over Africa, and trees, shrubs and various cacti worldwide, and planted them around a stream full of aquatic and marsh plants. The gardens are crowded on weekends but a haven during the week. Ewanrigg is at its best during the winter months (June to August) when all the succulents are in full bloom. The park is 40km (25 miles) north-east of Harare on the Shamva road and accessible by local bus.

The action of sun, wind and rain on Zimbabwe's granite hills has turned much of the country into a giant rockery and **Epworth Balancing rocks**, 13km (8 miles) south-east of the city, is one such fine collection. Some of the rocks balance on others, others have been eroded into bizarre shapes, giving the place something of a religious overtone. Fittingly, the area round about was named after Tshirembe, a famous spirit medium who lived there. There is a US$1 entrance fee and you are likely to be surrounded by hordes of kids from the mission school who will all want to be your guide.

Accommodation

Finding a hotel room in Harare is generally not a problem and there is something for all tastes and budgets. The selection starts at the top end with the five-stars like **Meikles Hotel**, the **Harare Sheraton** and the **Monomatapa**. Remember foreigners pay more than locals and in US dollars, too. Rates are usually in the US$100–US$150 range. Cheaper options are listed below.

Mid-price
Bronte Hotel 132 Baines Av, tel: 4 796631. Clean and quiet, with its own gardens and pool. You need to book well ahead, though. Single/double US$40/50.

Budget
Talk of the Town 92 Central Av. Spotless home-style accommodation aimed at business travellers. US$9
Palm Rock Villa 39 Selous Av, tel: 4 724550. A clean backpackers' hostel run by a new friendly manager named Jealous, which he isn't. Z$54 for a dorm bed.

Eating and drinking
As one would expect from a cosmopolitan city, there is a wide range of eating options. The usual American-style take-aways and pizzerias abound. If you are after *sadza*, try just about any café – they may look dodgy but the *sadza* will be excellent. Avoid 'Russians' – fat, red, deep-fried sausages which will not be Russian at all.

Coimbra, 61 Selous Av, is one of the nicer ethnic options, with superb Portuguese seafood and *peri-peri* chicken.

HARARE TO MUTARE
The ridge of mountains that runs down the east side of the continent, from Ethiopia in the north to the Cape in South Africa, creates a unique zone through all the countries it passes through. Here in Zimbabwe, on the edge of the escarpment, are the Highlands, with a climate and vegetation more like Scotland, and less like the bushveld and savannah plains one expects in Africa.

Zimbabwe's Eastern Highlands are a narrow strip of mountains which form a natural border with Mozambique. The mountains are the soul of the Highlands, stretching from Inyanga in the north to Chiredzi and Gonarezhou in the south. This agriculturally rich area is significantly cooler than the rest of the country, and is peppered with tea and coffee plantations. Large plantations of gum (eucalyptus) and pine trees, and granite domes which dot the edge of the plateau, make for some of the best hiking country in the region. The ridge, which is around 1,525m (5,000ft) high, is so narrow that you can see the descent into the low country on either side.

Getting around the Highlands demands a bit of ingenuity, planning and luck, as local transport here is not nearly as good as in the rest of the country. Cyclists, mountain bikers especially, are in for a treat – those relying on buses will have to be patient. Hiring a car in Mutare is a good way of getting to explore the region fully.

Although Mutare is a mere 250km (160 miles) from Harare, the daily train takes a full night to cover the distance, partly because of the twisting track as the railway winds its way into the mountains, but also because NRZ, eager as ever to please its customers, does not like dumping passengers on unknown station platforms in the wee hours. It is a pity that the train runs at night, for the scenery is often spectacular, especially at the eastern end of the journey. At least you will sleep well and arrive refreshed.

Being the service to the community that they are, trains will stop at almost any place with a platform. While the hours may be inconvenient, a little forward planning will enable you to get off along the way and explore a little.

Times
(main stops only)

	Eastbound Daily, all classes			Westbound Daily, all classes	
	dep	21.30	Harare	arr	05.20
	dep	23.41	Marondera	dep	03.28
	dep	00.39	Macheke	dep	02.21
	dep	01.48	Headlands	dep	01.06
	dep	02.54	Rusape	dep	00.04
	dep	03.30	Nyazura	dep	23.05
	dep	04.33	Odzi	dep	21.47
	arr	05.25	Mutare	dep	21.00

Fares
First class	Z$82.25
Second class	Z$67.50
Economy class	Z$31.85

Marondera
The first major stop after leaving Harare, Marondera is a bustling agricultural centre built around a central square. Unless you are really fond of agricultural towns, there is not a great deal to divert the casual traveller, apart from the local vineyards of which the country is very proud. Getting to the vineyards is difficult, but there are outlets in the town where you can taste the local product.

Accommodation is limited to the 25-room **Marondera Hotel**, tel: 79 4005.

Rusape
Also a farming town, Rusape is named after the Lesapi River which it straddles. The name means 'sparing of its waters', on account of the river's erratic flow. There is a dam on the river with a shaded campsite on the banks, but aside from good fishing, there is not much to do in Rusape.

The railway line now swings directly east and heads straight into the foothills. Granite outcrops and musasa trees dominate the countryside. About 70km (43 miles) from Rusape, the railway reaches the small town of **Odzi**, a tobacco and wine growing centre. Accommodation is non-existent in the town but you could try nearby Mapor Estates (tel: 204 3072), a working tobacco farm which has camping facilities as well as rooms in the main farm house. The nearby hills are full of caves and rock paintings. To get to Mapor, you will have to arrange a pick-up from the station in advance.

Mutare

Regarded as one of Africa's best situated cities, Mutare lies in the valley of the Sakubva River and is surrounded by the high granite mountains which make this part of the country so distinctive. The town is blessed with a warm but not overpowering climate and the surrounding slopes are covered with pines.

Locals will waste no time telling you that Mutare is the town that moved, thanks to the coming of the railway. The chief in the area in 1890 was one Chief Mutasa, a man whose goodwill the Portuguese and British competed to nourish so they could get on with prospecting for the gold in the area. Days after beginning their occupation of Mashonaland in 1890 the British South Africa Company built a fort in the area, effectively stopping any further overtures by the Portuguese. A boisterous but prosperous mining camp sprang up on the banks of the Mutare ('river of ore'), and was named Umtali by the hard-drinking miners.

By March 1896 the narrow gauge railway from Beira (being built by Rhodes, of course), had reached the far side of the surrounding hills. Rhodes visited the town and told the dismayed people that the engineers were going

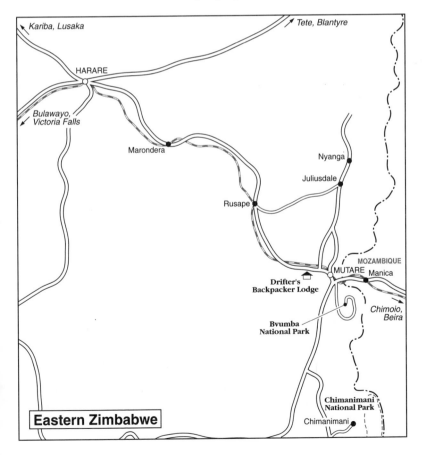

Eastern Zimbabwe

to take the railway through the mountains by the easiest route. This point happened to be 17km (10.5 miles) away in the valley of the Sakubva River, and separated from Umtali by a high granite ridge. Rhodes looked at the cost of building the line to Umtali and decided the town should be moved instead, which it promptly was. He paid £50,000 to the residents and laid out an exact copy on the site where the modern town stands today.

The city's name was changed from Umtali to Mutare in 1982, shortly after independence, in keeping with the move to correct the inaccuracies of the colonial era.

Today Mutare is a lovely place to spend some time in, although there is not a lot to do in the town itself. If you want to escape from the punishing mid-summer heat then this, and the surrounding Highlands, is the place to do it, and if you have come from Mozambique, where travel is significantly more arduous than in Zimbabwe, then a few days here will sort you out. The railway station is located at the south end of the town.

Practical details
Accommodation
Manica Hotel corner Aerodrome Rd/Third St, tel: 20 6 4431. Singles Z$1181, doubles Z$1536. Breakfast included.
Ann Bruce's 99 Fourth St, tel: 20 6 3569. Double room Z$80 per person, dorm bed Z$70. Good meals available, too: Z$50 for dinner and Z$40 for full English breakfast, Z$17 for a Continental breakfast.
Trevor's Place 119 Fourth St, tel: 20 6 7762. Singles Z$75, doubles Z$150.

Information
Manicaland Publicity Association Robert Mugabe St, Market Square; tel: 20 64711.

Climate
The region is unlike anywhere else in Zimbabwe and its elevation means the climate is pleasant all year round. The cool months between May and September have the most sun and least rain. The summer months are very hot. October is good as it is usually dry while February and March offer good, though wet, hiking weather.

Attractions near Mutare
The main attraction is the nearby **Bvumba Botanical Garden** (Bvumba has a silent 'B'), located 30km south-east of the town in the series of ridges known as the Bvumba. The garden is surrounded on three sides by farmland, some of which are commercial banana farms, and others worked by subsistence farmers in what is called the Zimunya Communal Land.

Despite the encroaching agriculture, there are still large tracts of indigenous forest on the hillsides. The natural afro-montane evergreen forest and high rainfall miombo woodlands are magnificent, with thick cover and trees ranging from 5m to 20m in height. There are some great day walks in the

Bvumba and the Bunga Forest, with distances ranging from 8km up to 14km (5–9 miles). This is excellent mountain biking country with loads of trails and paths, and landowners are said to be fairly relaxed about the presence of bikers. There is also good trout fishing in the area

You can camp here in a world-class **campsite**, perched on the side of a huge ridge and commanding a spectacular view to the east over the Burma valley hundreds of metres below and of the Chimanimani Mountains by the Mozambique border.

The Bvumba is tricky to get to unless you hire a car. There is a local bus service, but using it demands a fair amount of patience and luck.

If you find rugged landscapes thrilling, escape to the **Chimanimani Mountains** which form the border with Mozambique. It is a place of rocky gorges and cliffs, bizarre rock formations, tumbling waterfalls and crystal clear rivers and pools. The helpful Tourist Association in Mutare says of the area in its brochure, 'Footpaths are given as a guide only, they evolve, develop and even disappear.'

The quickest and most popular route in is the aptly named Bailey's Folly, a punishing two-hour climb from Mutekeswane Base Camp. The trail climbs through the musasa trees on the lower reaches to a dramatic sculpted-stone 'forest' on the upper slopes. You will know you are alive – the fire in your legs will tell you so. The view east to Mozambique, across the Bundi Valley, is stupendous.

The only **accommodation** in the park is in a stone mountain hut overlooking the valley. The hut has flush toilets and beds with mattresses. You can also camp or sleep in the nearby caves.

Park **fees** cost Z$100 for up to seven days (Z$20 for Zimbabwe residents). Camping costs Z$60 per person per night; the hut costs Z$200.

There is more **accommodation** in Chimanimani Village. Heaven Lodge (tel: 26 2701) is a clean backpackers' place with an outstanding view. The Frog and Fern Bed and Breakfast (tel: 26 2294) is a lot more expensive and they will not like your muddy boots.

Groceries are available at the Bottle Store. You can hire sleeping bags and other camping gear there too.

INTO MOZAMBIQUE
Mutare is a good jumping off point for Mozambique. Take a minibus-taxi to the border town of Machipanda, cross on foot and then pick up a train from there to Beira, Mozambique's second city. The journey from the border to Beira takes between 12 and 15 hours with stops at the border town of Manica (actually 20km east of the border), Chimoio, Gondola and Dondo. More details on this service are given in Chapter 17, page 265.

There are also numerous buses plying this route.

Warning Watch out for the money changers at the border – they are sharp operators and you will need to be vigilant if you wish to escape a scalping.

TO CHIREDZI AND SOUTH AFRICA

NRZ's fourth overnight service is the daily mixed train from Bulawayo to Chiredzi. All classes are available but there is no dining car. Instead on-board vendors sell biscuits, sweets, beer and cigarettes. First and second class accommodation is in sleeper coaches, economy is the standard cattle transport.

The Chiredzi mixed is really aimed at local people needing to get into the south-east part of the country and its appeal to the casual tourist is limited. However, its status as a 'people's train' makes it a journey worth undertaking if you want to meet real Zimbabweans.

The train runs east from Bulawayo on the main line to Harare before heading south at Somabhula, then swinging eastwards again at the junction at Rutenga. There are few towns of note on the way.

Times
(main stops only)

	Eastbound Daily, all classes			Westbound Daily, all classes	
dep	21.30	Bulawayo	arr	07.25	
dep	22.28	Heany Junction	dep	06.25	
dep	00.59	Somabhula	dep	03.23	
dep	07.50	Rutenga	dep	19.30	
dep	10.49	Triangle	dep	16.05	
arr	11.30	Chiredzi	dep	15.00	

Fares

First	Z$141.75
Second	Z$112.50
Economy	Z$59.15

Chiredzi

Chiredzi, founded in the 1960s as a supply town for sugar-cane farmers in the Hippo Valley, is the nearest access point for the **Gonarezhou National Park**. The 5,000km² park, whose southern boundary runs along the Mozambique border, is a difficult one to access without your own transport but persistence will pay off. There are walking trails lasting three to six days in the park – prices start at U$150 for a 3-day trail. Call 4 70 6077 for **information and bookings**. Game includes lion, buffalo, loads of elephant, rhino and antelope in abundance. The area's elephants have long been a magnet for poachers. One legend, an old bull named Dhlulamiti – 'Taller-than-the-trees' – was shot by a notorious poacher here in the 1920s. His tusks weighed in at 110kg, the largest 'taken' off any elephant south of the Zambezi River. The main visitors' areas are centred on Chipinda Pools in the north of the park and Mabalauta in the south. The latter is accessible off the Masvingo–Beitbridge road, while the former is an easier 55km from Chiredzi.

Chipinda boasts a campsite (with hot showers!) which is open year-round. There are no shops, hotels or restaurants in the reserve, however – take all your own provisions with you.

Accommodation in Chiredzi
Unfortunately there is little available. It is after all a sugar-cane town and not really a tourist spot as most of the lodges tend to congregate, like wild animals, near Gonarezhou itself. The best option in the town is the **Planters Inn** (tel: 31 2281).

Getting to the South African border
With the re-routing of the *Bulawayo* train from Johannesburg via Botswana and the withdrawal of the Johannesburg–Harare service, there are currently no scheduled passenger trains running between Beitbridge on the border and the small junction of Rutenga. If you are heading south from Chiredzi or Gonarezhou, you will be looking for a bus. You will need to get a local bus – of which there are many – to the main Beitbridge–Harare highway from where you can get another to the border. The fare should be no more than Z$40-60 for the latter section.

The train service south from Beitbridge is discussed in Chapter 6 page 80.

Namibia:
Background Information

Namib is a Hottentot word that means 'Thirstland', and that is the lasting impression most visitors have of this vast, arid country, one of the world's most sparsely populated. The Namib Desert runs north to south almost the whole length of the country's coast; inland, stark mountain ranges bake in the heat and life hangs by a thread for the animals and people who live here. Namibia is also astonishingly beautiful. The Namib has the world's highest dune; the fearsome Skeleton Coast is an untainted wilderness where the impact of humans is restricted to the rusting remains of a few ships which came too close; the northern savanna is alive with animals; and lush forests grow along the banks of the Kavango River in the far north.

BASIC FACTS
Location
The Republic of Namibia lies on the south-west coast of Africa, bordered by South Africa to the south, Botswana in the east and Angola to the north.

Size
Namibia covers an area of 824,290km² (318,260 square miles), yet its population is a tiny 1.5 million people, giving it a population density of roughly two people per square kilometre. As most of the country is desert, the population is based mainly around the major towns or in the more fertile areas to the north.

Capital
Windhoek, the capital, sprawls lazily across a wide valley, surrounded by hills. With its ubiquitous German architecture and pavement cafés, the city feels like a displaced piece of Europe.

Government
After independence from South Africa in 1990, Namibia became a nation-wide, multi-party democracy. The South West African People's Organisation (Swapo) controls the National Assembly, with its main support base among the people of Owamboland in the north. The main opposition is the centre-right Democratic Turnhalle Alliance (DTA), a coalition of 11 other parties.

Major towns
Windhoek is the largest town, followed by Keetmanshoop in the south, the coastal resort town of Swakopmund, and Walvis Bay, which is the country's port. Gobabis is a busy frontier town near the border with Botswana. The only town of any significant size in the north is Tsumeb, the centre of the country's copper mining industry.

Economy
Namibia's varied mineral resources – especially diamonds – make it the third-wealthiest country in sub-Saharan Africa. Its fishing grounds are also among the world's richest. Livestock rearing and tourism are other key sectors. Whites control most of the economy and unemployment among blacks remains high.

Languages
English was adopted post-independence as the country's official language in an attempt to dispel the colonial hangovers of both Afrikaans and German – still widely spoken – as well as to find a *lingua franca*. Namibia's population is made up of diverse tribes with different languages. The two main language and ethnic groups are the Bantu languages like Owambo, and the Khoisan languages of the San and Nama people. Whites tend to be either German- or Afrikaans-speaking, the latter language being widely used in the rural areas.

Currency
The unit of currency is the Namibian dollar which is divided into 100 cents. The Namibian dollar is tied to the South African rand on a one for one basis and its exchange rate with other currencies therefore reflects the rate for the rand. There is no market in Namibian dollars in most areas outside southern Africa and they therefore cannot be purchased by tourists before they leave home. Cash or travellers' cheques in US dollars are widely accepted in Namibia and may be a better option for visitors than other ways of carrying money.

Climate
Much of Namibia is desert or semi-desert which sees little rain. The north-east of the country is savannah and mopani forest, with heavy rains between November and March. The cold Benguela current which flows the length of the coast causes a thick, cold fog most days unless the hot *berg* (mountain) winds are blowing.

Average temperatures during the summer – October to April – can top 40°C (104°F) and go higher in the desert and canyons. In the north-east it gets very hot and humid. Winter temperatures are a more pleasant 25°C (71°F) on average. Nights in the desert are usually bitterly cold in all seasons.

Namibia's main holiday seasons are in December and January, and over Easter, and prices generally rise accordingly.

Geography

'Thirstland' is an apt name for this arid country. The northern parts are grassy savannah, but the overriding impression is of a land burned by the sun. The Namib Desert stretches the length of the west of the country along the coast. Eastwards, the escarpment rises to a central plateau before easing down into the Kalahari Desert. The north-east, however, is lush, covered with thick mopani forest in places. Two major rivers mark the northern border with Angola – the westward flowing Kunene and the Kavango which flows eastwards into the Caprivi Strip.

HISTORY

Little is known about the region's pre-Iron Age history. The harsh environment limited settlement for most peoples except the hardy San Bushmen who are at home in the desert. The San roamed freely over these huge expanses of desert – across the Namib, east to the Kalahari and south to the Karoo in South Africa.

Another group, the Khoi-Khoi (Hottentots) moved into the region around 40,000 years ago, putting some pressure on the San. The San were hunter-gatherers while the Khoi-Khoi were nomadic pastoralists. The Khoi-Khoi, ancestors of today's Nama people, eventually spread as far south as the Cape about 2,000 years ago.

The Wambo people, who today account for nearly half of the country's population, drifted into Namibia from the east some time in the 16th century. Settling in the north of the country, along what is today the Angolan border, they were farmers, growing melons, ground-nuts, millet, beans and pumpkins.

The Hereros, cattle herders and warriors, also migrated into Namibia from the east around the same time as the Wambo and settled in the good grazing lands in the north. Their devotion to cattle would later embroil them in a series of bitter cattle-rustling feuds with European colonists and settlers from the south. The Herero women wear a distinctive tribal costume of full length dresses, inspired by the wives of missionaries who spent decades among them in the 19th century.

The second biggest group, population wise, are the 'Damas' – 'black people' – whose origins and language have been forgotten. Their docile nature meant they were exploited as slaves and their languages have come down from their masters.

The Europeans arrive

When he landed to erect a crucifix at Cape Cross on the Skeleton Coast in 1485, Portuguese explorer Diego Cao became the first European to set foot in Namibia. Bartolomeu Dias reached what is now Lüderitz in 1487, but the barren landscape deterred any further Portuguese exploration or settlement. By the late 18th century Walvis Bay and Lüderitz had become favoured anchorages for whaling ships, however, prompting the Dutch to take possession of Walvis Bay in 1793. When France invaded Holland a few years later, Britain invaded the Dutch Cape Colony to prevent the French getting their hands on the strategic victualling station and hence the sea route around the Cape. Walvis Bay was annexed by the British in 1878 and control was transferred to the Cape Colony six years later.

Around this time a German merchant called Lüderitz began buying land along the coast and, in 1884, the German Colonial Company bought Lüderitz out and the area became German South West Africa. The Germans plundered the land from the locals, often using brute force. When the Hereros rebelled in 1904, they were massacred at Waterberg. Many Herero women were rounded up as sex slaves, while the surviving men fled across the border to the Bechuanaland Protectorate, now Botswana.

When World War I broke out, South Africa invaded German South West Africa, urged on by Britain, and defeated the Germans at Khorab after a short, sharp campaign. Under the terms of the Versailles Treaty at the end of the war, South Africa was given a mandate to govern South West Africa until such time as the country could become politically autonomous.

The South African guardians and the German population got on rather well and South Africa, recognising its strategic and economic importance, announced the annexation of the territory in 1947. The United Nations opposed the annexation until 1961 when it tried by legal means to establish the country's independence. South Africa, by this time something of a pariah state following its own full independence in 1961, religiously ignored UN Resolution 435 which declared that South Africa's occupation was illegal.

The independence struggle

Seeing that South Africa was unlikely to relent, the South West African People's Organisation (Swapo) took to the bush and so started a 27-year bush war which was to spill over into a bloody civil war in Angola. The UN General Assembly tried repeatedly to implement sanctions against South Africa and Namibia but the moves were vetoed by Western nations who had economic interests in the region.

Angolan independence from Portugal in 1975 changed the nature of the struggle as the new socialist government in Angola agreed to provide safe training bases for Swapo guerrillas. South Africa took the war to Swapo, pursuing its troops across the border in a series of large scale search-and-destroy missions. The situation was complicated by South Africa's material support for Jonas Savimbi's Unita, a growing band of well-armed, Western-backed rebels fighting the Cuban- and Soviet-backed MPLA government in Angola. Inevitably, South African forces clashed with Cuban reinforcements, by then pouring into Angola. The war dragged on until 1988, with South Africa now openly supporting Unita in large set-piece battles for towns in southern Angola.

The UN Security Council was powerless to stop the conflict but upheld its Resolution 435 anyway, calling for, among other things, an end to the fighting, the return of refugees, and democratic elections. A key point in the resolution was the repeal of racially discriminatory legislation.

The black population of Namibia accounted for 90% of its people, yet into the 1980s whites had almost total control of the economy – white farmers for example accounted for three-quarters of agricultural output. South Africa, intensely fearful of the Communist countries sitting on its northern borders, played for time against UN pressure by refusing to negotiate on independence until Cuba withdrew its troops from Angola. Both South Africa and white South-Westers were terrified of what might happen when socialist Swapo came to power. With Mozambique and Zimbabwe both firmly in the socialist camp, South Africa's leaders believed they could not afford to have another neighbouring country follow suit.

By 1988 the war was costing South Africa over one million rand a day, straining its resources. Angola was ruined. It was time to settle. Mikhail Gorbachev's advent on the Soviet political scene changed everything – the Soviet Union stopped its expansionist ambitions in the Third World and, following US-mediated talks, phased troop withdrawals – Cubans from Angola and South Africans from South West Africa – began the same year.

Implementation of Resolution 435 followed. Independent bodies arrived to teach people about the voting process. The UN sent a peace-keeping force to monitor the elections, which took place in November 1989. Swapo won clearly but without its hoped-for two thirds majority.

GETTING THERE
By air
With Johannesburg pulling most of the region's international air traffic these days, just three major airlines connect Windhoek with the world, the national carrier Namib Air, South African Airways and Lufthansa. Namib Air flies to London and Johannesburg, one SAA flight to London stops over, and Lufthansa flies to Frankfurt.

Flying Johannesburg–Windhoek costs around R1,600 one way, while tickets from London range from £450–£600 return. There are no direct flights from the US – the best option is to fly to Johannesburg and fly to Windhoek from there.

The international airport is 30km from the centre of town. You can catch an Intercape bus to the terminus in town on Independence Av. The fare is R30 one way. You can also hitch a lift – remarkably easy in Namibia. Taxis are expensive.

By train
At the moment, the only train service to and from Namibia runs between Windhoek and Upington in South Africa (see pages 234–7). Facilities in Upington and how to get there from elsewhere in South Africa are discussed on pages 116–7.

By ship
Unicorn, a South African-based shipping line, has regular sailings between Durban, Cape Town and Walvis Bay. The freighters, which have

accommodation for six passengers in three cabins, sail twice monthly on a schedule which depends on cargo and weather. The fare from Durban to Walvis Bay is R3,000 and the journey takes 12–14 days. All meals are included.

By bus

Intercape Mainliner operates buses from Cape Town and Johannesburg to Windhoek. The one way Cape Town–Windhoek fare is R330. These buses can get uncomfortably full during the summer holiday season. There is also a weekly service between Windhoek and Victoria Falls in Zimbabwe, see page 192.

TRAVELLING IN NAMIBIA
Cost of living

Anyone travelling in southern Africa on hard currency – and this means just about any European currency, as well as the mighty dollar – will find Namibia fairly cheap. Although the Namibian dollar is on a par with the South African rand, the cost of living in Namibia is slightly higher. Hotels and meals are reasonable value; a double room in a good city hotel in Windhoek costs around N$425 a night, but a soft dorm bed in a clean backpackers' hostel will set you back only N$35 per person.

The main tourist attractions such as the game parks and hiking trails are remarkably inexpensive, especially when compared to the cost of similar attractions in East Africa. Tourism is one of the country's fastest growing economic sectors and this will ultimately boost prices. Go soon.

Independent travellers using public transport will be able to get by quite cheaply. However, some of the best parts of the country are not served by train or bus and, to get there, you will need to get a lift or hire a vehicle. Hiring a small car for two weeks would cost around N$285 per day; a fully equipped 4x4 would cost about N$930 per day.

Visas

The visa situation in Namibia was in flux during the early 1990s. It now seems to have settled down and currently visas are not required for visitors from the US, Canada, Australia, the UK and most EU countries. It is always worth checking, however, either with the Namibian embassy in your home country or the Department of Civic Affairs in Windhoek, tel: (+264) 61 33 398111.

Namibian Embassies overseas

UK 6 Chandos St, London W1M 0LQ, tel: 0171 636 6244.
USA 1605 New Hampshire Av, N.W. Washington DC 20009, tel: 202 986 0450.

Foreign Representatives in Namibia

British High Commission 116 Robert Mugabe Av, Windhoek, tel: 061 223022.
US Embassy 14 Lussen St, Windhoek, tel: 061 221601.

Banks

Banking hours are 08.30–15.30 on weekdays and 08.30–11.00 on Saturdays. Cashing travellers' cheques is straightforward; US dollar, sterling or rand denominations are all usually fine, but dollars may be best off the beaten track. Visa, Mastercard and American Express credit cards are widely accepted, but cannot be used to buy train tickets.

Driving

The roads here are generally wide, well-maintained and, by European standards, devoid of traffic. Major roads are tarred, secondary roads usually gravel. Most of the sites can be reached in an ordinary passenger car. You will need a 4x4 if you want to go deep into the Namib or up the Skeleton Coast, however. Namibia drives on the left.

Cycling

Apart from the punishing heat, Namibia is a cyclist's paradise with wide, empty, pollution-free roads. Distances are long, though, and you would be better off using the trains for major journeys, where you can, and cycling shorter distances. If you do cycle, remember to take plenty of water. This is a hot, dry, place and it can hurt you really quickly.

Hitchhiking

Most travellers report astounding success hitching around Namibia. The people are pretty friendly and you will find many drivers eager for company on those long desert drives. You should be prepared for long monologues on the state of the country – we suggest you remain polite and silent as being dumped hundreds of kilometres out on a quiet desert road is bound to be an unnerving, and probably a dangerous, experience. The usual precautions apply – if at all in doubt, do not get in the car.

Telephones

Most post offices have public telephones and phone cards are available at the counter. The international dialling code for calls to Namibia is 264. If you are calling from abroad you should omit the initial '0' of the Namibian area code in the usual way. To make international calls from Namibia first dial 09 then the appropriate country code and number as normal.

Accommodation

Hotel and backpacker standards are very high. Hotels tend to be quite expensive, but more and more B&Bs and backpackers' places are opening up as independent travellers discover Namibia.

Camping

Outside the towns, you can bush camp just about anywhere; in towns, you will never be far from some sort of campsite. All campsites have ablution blocks of some sort. Some are immaculate, with hot running water, others are utterly repellent. Campers are normally charged for the site, and not per person, though trying to cram eight people onto one small pitch is sure to displease the management. Prices vary and may not reflect the facilities available.

Food and drink

The country's colonial past is quite evident in the lack of anything that could be called a unique Namibian cuisine. Food tends to be European in style although you will find *sadza* just about everywhere. With large-scale cattle and sheep farming being major economic activities, it is a very meat-oriented society, but most restaurants will have some vegetarian options.

There are few fresh vegetable and produce markets such as those in Zimbabwe or South Africa, but where they do exist, prices are lower than in supermarkets. A lot of food such as pasta, rice and canned goods is imported from South Africa, and supermarkets are generally well-stocked and fairly cheap.

Alcohol

As one might expect from a former German colony, Namibia has some great locally-brewed lagers which are gradually spreading beyond their homeland. Wine and spirits tend to be imported, once again from the south.

Water

Tap water everywhere is safe to drink. If the source is a waterhole or well, it should be purified before drinking. In the north, any water taken from the rivers should be boiled or purified chemically before drinking.

Public holidays

January 1
Good Friday
Easter Monday
Independence Day – March 21
Workers' Day – May 1
Ascension Day
Day of Goodwill – October 1
Human Rights' Day – December 10
Christmas Day – December 25
Family Day – December 26

National parks

The national parks are all controlled by the rather bureaucratic Directorate of National Parks, situated on Independence Av in Windhoek. All advance bookings must be made through them and not the specific park you wish to visit. You can book by writing to Directorate of Nature Conservation and Recreation Resorts, Reservations, PO Box 13267, Windhoek. Telephone bookings: 061 33875; information tel: 061 36975. Prices vary from N$90 to

N$130 per night camping, and from N$280 to N$360 per night for bungalows.

Post

Namibia's postal service is safe, cheap and efficient, if a little slow. An airmail postcard dropped into the main station letter box will reach the UK within two weeks.

Electricity

Power is 220/240V, 50Hz. You will need to bring an adapter to use British or American equipment of any kind.

Media

The radio and television services are operated by the state-owned Namibian Broadcasting Corporation, but there are no restrictions on the press. There is quite a vibrant free publishing scene, although the pro-government *Namibian* seems to be the most popular paper.

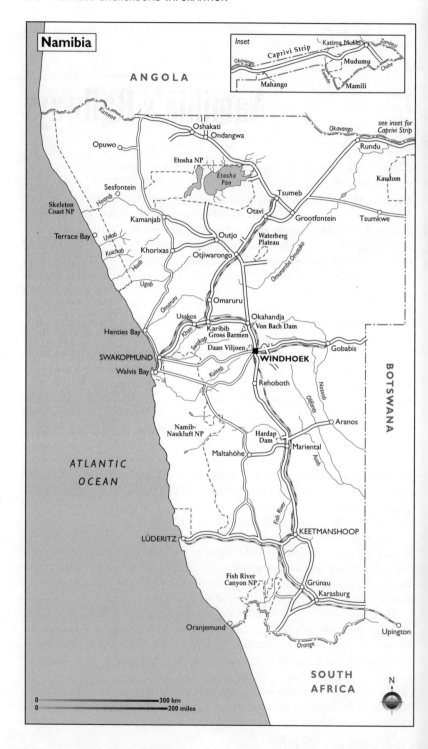

Namibia

Inset

Caprivi Strip
Okavango
Katima Mulilo
Zambezi
Mudumu
Chobe
Mahango
Kwando
Mamili

ANGOLA

Kunene

see inset for
Caprivi Strip

Oshakati
Ondangwa
Okavango
Rundu

Opuwo

Etosha NP

Etosha
Pan

Kaudom

Sesfontein
Hoanib

Tsumeb

Tsumkwe

Skeleton
Coast NP

Kamanjab

Otavi

Grootfontein

Terrace Bay
Uniab
Hoanib

Khorixas

Outjo

Waterberg
Plateau

Koichab
Huab

Otjiwarongo

Omuramba Omatako

Ugab

Omaruru

Omaruru

Usakos

Okahandja

Henties Bay
Khan

Karibib
Gross Barmen

Von Bach Dam

Gobabis

Swakop

Daan Viljoen

WINDHOEK

SWAKOPMUND

Walvis Bay

Kuiseb

Rehoboth

Nossob

Aranos

ATLANTIC
OCEAN

Namib-
Naukluft NP

Hardap
Dam

Olifants

Maltahöhe

Mariental

Auob

Fish River

KEETMANSHOOP

LÜDERITZ

Fish River
Canyon NP

Grünau

Karasburg

Oranjemund

Upington

Orange

SOUTH
AFRICA

N

BOTSWANA

0   300 km
0   200 miles

Namibia's Railways

Namibia has one of the shortest railway systems on the continent, with just 2,382km (1,480 miles) of frail steel ribbon crossing the desert. The Germans did not bother doing much railway building in the colony – there were not many places to go once the rails from the sea reached Windhoek and opened the way to the copper deposits around Tsumeb.

The first track was laid in the 1890s when the German Colonial Company started building a narrow gauge line from the harbour at Swakopmund to Windhoek. As with many colonial railways, the narrow gauge was chosen not only for its cheapness of construction but also because it was easier to push such a line over the terrific physical obstacles.

The railway heads north-east out of Swakopmund, skirting the mountains. The blowing sand made life hell for the track gangs and railwaymen. Sand-storms would often bury the line completely and locomotives had to have metal covers over their wheels and valve gear to prevent sand fouling the moving parts. The line reached Windhoek in June 1902. For years thereafter the little *Zwillinge* (or 'twin') locomotives, two engines joined back-to-back, struggled with their loads up to the capital.

When copper was discovered around Tsumeb, a second railway, the Otavi, was built from Kranzberg on the Windhoek–Swakopmund line to bring the copper out to the sea. When completed in 1907, this was the longest narrow gauge railway in the world, 225km (360 miles) of 61cm (2ft) gauge track which survived until re-gauged to 107cm (3ft 6in) in 1960.

The ride from Swakopmund to Tsumeb took two days, for it was considered unsafe to travel at night. Some of the little coaches were fitted with bunks, built fore-and-aft as there was not enough room to place them across the compartments. Passengers had to supply their own food, though, and most stayed in hotels when the train stopped for the night.

The Otavi itself was a profitable railway, enjoying the economic benefit of carrying only one commodity and downhill, too. Excellent 2–8–2 steam locomotives were built in Germany by Henschel & Sohn and at least one of these survives in Port Elizabeth, South Africa, being used to haul the *Apple Express*.

The discovery of diamonds in the desert not far from the little whaling harbour of Lüderitz on the country's southern coast, saw the town boom. A railway was built from the coast right through the dunes to Aus, reaching there in 1907. Building the Lüderitz line was a terrific struggle. The massive shifting sand dunes were even more of a problem than at Swakopmund, and there was absolutely no water for the steam locomotives. To overcome this deficiency, deep wells were sunk at Garub, half-way along the line. While steam disappeared from the line decades ago, the water tanks are still there. The same spring which filled the tanks during World War I is vital to the survival of a herd of wild horses, descendants of German military chargers which bolted into the desert. Not much traffic moves on the Lüderitz line today and passengers are carried by buses contracted to TransNamib. While the diamond strike petered out, leaving a fabulous ghost town at Kolmanskop, the fishing industry ensured Lüderitz's own survival.

The line from Lüderitz was extended inland from Aus and reached Keetmanshoop, the largest town in southern Namibia, in 1908. When German South West Africa was handed over to South Africa's 'protection' after World War I, a line was built to the south from Windhoek through Keetmanshoop and across the Kalahari Desert, to connect with the South African system at De Aar junction.

In fact, from that time, South African Railways ran the whole South West African system almost like a branch line. The track was mostly light 60kg/m (45lb/ft) rail and, for many years, the locomotives employed were ageing hand-me-downs from secondary lines in South Africa.

During the long war on the northern border through the 1980s, the railway was a vital supply line for the South African forces. Troop trains rolled monotonously across the empty landscape, and it was no accident that South Africa's largest ammunition dump was and is situated in De Aar, at the southern end of the line.

After Namibian independence in 1989, South African Railways relinquished, possibly with some relief, its administration of the Namibian system to the new national carrier TransNamib. However, SAR did leave a range of wagons and a reasonable fleet of diesel locomotives behind. For some time afterwards, the *Southwester*, a weekly passenger train from De Aar to Windhoek, continued to run. However, it was one of the first trains to be axed when South Africa's passenger trains were rationalised a few years ago.

Today TransNamib is a relatively successful railway company, having cut costs to the bone. However, like elsewhere in Africa, a lot of its business has bled away to road competition and its survival will ultimately depend on the management's ability to win it back.

NAMIBIA BY TRAIN

Staying at a backpackers' place in Windhoek, I mentioned I was travelling by train to Swakopmund. There was a stunned silence. 'But there are no trains in Namibia,' someone said. My acquaintance was right in a way for, although there are passenger trains in Namibia, they are not like most others in Africa.

As part of the urgency to cut costs, the passenger train as we know it was one of the first things to go, and the country no longer has any fully dedicated trains aimed at the general travelling public. Instead, TransNamib operates

Starline, a sparse but fully adequate service on five routes, four out of Windhoek and one between Walvis Bay and Tsumeb, using refurbished, open-plan passenger coaches attached to reasonably fast freight trains. Mixed trains like this are an old concept, usually a way of satisfying demand for trains along sparsely populated or under-served railways, and here they are taken to a nineties conclusion. Disturbingly, only one passenger coach is coupled to each freight train, although a second coach is added at times of peak demand. Moreover, none of the trains runs every day so you will need to plan carefully.

Accommodation

Accommodation is in aircraft-style seats in sealed, fully air-conditioned coaches, in two classes. The business class section, with wider seats and more leg-room, seats 20 passengers, while economy class is more of a cattle-boat experience with 64 passengers seated two-abreast in two rows of seats.

The two classes are divided by an area with toilets and a vending machine and the economy class passengers spend their whole journey straining for a brief look into the relative opulence of business class. Apart from the vending machine, which sells soft drinks, crisps and chocolate, there is no other food in the coach. Bring plenty of provisions, especially if you are doing the long haul between Upington and Windhoek. Unlike in other parts of Africa, food and drink vendors do not excitedly storm TransNamib trains when they pull into a station, most likely because the business generated by a single passenger coach is bound to be paltry.

If you get bored of watching the desert slide past at freight train pace, there is a constant, sometimes diverting, stream of videos – some were months ahead of Windhoek's main cinema on a recent trip. The only train crew is a conductor whose other duties include helping with shunting and changing the video.

Most of the trains run overnight, departing in the afternoon or early evening and arriving at their destinations around dawn. The one exception is the Windhoek–Upington service which takes over 24 hours to cover the distance.

Fares

With fares subsidised by the government, train travel is a bargain. Fares are worked out on a zone basis. Prices vary, however, according to the travel period. High-peak times are at the beginning and end of school holidays and over Christmas, New Year and Easter, while peak periods tend to be over most weekends. The price difference between high-peak and off-peak is only a few Namibian dollars – hardly enough to strain your travel budget.

Sample one-way fares for Windhoek–Walvis Bay are as follows:

Business class	N\$55
Economy class	N\$40

Concessions

Though local students and scholars can travel at 33% off at the beginning and end of university terms an international student card is unlikely to score visitors any discount but it may be worth a try. Family groups of more than two people can buy an excursion package in off-peak periods. Discounted tickets are granted on return journey reservations made at least a week in advance. Pensioners also qualify for a 33% reduction for reservations made before 16.00 on the day of departure. You will need ID or a pension card to prove your venerable status.

On the Windhoek–Keetmanshoop service, the discount is only available on Tuesdays and Wednesdays. On other routes, discounts apply any day the service is available.

Cancellation fees

None if you give more than 48 hours notice, 50% between 47 hours and departure time. Cancel after the train has gone and you forfeit the whole fare.

Booking

A new reservations system has been in place since 1995, and you can now book tickets by telephone or fax. However, since credit cards are not acceptable, you cannot actually buy your ticket over the phone, so you are still going to have to get to the relevant station in time to buy the ticket. For bookings, phone Central Reservations on 061 298 2032, or fax 061 298 2495. Business hours are 08.00–16.00.

Baggage

The baggage allowance in economy class is 20kg (44lb) and 30kg (66lb) in business class. Luggage has to be able to fit in the overhead racks which, it must be said, are fairly cavernous. Extra baggage has to be booked in at the parcels counter – it will be sent on a parcels train and will be there when you arrive at your destination.

Lost baggage

Call 061 298 2533 between 07.30 and 16.00, Monday to Friday.

Bicycles

There is no room for these on your train – they are treated as parcels and will be sent ahead of you, if not actually in a goods wagon on the same train. The cost of sending a bike is more or less the same price as an economy class fare for the same distance. TransNamib will cheerfully send your car or motorcycle by overnight train, but this is expensive.

LUXURY TRAINS

The *Desert Express* is Namibia's answer to South Africa's *Blue Train*. It is a concept train, built from scratch in TransNamib's Windhoek workshops. The train runs between Windhoek and Swakopmund and the first service ran in 1998.

It is a mellow journey which includes two excursions off the train, one to the awesome Spitzkoppe – the world's second largest granite formation – and the other to an Okapuka game ranch near Windhoek to watch lions being fed. The Spitzkoppe, near Swakopmund, is seen at its best around sunset and sunrise, and trains in both directions are timed to take advantage of this. You will also get to see a little more general desert scenery than on normal TransNamib services and the food is better, too. But the price puts the *Desert Express* beyond the reach of most budget travellers.

TransNamib boasts that the *Desert Express* offers 'sheer luxury'. There are two types of accommodation. The sleeper coaches each have 24 compartments, with en-suite showers and toilets, to accommodate one, two or three people. Each sleeper converts to a sitter during the day. Starview sitter class is basically luxury airline travel with 35 wide seats in a glass-domed coach. You can actually watch the stars through the roof, and they are like fire in the clear desert night. Music and videos complete the entertainment. The *Desert Express* is air-conditioned throughout and the windows do not open. The design of the train is based on Europe's ICE trains which solve the problem of creating luxury in severely limited space in a highly efficient, if somewhat antiseptic, way.

Sleeper passengers have their own lounge, the Spitzkoppe Lounge, and dining car. Breakfast and dinner are included in the fare. Starview passengers can get light meals and drinks in the Starview Bistro, the next coach along from theirs. The only time the passengers from each class will mix is on the off-train excursions.

Fares
Sleeper class

		Starview class	
Single occupancy	N$1,380	Sitter	N$600
Double	N$1,080		
Triple	N$780		

Times
dep Windhoek   14.30 Sunday, Tuesday, Friday
arr Swakopmund 10.00 the next day

dep Swakopmund 14.30 Monday, Wednesday, Saturday
arr Windhoek   10.00 the next day

The train departs and arrives an hour later in summer because of the fierce temperatures.

Bookings
Tel: 061 298 2600; or fax: 061 298 2601; or contact TransNamib on email: <dx@transnamib.com.na>; or you can visit the company's website at <http://www.transnamib.com.na/dx>.

Shongololo
Named after a millipede found just about everywhere in Africa, the *Shongololo*

is a sort of rail-drive cruise where passengers alternate between travelling on the train and going off on side trips in mini-buses driven by tour guides. The train part of the *Shongololo* is a conventional passenger sleeper, cleaned up and decorated a little, which runs only at night. In the morning, the mini-buses, carried in dedicated vehicle carriers attached to the back of the train, are unloaded and the day is spent sightseeing, before the train moves on to the next location while the passengers sleep. Each of the six coaches on the train has five double compartments and two single cabins. There is a basin in each compartment and one communal shower in each coach. The train has a full dining car and a separate lounge car.

The operation is basically a package tour. At the moment there is just one 13-day-tour covering the whole of Namibia (plus various tours in South Africa), from the Fish River canyon in the south to Epupa Falls on the Angolan border. There are two connecting excursions – a six day tented safari through Botswana to Victoria Falls in Zimbabwe, and a five day tour from Cape Town to connect with the train at Windhoek. Camping on safari is in tents with fold-up beds, set up by an advance team.

The cost for the standard trip is N$7,510 per person, sharing a double compartment. The price includes all meals, daily excursions and game park fees. Drinks and other optional activities are not included. Tours run approximately once every month. For bookings phone (+264) 061 246 428 or (+264) 061 298 111; or fax (+264) 061 298 2160 or (+264) 061 250 378. Alternatively, contact the Cape Town office on (+27) 021 216 685; or fax: (+27) 021 419 6868.

Routes in Namibia

WINDHOEK

One gets the impression that Windhoek, Namibia's largest city as well as its capital, has been left in the oven too long, and baked itself to a standstill. The city lies at 1,654m (5,425ft) above sea level, at the head of a valley made by a tributary of the Swakop River. Hills and mountains covered with grass and trees surround the town. The Herero people called the site *oTjomuuse*, 'the place of steam', because of the hot springs which bubble at the top of the valley. A group of Nama people, who called the place /Ai/gams, 'fire water', settled here in 1840. Their leader, Jonker Afrikaner, named it Winterhoek, a name which stuck.

Rhenish missionaries came to Winterhoek in 1842, building a school and church, while Wesleyan missionaries followed shortly afterwards. The settlement grew as traders began passing through the area, bartering alcohol and guns for cattle. The region's tribes had quickly resorted to cattle rustling to pay the traders, resulting in a brutal cattle war. On August 25 1880 a Herero raiding party attacked and burned the settlement in retaliation for Jonker's theft of 1,500 sacred cattle. Jonker and his people fled southward and the missionaries were left with no-one to mission to. The settlement stayed empty for 10 years until a German column, led by Major Curt von François arrived in October 1890. Von François immediately started building a hill-top fort which became the headquarters of the *Schutztruppe*, the German colonial army, when it was finished two years later. The *Alte Feste* (Old Fort) survives today as a museum.

Von François renamed the place Windhoek and watched it grow. The German Colonial Company began building a 2ft 6in (76cm) narrow gauge railway from the port at Swakopmund across the desert to Windhoek, reaching the town in 1902. Windhoek got its town council in 1909 and became the seat of the colony's Legislative Assembly in 1910. The city remained the seat of the administration after World War I when the League of Nations granted South Africa the mandate to watch over South West Africa.

Windhoek has a pleasant, calm feel about it. Pavement cafés bustle during the day, people move slowly in the wide streets. Much colonial architecture survives and it is worth taking a long walk around the town, especially towards the hills in the east. Just watch out for the heat in summer – you will bake yourself if you do not take water and a hat.

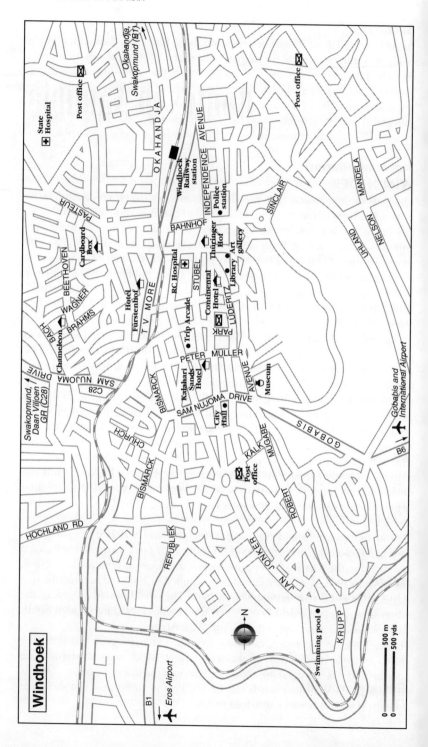

Windhoek

Security

As African capitals go, Windhoek must surely be the safest. Although crime is rising, it is still uncommon for tourists to be robbed. Use your common sense, though. Like any city, there are no-go areas. The sprawling township at Katutura, whose name translates as 'the place where we do not live', may offer a revealing look into Namibian life. Like all townships, it is not particularly safe and it is certainly best to go there with someone who knows their way around. Walking about looking lost in any township at night is a terrible idea.

Accommodation

Windhoek has the usual range of accommodation options one would expect in a capital city. Standards are high and it is very rare to see the kind of run-down, laissez-faire establishments found elsewhere in parts of southern Africa.

Luxury

Hotel Thüringer Hof Independence Av, Windhoek, tel: 061 226031; fax 061 232981. Right in the city, near the station, with 39 rooms and a cool garden to hide from the heat. Doubles N$425, singles N$320.

Windhoek Hotel and Country Club Just off the B1 Western by-pass, five minutes drive from centre, tel: 61 2055911. Facilities include swimming pool, tennis and 18-hole golf-course. From N$550 for a single to N$630 for a double.

Villa Verdi On Verdi Street, tel: 61 221994. Situated in the centre of Windhoek, but peaceful and intimate. All rooms have en-suite facilities. From N$495 for a double, N$295 for a single.

Hotel Heinitzburg Heinitzburg Street, tel: 61 249597. Quite a spectacle – most rooms have four-poster beds. A modern castle (built in 1914) which overlooks Windhoek. From N$560 for a double, singles from N$390.

Mid-price

Airport Lodge Situated between the airport and Windhoek, it's 18km east of the city on the B6, tel: 61 231491. Consists of six African thatched cottages with facilities to self-cater, although there is a restaurant. N$260 for a double, N$190 for a single.

Jan Jonker Holiday Apartments 183 Jan Jonker Road, tel: 61 221236. Apartments have 1 or 2 bedrooms, lounge, kitchen and bathroom. One person N$200, 2 persons N$350, 3 persons N$450, 4 persons N$550.

Budget

The Cardboard Box 15 Johann Albrecht St, tel: 061 228994; fax 061 245587. Friendly, spotless backpackers' hostel overlooking town. Swimming pool. Dorm beds N$30.

Backpacker 5 Greig Street, tel: 61 25 9458. New hostel, 10 minutes from city centre. Swimming pool, sauna and free pick up. A number of safaris available.

Getting around

This is a walking town. There is not much public transport bar a handful of expensive cabs. Minibus taxis serve Katutura and Khomasdal townships.

What to see

The *Alte Feste* on top of the hill is worth a look. The building has a Foreign Legion feel about it with its shady verandahs and open courtyard. A complete narrow gauge train of locomotive and coaches is preserved outside the fort. A small museum on Namibian natural history, people and animals is situated just behind the library near Lüderitz St. There is also a tiny art gallery on Leutwein St. The old *Tintenpalast*, 'palace of ink', built during the German occupation, is still in use as the administration building.

The **railway museum** is on the top floor of the main station building. Apart from the little *Zwillinge* locomotive and an armour-plated personnel carrier preserved outside, the museum is a little short on rolling stock exhibits. However, its supremely dedicated curator, Walter Rusch, has collected a staggering array of photographs, maps, documents, tools, models, signalling equipment and the like and spread this around the offices which serve as the museum.

The history has been meticulously documented and it is worth spending a good few hours here if railways are your thing. With any luck, you will be met at the top of the stairs by a jovial German-Namibian who will give you an initial rush tour, pointing out artefacts such as conductor's badges and saying 'and here we have a conductor's badge'. You can then wander around at leisure. Walter Rusch himself is a human library and, given time, will tell you amazing stories of the old days.

Many of the towns around Namibia, at least those connected with the history of the original Otavi Railway, have preserved locomotives and coaches, either at the station or somewhere in the town.

Nightlife

Windhoek is not famous for its after-hours activity. There are a few clubs and pubs, ranging from slightly trendy to very dodgy. The only cinema is the Kine 300 on Klein Windhoek. If you missed seeing anything months before on the big screen at home, chances are you will get to see it here.

Shopping

You will find a good spread of overpriced curio shops in the malls and shopping centres along Independence Av. It might be worth waiting until you get out of Windhoek to buy this sort of thing. For rocks and gem stones, however, it is hard to beat the House of Gems on 131 Stubel St. The place is full of rocks and precious stones and prices are excellent.

The best camping store and bike shop in town is Cymot at 60 Mandume Mdemufayo Av, tel: 061 23 4131.

Information

The city's tourist information bureau in Post St Mall is helpful as is the Namibian tourist bureau on Independence Av. The privately-run information centre on Peter Müller Strasse is good for information and bookings for tours and transport.

Post office
The main post office is on Independence Av. Postage rates are still a bargain in this part of the world and the service is efficient and safe. Most post offices have public telephones and phone cards are available at the counter.

WINDHOEK TO SWAKOPMUND AND WALVIS BAY
The railway down to the sea is the most popular of all the routes among travellers, linking Namibia's seaside holiday town to the nation's capital. In winter, the arrival times in Windhoek and Swakopmund may seem a little bleak but at least it won't be raining or snowing. The service runs daily, except Saturdays.

Times

Train 6606 Windhoek–Walvis Bay			Train 6607 Walvis Bay–Windhoek	
dep	20.00	Windhoek	arr	05.48
arr	21.56	Okahandja	arr	04.19
arr	00.32	Karibib	arr	01.52
arr	00.58	Kranzberg	arr	00.40
arr	01.47	Usakos	arr	00.20
arr	03.40	Arandis	arr	22.09
arr	04.54	Swakopmund	arr	20.10
arr	06.54	Kuiseb	arr	18.58
arr	07.00	Walvis Bay	dep	18.50

Fares
Windhoek–Walvis Bay, one way, full price:

Business	N$55
Economy	N$40

In addition to this standard TransNamib service there is also the luxury *Desert Express* which runs on the Windhoek–Swakopmund route three times a week in each direction. Full details are given in Chapter 15 page 222 above.

Okahandja
Traditional home of the Herero people and the place where most of their chiefs are buried, the modern town started out as a Rhenish mission station in 1850. Now a road and rail centre, it is still a quiet place, although in August the Hereros gather in the park where their leaders are buried to hold a memorial service.

Karibib
Once an important railway town, Karibib is better known for its marble deposits and the gem stones, aquamarines, golden topaz and tourmalines, which are mined nearby. The town bakes in the summer. If you

do find yourself here, there are some superb examples of German colonial architecture, including the classic Hotel Kaiser.

Usakos

Usakos used to be a watering point for steam locomotives panting across the desert, but has accordingly slipped in importance as a railway town more recently. Passengers would formerly de-train gratefully and repair to the hotel to hold the desert at bay with what must have been fine, chilled lager.

Just 30km (19 miles) north of the town are the **Erongo Mountains** with caves, such as the 50m (164ft) deep Philipp Cave, containing some of the country's finest San rock art. Hard and hot to get to without transport, though.

Swakopmund

Generally known as Swakop, this is Namibia's seaside playground, very European in style with beach-front cafés, a pier and paddle boats on the bay. It is a bit like an English seaside town without the inclement weather. Swakop was founded in 1892 as part of a German attempt to avoid using the port facilities of the British-held enclave at Walvis Bay which had been annexed to the Cape. The new port was exposed, but it was good enough, and the settlement began to flourish after building of the railway to Windhoek began in 1896.

Eventually, however, Swakopmund failed as a port — it could not compete with the safe, natural anchorage at Walvis Bay. But it is a much nicer town to spend time in. Many of the original colonial buildings are intact, including the magnificent old railway station, which, sadly, is no longer the railway station. In a mark of Swakopmund's tourist boom and the decline in passenger train traffic, the station, past which trains still thunder, has been turned into a hotel and entertainment centre.

The **beaches** are great, though the water is a numbing 12°C (54°F). There is good surfing and brilliant fishing. The old metal pier, built in 1911, is the best place to fish off. The desert is never far away, however. The hot east winds bring the Namib shuffling through the streets.

The **Swakopmund Museum**, once the customs house, is full of Swakop memories and exhibits on the Namib Desert. Hours are 10.30–12.30 and 16.00–18.00 every day. One of the town's most evocative relics is *Martin Luther*, a steam tractor which was brought to haul goods inland. Boiler problems, however, resulted in it being left in the sand where it stopped, just outside the town. 'Here I stand; God help me, I cannot do otherwise,' said Luther. The engine is just as immovable, on a plinth now, looking out across the Namib.

Swakop is the jumping off point to explore the Skeleton Coast and Namib, although you will need to hire a vehicle to do this. The tourist authority located at Woermannhaus, near Kaiser Wilhelm Strasse, tel: 64 405634, is a useful, friendly place and will help with car hire.

Accommodation
Mid-price
The Strand Hotel on beach front, tel: 64 400315. N$425 for double, single N$325. Under-12s go free if sharing with parents, 12–18-year-olds, if sharing, pay for breakfast only.

Budget
Jay Jay's 8 Brucken St, tel: 40 2909. Central location with friendly hosts. Good cheap food and happening bar. Dorm N$20pp; single N$27.50 without bathroom, N$36.50, with bath; double N$56 without and N$68 with bath.
Alternative Space Backpackers 46 Dr Alfons Weber St, tel: 40 2713. It's good, popular and out of town, so ring first. Dorm N$30, double N$60.

The railway line south from Swakop to Walvis runs through the coastal dunes of the Namib, one of the most dramatic rail trips in Africa. You get the feeling that if you turned away for a second, the desert would just come sliding in and bury the railway.

Walvis Bay
Walvis or 'Whale' Bay might be a working harbour but it is an exquisite one, with a sweeping bay and pleasant shallow lagoon among its plus points. Aquatic birds, including flamingos and pelicans, thrive in a protected bird park, with the flamingos often providing an elegant sweep of pink at sunset.

A naturally-protected harbour regularly used by whale ships during the 19th century, the port was annexed by the British in 1878 and became part of South Africa after Union in 1910.

WINDHOEK TO GOBABIS
A branch railway was built east from Windhoek to Gobabis, near the Botswana border, in 1930. Trains run from the capital on Sundays, Tuesdays and Thursdays, returning on Mondays, Wednesdays and Fridays.

Times

Windhoek–Gobabis Train 2403 Sun, Tue, Thu		Gobabis–Windhoek Train 2404 Mon, Wed, Fri	
dep 21.50	Windhoek	arr 04.45
dep 23.05	Hoffnung	dep 03.47
dep 23.45	Neudamma	dep 02.46
dep 02.34	Omitara	dep 00.06
dep 04.23	Witvlei	dep 22.24
arr 03.43	Gobabis	dep 21.00

Fares
Business	N$25
Economy	N$15

Gobabis

There is not a lot going on in Gobabis, 'the place where elephants drink', although it is a nice enough town. It has boomed in the past few years as a cattle ranching and frontier town, following the completion of a decent trans-Kalahari road through Botswana. A lot of travellers pass through here on their way to or from Namibia – it is much quicker to get to the Okavango Swamps, Zimbabwe or even Johannesburg this way, instead of the long haul around through the Northern Cape.

The new road has really improved transport options east of Gobabis. A few years ago, anything less than four-wheel drive would not make it very far into Botswana. The usual precautions apply if you are planning to hitch. Remember, too, that it is a lonely, hot road into the desert so be prepared — take as much food and water as you can.

WINDHOEK TO TSUMEB

The building of the railway to Tsumeb was motivated purely by the need to get copper ore from the mines to the sea. Tsumeb remains the centre of the copper mining industry and not much else. But it is a useful place from which to explore the magnificent **Etosha Pan National Park**, though you will certainly need to hire a car to do so. Trains run to Tsumeb from both Windhoek and Walvis Bay. Both services begin on the regular route between the two, but half-way between Windhoek and Swakopmund they swing north-east at the junction of Kranzberg. The countryside throughout the routes is open, flat and basically empty.

Times

Windhoek–Tsumeb Train 6666 Sun, Tue, Thu		Tsumeb–Windhoek Train 2213/2615 Mon, Wed, Fri	
dep 17.30	Windhoek	arr 0520	
dep 20.25	Okahandja	dep 03.40	
dep 23.00	Karibib	dep 00.50	
dep 23.45	Kransberg	dep 23.55	
dep 01.40	Omaruru	dep 21.35	
dep 05.35	Otjiwarongo	dep 17.50	
dep 08.20	Otavi	dep 12.15	
arr 09.40	Tsumeb	dep 10.30	

Walvis Bay–Tsumeb Train 2603/2200/6666 Sun, Tue, Thu		Tsumeb–Walvis Bay Train 2213/2201/2612 Mon, Wed, Fri	
dep 16.25	Walvis Bay	arr 04.00	
dep 16.35	Kuiseb	dep 03.50	
dep 18.05	Swakopmund	dep 02.35	
dep 19.45	Arandis	dep 00.50	

dep	21.55	Usakos	dep	22.55	
dep	22.30	Kransberg	dep	22.30	
dep	00.25	Omaruru	dep	20.35	
dep	05.35	Otjiwarongo	dep	16.45	
dep	08.20	Otavo	dep	12.15	
arr	09.40	Tsumeb	dep	10.30	

The Windhoek and Walvis Bay coaches are attached to the same train between Otjiwarongo and Tsumeb. There is therefore a long stopover at Otjiwarongo in both directions.

Fares
The fares for the full distance on both routes are the same.

Business	N$35
Economy	N$30

Otjiwarongo
An agricultural town which has picked up a little since tourists started coming to Namibia. This is an alternative base from which to explore Etosha.

Tsumeb
Ancient prospectors discovered copper centuries ago and worked the deposit as much as they could with prehistoric tools. But it was the Europeans who really opened up the richness of Tsumeb's 1,500m (5,000ft) deep copper pipe, which also contains zinc, lead, silver, germanium, cadmium and crystals. The town is quite pretty with streets lined with jacaranda trees and bougainvillaea.

You will really need a car if you want to explore Etosha fully and Tsumeb is the best place to organise this. Car hire agencies which have offices here include Avis, tel: 067 220520, and Imperial Car Rental, tel: 067 220728.

Accommodation
Hotel Makalani Tel: 67 221051. Singles N$192, doubles N$219.
Hikers Haven Tel: 067 243101 is a budget alternative.

Etosha Pan
Etosha, 'the place of mirages', is a vast pan of white sand, about 130km (80 miles) from east to west and 72km (45 miles) from north to south, the remains of a large inland lake which dried up after the rivers which fed it changed their courses. The country around the pan ranges from open plains to thick mopani forest, and the area is overrun with wild animals. Etosha is one of Africa's great game spectacles and is available for a fraction of the cost of other parks in the region. The pan fills with water when the rains come between December and March, attracting thousands of flamingos and other water birds. There are altogether 300 species of bird in the park.

The water holes around the southern edge of the park are the key to survival

234 ROUTES IN NAMIBIA

for the many animals which live there, with the game drawing closer to the water as the dry season bites, providing some of Africa's best game watching. Herbivores include elephant, black rhino, wildebeest, zebra, roan antelope, kudu, eland, oryx, giraffe and springbok. Rare mammals include black-faced impala, Hartmann's mountain zebra and the Damara dik-dik, a tiny antelope endemic to Namibia. Etosha has an abundance of carnivores – lion, leopard, cheetah, brown and spotted hyena, jackal, bat-eared fox and wild dog.

When to visit
Average temperatures during the rainy season hover around 40°C (104°F), falling to 30°C (86°F) in winter, the best time to visit. The nights can be cool, but it beats being cooked alive in a car. Etosha gets busy over Easter and the South African school holidays and booking is essential then. At other times it is relatively empty.

Accommodation
Etosha has three camps, Namutoni, Halali and Okaukuejo. The accommodation ranges from camp sites to luxury bungalows. **Namutoni** camp, at the park's eastern entrance, is actually a beautiful old white fort. Formerly a German police post, and later an army base, it was converted into a tourist resort in 1957. The rooms inside the fort are not much changed from police post days. If Foreign Legion living turns you on, you will be happy here. There are newer, air-conditioned bungalows outside the main fort. **Okaukuejo** is a standard rest camp near the Andersson (western) entrance to the park.

Prices in Namutoni and Okaukuejo range from N$40 for a campsite to N$230 for a luxury bungalow. A room in the fort costs about N$160. Halali is the newest and smallest of the Etosha camps. It has a restaurant, shop and swimming pool. Double chalets start at about US$35 or you can camp at US$10 per site. For **bookings**, contact the Directorate of Tourism in Windhoek, tel: (+264) 61 236975.

There is also the **Mokuti Lodge**, (216 beds) Namutoni Gate, Etosha; tel: 067 229084, or fax 067 22909. This is a luxury Namib Sun hotel just outside the park, pricey but nice. Singles from N$400, doubles N$560.

Getting there
Namutoni gate is 106km (66 miles) from Tsumeb, Okaukuejo is 121km (76 miles) from Otjiwarongo. Gates open at sunrise and close about 20 minutes before sunset. Night driving is forbidden. There is a N$30 entry fee but it is included in the accommodation rates if you stay over.

WINDHOEK TO KEETMANSHOOP
This line links the Namibian capital with Keetmanshoop, southern Namibia's business and agriculture centre. Twice a week, the train continues to Upington in South Africa, thus forming Namibia's only scheduled rail link with the south. Accordingly, it pays to plan this leg carefully.

Times

		Train 6607 Windhoek–Keetmanshoop Daily, except Sat			Train 6666 Keetmanshoop–Windhoek Daily, except Sat	
	dep	19.10	Windhoek	arr	06.15	
	dep	21.45	Rehoboth	dep	03.55	
	dep	23.30	Kalkrand	dep	02.00	
	dep	01.55	Mariental	dep	23.50	
	dep	03.02	Gibeon	dep	21.50	
	dep	03.44	Asab	dep	21.03	
	dep	04.42	Tses	dep	20.10	
	arr	06.27	Keetmanshoop	dep	18.30	

Fares

Windhoek–Keetmanshoop, one way

Business class	N$60
Economy class	N$45

The southbound train leaves Windhoek in the early evening. In summer, there is enough light to experience the twisting climb out of the capital into the sun-baked mountains surrounding the city. The remainder of the journey is at night, a pity as one does not really get a sense of the vastness of this country.

Stops are made at every hamlet with a siding which, considering the emptiness of this land, is not that many. Progress is slow but fairly relaxing.

Some 84km (52 miles) south of Windhoek, **Rehoboth** is famous for its *Baster*, 'half-breed', community. They are descendants of 30 European trek farmers who settled north of the Orange River at the end of the 18th century and married Khoi-Khoi women, forming a new clan. Part of the clan settled here in 1868 on the site of an abandoned mission station. Rehoboth is a definite oasis in the desert but there is not much to do.

Mariental lies on a grassy plain, near the Hardap Dam which boasts a tourist resort. The area is famous for its hardy Karakul sheep, 36 of which were imported from Iran by a German businessman at the turn of the century. The Karakuls, prized for their pelts, are now everywhere.

Keetmanshoop

Founded in 1866 by a German industrialist called Johan Keetman as a mission station for the Nama people, a town grew up rapidly around the church. The horizon stretches away on all sides, giving the town a somewhat tenuous feeling. Even so it has some beautiful colonial buildings, all with thick walls to beat the heat, and a decidedly slow atmosphere. If you are heading for Lüderitz get off the train here.

West to Lüderitz

A landlocked natural harbour, Lüderitz has been a favoured refuge for sailors since the time it was discovered by Portuguese navigator Bartolomeu Dias in

1487. He called it *Angra dos Ilheros*, 'Bay of the Islets'. The arid interior deterred any development other than that related to the fishing, seal-hunting and guano industries. However, in 1883 businessman Adolf Lüderitz set up a trading station . The Khoi-Khoi people sold land to him and a settlement grew up.

The discovery of diamonds in the desert in April 1908 heralded a boom time. Diamond hunters poured into the area and a mining town quickly flourished at Kolmanskop, 9km (5 miles) to the east. The railway, meanwhile, was extended inland to Keetmanshoop by 1908, having taken just two years to build. Regular passenger trains stopped running on the Lüderitz line some years ago but TransNamib operates a daily bus service instead, departing Keetmanshoop at 07.30, arriving Lüderitz at 12.15. The return service departs at 12.30, arriving in Keetmanshoop at 17.30.

Kolmanskop has turned into a ghost town. At its peak, it was home to about 700 families. Ice vendors roamed the streets delivering the daily ice ration, while a team of street sweepers kept the desert at bay with brooms – until diamond yields fell. The town is still basically intact, although the sands of the Namib now blow through open doors and fill the houses. Tours can be arranged – ask at the Consolidated Diamond Mines (CDM) office in Lüderitz.

Lüderitz

While the diamond area extends north and south from the port, Lüderitz itself makes more money from tourism and fishing, specifically crayfishing. The sea really is cold here but good fishing lures anglers from everywhere. The usual colonial buildings predominate and it is well worth taking a walk around the town to view some of them. The contrast between its European architecture and the awful bleak beauty of the Namib nearby is actually quite bizarre.

Accommodation

Hotel Zum Sperrgebiet tel: 063 203411, or fax: 063 203414. Doubles from N\$410, singles from N\$245.

KEETMANSHOOP TO UPINGTON

At the time of writing, there were only two through trains a week between Windhoek and Upington. It took TransNamib two years to persuade the South Africans to let the train run as far as Upington. In recent years, the service had been ending at the border, at a horrendous little town called Ariamsvlei. From there passengers had to entrust themselves to dodgy minibus taxis to Upington and onward.

TransNamib hopes to restore the service all the way to De Aar on the main line between Cape Town and Johannesburg. A through rail service to and from De Aar would at least allow passengers the relative opulence of rail travel and the choice of northbound and southbound rail connections. For the moment passengers coming from Namibia have to overnight in Upington and then catch a bus or minibus taxi on to Cape Town, Johannesburg, Kimberley or De Aar the following day.

One advantage of taking the train across the border is that customs and immigration formalities are done on the train. The train invariably arrives in Upington after dark, but it is not too far to walk into the centre of town – just stay on the main drag with the glaring sodium lights. There may be taxis at the station when the train gets in.

Times

	Train 2607 Wed, Sat		Train 6666 Thu, Sun	
dep	08.10	Keetmanshoop	arr	16.31
dep	12.45	Grünau	dep	12.38
dep	14.30	Karasburg	dep	11.25
dep	18.30	Ariamsvlei	dep	09.00
arr	21.30	Upington	dep	05.00

Fares

Keetmanshoop–Upington, one way:

Business class   N$50
Economy class   N$40

The Keetmanshoop–Upington journey (in either direction) offers the longest daylight passenger train service in Namibia and you get a real feeling for the vastness of the country as it slips past at the ambling gait of the freight train. There is little to break up the openness of the terrain other than rock formations near Grünau and a twisting and turning section through a canyon near Ariamsvlei.

Upington itself is described in Chapter 7, page 116–7, along with details of bus and minibus taxi services linking it with other locations in South Africa.

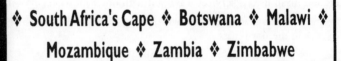

Journeys for the Adventurous

It is still possible to ride a train through the African bush and see wild animals galloping for the horizon on both sides, or take a train to the shore of an inland sea and catch a lake steamer to another country, or ride on the barking steam locomotive of a train going nowhere but just ambling through the bush, picking up the odd passenger or bundle of wood at some half-forgotten siding.

Some of the train rides described here are strictly for the hardy, some for the romantic, others for confirmed train junkies. There is a common thread on all the journeys which follow – they are uniquely African in their pace, operational quirks, and soul. You will also be doing yourself a big favour by taking food, water, malaria pills and a deep well of patience.

BOTSWANA

Botswana is largely a desert country, and thus sparsely populated, with most of its people living along its south-eastern border with South Africa. It is however rich in minerals and along with large scale cattle ranching and tourism, this has helped make it one of Africa's few economic successes.

The Okavango Delta, a unique swampland in the north where the Okavango River soaks into the Kalahari Desert, unable to reach the sea, is its biggest tourist attraction along with the superb Chobe and Moremi game reserves in the north east.

Getting there
By air
There are flights from Johannesburg to Gaborone, the capital, and Maun, gateway to the Okavango Delta, and also from Maun to Victoria Falls, Zimbabwe, and Windhoek, Namibia.

British Airways' twice weekly flight between Gaborone and London is the only direct service to a destination outside Africa. The return fare is around £660 low season and £1,100 high.

By rail
There are just two international rail connections. The *Bulawayo* travels weekly between Pretoria and Bulawayo via Gaborone (see page 84) while the *Botswana Blue* (see below) runs daily each way between Lobatse in the south and Bulawayo.

Currency

The pula is one of the strongest currencies in the region. The rate of exchange at the time of writing was US$1 = 3.60 pula. You can change currencies at any bank. US dollars and South African rands are also widely accepted.

Language

Setswana is the official language. English is widely spoken, however.

Visas and red tape

Visas are not required by nationals of the US and citizens of most EU and Commonwealth countries. Most visitors are granted a 30-day stay on arrival. Nationals of other countries should check with the nearest Botswana High Commission.

Phone codes

The country code for calls to Botswana is 267 but there are no area codes.

Further reading

Chris McIntyre and Simon Atkins *Guide to Namibia and Botswana* (Bradt), is the most comprehensive guide yet written on Botswana, describing in some detail parts of the country which other travel guides tend to ignore. Unfortunately it is currently out of print but you may be able to track down a copy. *Zimbabwe & Botswana: The Rough Guide*, Barbara McRae and Tony Pinchuck is also worth trying.

The Botswana Blue
Lobatse–Gaborone–Bulawayo

The *Botswana Blue* is, by any developing world standards, a swish train. Its blue, air-conditioned coaches have comfortable accommodation in first and second classes and the food from the dining car is generally good, as long as it does not run out. Botswana Railways was so proud of this train that in the last days of steam locomotive line working in Zimbabwe, they insisted NRZ haul the train from the border to Bulawayo behind diesels – steam was obsolete and would tarnish the train's image. The result was repeated chaos and appalling delays at the border station and shunting yard of Plumtree.

Ironically, the train, now diesel-hauled throughout its journey, has begun showing its age and is not quite the rolling advertisement Botswana Railways would like it to be. The *Botswana Blue* is a travellers' train, linking Lobatse, near the South African border, to the capital Gaborone and on to Bulawayo, one night's journey away in Zimbabwe. Your train companions will likely be a mix of travellers making their way up from the south, merchants with suitcases of curios and businessmen heading to and from Zimbabwe.

The train – and the railway it runs on – serves the well-developed eastern strip of the country where over 80% of the Botswana population live. The ride is smooth and relaxed and you will get to meet the people. It generally runs on time and it has the advantage of being a fairly cheap and comfortable daily

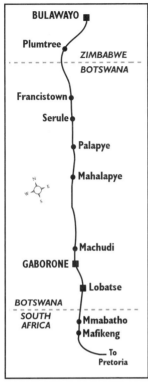

connection between Botswana and Zimbabwe.

As a tourist train, however, it is not much cop, for several reasons. Firstly, while the eastern border may be the most densely populated part of the country, it has got very little in the way of attractions. **Gaborone** is a quiet, dusty place, strictly for people who feel the urge to visit every capital of every country they travel to (though the national museum is a major treasure with exhibits on the history, people and geography of the country, showing how humans have lived here from earliest times). Botswana's real attractions are the wilderness areas in the centre and north-east.

The *Blue* also runs south only as far as Lobatse, 75km (90 miles) short of the South African border town of Mafikeng, where you can get trains to the south and east. (Lobatse is also a few kilometres east of the South African border post of Skilpadsnek, but you can only get to and from there by road transport.) It is a bit of a drag arriving at Mafikeng at night as the trains from Johannesburg do, kipping in the station and then having to hitch through flyblown desert in the early morning to try and catch the northbound *Blue* at 09.00. A few people do it; most, however, opt for one of the many minibus taxis which have competitively filled the gap left by the *Blue* and, once on, why not go all the way to Gaborone?

Times

	Lobatse–Bulawayo *Botswana Blue* Northbound			Bulawayo–Lobatse *Botswana Blue* Southbound	
	dep	19.10	Lobatse	arr	08.30
	dep	20.20	Gaborone	dep	07.20
	arr	12.25	Bulawayo	dep	14.30

Other stops include Mahalapye, Palapye, Serule, Francistown and Plumtree.

Fares

Lobatse–Bulawayo, one way:

First class	P135
Second class	P112
Economy	P38

Tickets

Buy them at the stations in Lobatse, Gaborone, Mahalapye, Palapye or Francistown. For information, phone 411375.

The Gaborone station is on Station Rd, west of the centre of town, tel: 411375 as above, and is open 07.30–13.00 and 14.00–19.00 Mondays–Fridays, 16.00–19.30 Saturdays and Sundays The left luggage facility at Gaborone station is open 08.00–13.00 and 14.00–16.00, Monday–Friday.

Botswana's game parks

Foreign travellers to Botswana are invariably attracted by the country's outstanding game parks of **Chobe** and **Moremi** which are overrun with wildlife. The **Okavango Swamps**, a magnificent wetland created where the Okavango River fans out into the Kalahari Desert, is the true incarnation of an oasis. The Makgadigadi Salt Pans in the middle are fabulous expanses of nothingness, dry for months, even years on end, then bursting with life after the infrequent rains. In keeping with the country's ethos of low-density, high-cost tourism, visiting the game parks, however splendid they may be, is quite expensive with daily park fees around US$14 per person being charged.

Unfortunately, the railway goes nowhere near any of these places. You need a vehicle to get into the parks and the salt pans, although there are regular buses between Francistown in the eastern corridor, and Maun, the jumping off point for the Okavango Swamps.

Getting there

If you want to get into the game parks, you will need to hire a vehicle – preferably a 4x4, although two-wheel drive vehicles with high clearance are adequate for many parts of the country. Vehicles can be hired in Francistown and Gaborone. The alternative is to try and get a lift into the parks with other visitors. You will more than likely have to share costs.

Francistown

This, the country's second largest town, is fine for cooling heels in, although some might not like its transient atmosphere. It is the junction between the main north–south road and the roads to Maun and Kasane, so there are always plenty of vehicles passing through. Vehicles can be hired here but it is expensive – shop around, or start looking for that lift. The **Marang Motel**, 4km (2.5 miles) out of town, is a popular hang-out for overlanders and tourists and a good place to look for lifts. The station is on Haskins St, tel: 213444, and the booking office is open 08.00–13.00 and 14.00–16.00, weekdays only.

ZAMBIA

Landlocked and massive, Zambia has developed along its central railway line which links Zimbabwe, at Victoria Falls, and the Copper belt, via Lusaka, the rough and tumble capital.

It is mostly bush country, off the beaten track, stretching from the source of the Zambezi River in the west to Lake Tanganyika in the east. Zambia has some of the continent's most prolific wildlife in awesome areas such as the Luangwa Valley. The people are some of the friendliest in Africa, smiling through fairly arduous economic hardship. The country has been largely undiscovered by travellers, possibly because it is difficult to get to many places on public transport. It is also not a cheap country by regional standards, but many travellers – stung by soaring prices in Zimbabwe – are discovering that the Victoria Falls can be experienced as movingly from the Zambian side of the river.

Travellers in Zambia will benefit from its early independence policies – good education means English is spoken well enough to make every train ride a good way to meet the people.

Getting there
By air
At least ten major regional and overseas airlines fly to Zambia including Air France, British Airways, Kenya Airways, South African Airways and Aeroflot. Once again the lack of direct competition on the long-haul route means that it will probably work out cheaper to fly to Zimbabwe first and make your way overland. Direct flights from Johannesburg to Livingstone, Lusaka and Ndola are operated by SAA, Aero Zambia and Zambian Express.

By rail
The weekly *Bulawayo* train will get you from Pretoria or Johannesburg to Bulawayo in Zimbabwe from where National Railways of Zimbabwe's daily overnight service runs to Victoria Falls. A shuttle is supposed to run over the Zimbabwe–Zambia border every week but does not always do so, but Livingstone is a short taxi ride away from Victoria Falls. There are trains daily between Livingstone and Lusaka and the Copper Belt.

A second route, the Tazara Railway, links Zambia with Tanzania. Expresses run twice weekly each way between Kapiri Mposhi and Dar es Salaam while there are three local trains a week running as far as the border from each side. Details below.

By ship
The MV *Liemba*, a converted German World War I warship, sails a weekly schedule on Lake Tanganyika between Bujumbura in Burundi, Kigoma in Tanzania and the Zambian port of Mpulungu on the southern shore of the lake. The ferry takes passengers, cargo and vehicles and offers three classes of accommodation. Meals are available but you might be wise to supplement these with your own emergency stash. See also page 255–6.

Visas and red tape
Citizens of most Commonwealth countries, Ireland and Denmark do not need visas but UK passport holders and the nationals of most other western countries do. It is cheaper to buy your Zambian visa in a neighbouring country but if you are flying straight in then get it before you leave from the nearest

embassy. UK citizens are inexplicably singled out for a US$50 visa fee. South Africans do not need visas.

Currency
The Zambian Kwacha is soft and getting softer. The exchange rate in mid-1998 was US$1 = Kw1,400. Foreign currency is eagerly exchanged by most banks and larger hotels and US dollars are readily accepted almost everywhere.

Language
English is widely spoken.

Telephone
The country code is 260. Important area codes are Lusaka 01, Livingstone 03, Mpulungu 02 and Kapiri Mposhi 05.

Tourist information
Zambia National Tourist Board has offices in Lusaka and Livingstone. The Lusaka office is on Lusaka Square, Cairo Rd, tel: 01 22 9087. Livingstone's tourist office is called the Tourist Centre – just ask and you will be pointed in the right direction, tel: 03 32 1487.

Rail information
For Tazara bookings phone the reservations office in Lusaka, tel: 01 22 8125/8, or fax: 01 22 3621. For bookings on Zambia Railways' expresses and local trains, it is best to go to the station yourself at least the day before departure.

Further reading
Guide to Zambia, Chris McIntyre (Bradt,). *The Spectrum Guide to Zambia* (Camerapix), is more of a pictorial guide but inspirational nonetheless.

The Livingstone–Lusaka–Ndola/Kitwe route
'*Bado kibogo*' is a Swahili phrase which loosely translated means 'maybe tomorrow'. It is a useful attitude to cultivate if you plan to travel on Zambian trains, which should win medals for being among the slowest on earth. All things are relative, however, something I found myself thinking over and over when, in a moment of weakness, I once chose to ride a night bus south from Lusaka. One of life's certainties is that Zambia's trains are safer than its buses, and I will never be weak again.

There is really only one railway in Zambia, running from Livingstone in the south, via the capital city Lusaka, and on up to the Copper Belt in the north. The line continues north into the Democratic Republic of the Congo (until recently Zaire), but travel beyond Zambia is not recommended, at least for the time being.

Construction of the railway was driven by the discovery in the early 1900s of copper and lead deposits in the far north of present day Zambia. The now familiar face of railway builder extraordinaire George Pauling was on site,

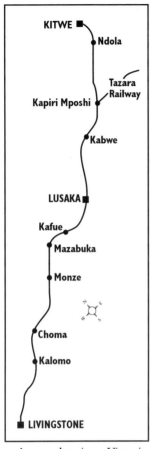

urging the line on at the one mile per day rate stipulated in his contract. Pauling had many rivers to cross, including the mighty, sluggish Kafue. It took him just six months to cross the Kafue, building a bridge of thirteen 30m (100ft) spans. Such was the urgency that all thirteen 56-tonne structures were placed in position in eight days. At that time the Kafue River bridge was the longest bridge in Africa. Broken Hill was reached ahead of time in January 1906.

A second line, the post-colonial Tazara Railway, built in the 1970s to relieve Zambia's dependence on a rail link through apartheid South Africa, leaves the north line at Kapiri Mposhi and runs east across Zambia and Tanzania to Dar es Salaam.

Livingstone

Heading north from Victoria Falls, the journey begins in Livingstone, the former Zambian capital until independence in 1967. From then until recently the town was in danger of becoming a terminal backwater on the banks of the Zambezi, abandoned by its citizens who either went north to the new capital or south to escape economic and political turmoil as Zambia slid into chaos in the 1970s.

Across the river, Victoria Falls started booming after Zimbabwe became genuinely independent. However, people who came to see the falls almost all stayed on the Zimbabwean side. The tourist boom which has had such a marked effect on Victoria Falls town, has another, quietly pleasing aspect – Livingstone is waking up and offering a significantly cheaper alternative to some of the extortion on the other side of the river. Many travellers still rush through, which is a pity, because Livingstone, quiet, pretty, shaded and cheap, is a good place to prepare for the rigours of the train ride north to Lusaka, and beyond. Dollar tourism will doubtless change this but for now, Livingstone is enjoying a backwater renaissance. Go soon.

Livingstone railway **station** is south of the centre, off Mosi oa Tunya Rd, the main road heading towards Victoria Falls.

Railway Museum

Zambia's railway museum is situated in the old locomotive shed of the Zambezi Sawmills Railway (ZSR), just off the main road which runs through the town. It houses locomotives, carriages and wagons in all kinds of decay and

an inside display of railway history and artefacts. The 1950s-era claims book
tells the story of a few days in the life of the town:

| 19.1.57 | Bodalia & Co | four bars of blue soap missing value 4s 2d |
| | Ankleshwar Trading | 61 packets of biscuits short value 5s 3d |

But there was an even bigger blow later that week:

| | J.F. Couvais | 11 bottles of milk stout missing value 10s 4d |

Some of the locomotives are thought to be operable and many enthusiasts
pass through here dreaming of rekindling the old days of the ZSR. But with
most of the rolling stock in dire straits, any future train service will rely on the
outside world. The museum devotes the largest part of a shed to the story of
the Tazara Railway, complete with compelling pictures of the thousands of
Chinese workers who were brought in to drive it through the bush.

The US$5 entry fee is a little steep by local standards, but then this is a
museum which needs the money. Afterwards, I highly recommend the
railway club across the tracks outside the main gate for a drink and a chance to
meet Livingstone.

Accommodation
Luxury
Wasawanga Lodge On the airport road, about 5km from the centre, tel: 03 324 066.
This is quite basic luxury by many standards, but one of the best nevertheless. Being
out of town, it is also a quiet place to stay. Singles US$80, doubles US$110.

Mid-price
The New Fairmont Hotel Mosi-oa-Tunya Rd, tel: 03 320 075. Probably the
cleanest hotel in town. Self contained rooms are US$30–$35.

Budget
Jolly Boy's Backpackers 559 Mokambo Road, tel: 03 324 278. This is *the* place to
stay in Livingstone if you are a backpacker. There is a pool, sauna (often used till the
early hours), cooking facilities and bike hire here and the friendly owner will help you
organise whatever you need. Dorm beds are US$9 and camping is US$4.
The Red Cross Hostel Mokambo Road, tel: 03 322 473. Double rooms are clean
and cost US$7.

Heading north
There are two trains with little to choose between them as far as comfort goes.
The 'Ordinary' trains leave daily for Kitwe on the northern border. The more
luxurious *Zambezi Express* runs three times a week between Livingstone and
Lusaka only. Another express train, the *Kafubu*, runs north from Lusaka to
Ndola in the Copper Belt, also only three times a week. In theory the two
expresses are meant to connect at Lusaka so that all you have to do is change

THE ZAMBEZI SAWMILLS RAILWAY

The forests north of Livingstone had stood for centuries, untouched sweeps of teak and whitewood, for thousands of square kilometres. It was not long, though, before the Zambezi Sawmills Company had pushed a railway from Livingstone into the heart of the forest. Rickety feeder lines soon branched off the main line into the trees. From 1928 the mills were producing 85,000 cubic metres (3 million cu ft) of rough timber and a million tonnes of sawn timber a year, all moved by rail. Since the railway was the only transport in the region, passengers were carried too – some 25,500 of them annually.

A motley collection of steam locomotives was slowly built up over decades, ageing, wood-fired beasts who had done their time on the 'real' railways of the south. The first engine, No. 69, cost £200 in 1926. The railway gradually took on a mythical status for train enthusiasts. The tracks running through unscarred bushveld, the trestle bridges, the whole untamed aura of it, drew people from all over the world to have a look. Some of the rails dated back to 1874, cast-offs from the old Cape Government Railway in South Africa.

Against all the odds, the ZSR held on into the 1970s. There were still vast areas of untouched forest, and the locomotives – with plenty of firewood to hand – were economical to run. The end came when the mills were nationalised in the 1970s. The ZSR stopped running trains soon afterwards and the mills closed.

Somewhere in the forests it is said that there is an abandoned locomotive and its train. According to legend it is guarded by a vicious snake. Some say there is gold on the train, others that the company merely stopped the locomotive in the bush and forgot about it – strange things happen in Africa.

The tracks to the forests are still in place and a twice-weekly Zambia Railways passenger train ambles up to Mulobezi, half-way up the line about 90km (50 miles) north-west of Livingstone. The return journey takes two days and there is no food or water provided on the train. Derailments are frequent. The line passes by many silent stands of ancient and valuable teak and in Livingstone the dreamers are running about with schemes to re-open the mills, repair the tracks and start running log-trains on the ZSR once more. *Bado kibogo.*

trains if you want to continue in the same direction. However, the timetables should be viewed as a rough guide only. Late running is standard.

The express trains do not stop except at major towns although, given the appalling mechanical state of many of Zambia Railways' diesel locomotives, it is likely the train will stop anywhere and often. The ordinary trains are known as '*Kaufelas*' or '*domba-domba*', which literally means 'picking-up'. They stop anywhere to pick up passengers.

Accommodation on the *Zambezi Express* consists of first class seat (airline-style, reclining seats), first class sleeper, standard seat (supposedly akin to business class in airline travel) and economy. There is no sleeping accommodation on the *Kafubu Express* as it runs during the day. Ordinary train accommodation comprises first, sleeper, standard and economy, but the fares are significantly lower on these trains. First, sleeper and standard tickets should be booked well in advance (best done by a personal visit to a station), economy class tickets can be bought on the day of departure.

Excess baggage is no problem either, with a baggage van attached to all trains. A Zambia Railways leaflet says, 'We handle all sorts of parcels from your household effects, pets, chickens and your mail. Our prices are cheaper than you think.'

Times

In view of the uncertainty of the timings these are only given for the scheduled starts and ends of the *Kaufela* journeys and for major stops on the 'expresses'.

Kaufela

Northbound Daily		Southbound Daily
dep 09.00	Livingstone	arr 18.00 next day
arr 09.00 next day	Kitwe	dep 18.00

Zambezi Express

Northbound Train 5 Down Sun, Tue, Thu		Southbound Train 6 Up Mon, Wed, Fri
dep 18.30	Livingstone	arr 06.10
dep 21.45	Kalomo	dep 03.05
dep 23.10	Choma	dep 01.55
dep 01.15	Monze	dep 23.35
dep 02.45	Mazabuka	dep 22.05
dep 04.05	Kafue	dep 21.00
arr 05.15	Lusaka	dep 19.30

Kafubu Express

Northbound Train 5 Down Sun, Tue, Thu		Southbound Train 6 Up Mon, Wed, Fri
dep 07.45	Lusaka	arr 15.15
dep 10.55	Kabwe	dep 12.25
dep 12.25	Kapiri Mposhi	dep 10.55
arr 15.15	Ndola	dep 07.45

Fares

All fares are single (one way). The *Zambezi Express* is almost always full so book your ticket at least 48 hours in advance.

Zambezi Express
Livingstone–Lusaka

First class seat	K21,000
First class sleeper	K26,000
Standard	K10,500
Economy	K9,000

Kafubu Express
Lusaka–Ndola

First class	K15,000
Standard	K9,000
Economy	K7,500

Kaufela
Livingstone–Kitwe

First class seat	K24,000
First class sleeper	K26,000
Standard	K20,900
Economy	K17,100

The journey

The overland rail route north from Victoria Falls has long been popular with backpackers. It is cheap and, in terms of suffering, a whole lot nicer than being at the mercy of Africa's bus system. The route is part of one of Africa's most useful train journeys, allowing reasonable access to game parks in southern Zambia, a jumping off point for northern Malawi, and a reasonably easy ride on to Dar es Salaam in Tanzania.

The track north from Livingstone is in abysmal condition, however, and trains crawl along at about 24km/h (15mph). While it may seem excruciatingly slow, there is a lot to be said for letting Africa drift past at that pace – the mind empties and the journey becomes something of an ambling meditation. Meals are available on the 'expresses' and snack food on the ordinary trains, but take along a supply of comfort food and bottles of water.

If it is scenery you want, you may do better to take the ordinary day train from Livingstone. The area around the Kafue River is especially beautiful. Bear in mind, however, that you are almost as likely to see a good deal of the countryside from the overnight trains in the common event of the service running late.

Lusaka

The Zambian capital since independence in 1964, Lusaka is not a diverting place. A mixture of African urban and high-rise architecture, it has not really made itself friendly to travellers, although this is slowly changing as Zambia becomes more of a place to travel in, rather than just pass through.

The main strip is Cairo Rd, along which you will find the **tourist information** office (tel: 01 22 9087) and **banks** like Standard Chartered and Barclays where you can change money fairly quickly and painlessly. Most of the embassies and travel operators seem to have moved out into the suburbs. If you need to get to either, ask tourist information for directions and take a taxi.

Lusaka's **station** is off Kimathi Rd, behind the bus station, but be extremely vigilant here as muggings are rife.

Lusaka is known for its high crime rate, so take care if you do stop over. Note that the western side of Cairo Rd is a notoriously dangerous area. Pickpockets and muggers abound. There is a heavy police presence around the railway station, especially when trains are arriving or departing, but do not be complacent.

Accommodation
Luxury:
Intercontinental Hotel Haile Selassie Ave, tel: 01 250 600. This is the top hotel in Lusaka. It has a swimming pool and tennis courts. Single rooms US$130. Doubles US$150.

Pamodzi Hotel Church Road, tel: 01 254 455. The Pamodzi also has a swimming pool, plus a fully equipped gym and massage room. US$120 for a single. US$130 for a double.

Mid-price:
Ndeke Hotel corner of Haile Selassie Ave and Los Angeles Boulevard, tel: 01 252 779. En suite doubles cost US$56, (single US$32), but are often half price if available after 6pm. Includes breakfast.

Belvedere Lodge Leopard's Hill Road, tel: 01 263 680. En suite rooms are US$36. This includes three full meals.

Budget:
Emmasdale Lodge Great North Road, 2km past North End roundabout, tel: 01 243 692. Single rooms cost US$15.

Camping
Pioneer Campsite is 18km east of the city centre, and 5km south of the Great East Road. They charge US$5 to camp and have chalets for US$10.

Eureka Camping Park on a farm 10km south of the city is the same price.

North from Lusaka
Unless you like copper mines or are bravely heading for the Congo, attractions along the border with what was Zaire are limited. Most travellers get as far as **Kapiri Mposhi** and change there for the Tazara Railway. Kapiri itself is little more than a junction town, with a few dusty streets, presided over by some dodgy motels. While careful planning is recommended to minimise your stay here, remember that you are at the mercy of the railway system.

The eastbound expresses for Dar es Salaam depart Kapiri on Tuesday and Friday at 14.16, while the westbound trains are supposed to arrive in Kapiri at 07.14 on Thursday and Sunday.

The *Kafubu* timetable shows a few possible connections with Tazara expresses. These look terrific on paper – the Friday northbound train arrives in Kapiri at 12.20, well in time for the *Kilimanjaro Express* departure for Dar es Salaam. Do not be deluded – planning like this will only cause much sadness. Make huge allowances for the inevitable delays. On the other hand, you may arrive so late that you will be able to make an unexpected connection with a train going in your direction. Be super alert to the possibilities of this happening if you need to keep to a reasonably tight schedule.

The daily *Kaufela* trains are possibly a much better bet if you want to connect to or from the Tazara Railway. The northbound train is due in Kapiri around 03.30, while the southbound train from Kitwe arrives at 23.30.

Bear in mind also that changing trains in Kapiri Mposhi means changing stations as well. For reasons long since obscured in bureaucratic musings, the two railway stations are over a kilometre apart. On arrival at either, you will either have to walk or take a taxi. If you arrive late at night, do not walk around, rather get a taxi to take you to one of the motels. Being a transit town, Kapiri is awash with thieves and conmen.

If the Tazara express arrives late in Kapiri, the train crew will often let passengers stay on the train for the night as this is the terminus. This is a far better idea than blundering into Kapiri's streets.

TANZANIA

Think of the best of Africa in one country and you have Tanzania. The country's eastern seaboard is a coral coast, while its northern and western borders are marked by East Africa's three inland seas – Lakes Victoria, Malawi and the electric blue Tanganyika. As yet untrampled by tourism, mainly owing to the difficulty of getting around, a quarter of Tanzania is conserved territory and sanctuary to millions of Africa's wild animals. Add to the mix a tropical coast, jungles and then savanna grassland farther west and Mount Kilimanjaro on the border with Kenya.

The romantic island of Zanzibar is a few hours boat-ride from the capital, Dar es Salaam. Few countries in the region have more to offer.

Getting there
By air
Overseas airlines flying into Tanzania include British Airways, Air France, KLM, Air India, Swissair and regional carriers such as Zambia Airways (ex-Lusaka), Air Zimbabwe (ex-Harare) and Royal Swazi (ex-Mbabane). There are few bargains to be had on long-haul flights and most budget travellers tend to pick up bucket shop tickets routed through Nairobi in Kenya. There are direct flights between Johannesburg and Dar es Salaam, as well as to Kilimanjaro International Airport, near Moshi..

By rail
There is only one way to get to Tanzania by train, on the Tazara line between Kapiri Mposhi in Zambia, and Dar es Salaam, entering Tanzania at Tunduma.

By sea

The most romantic way of travelling the African coast is by dhow, just as traders have done for centuries. To do this though, you will need luck and a deep ocean of patience. Realistically, the only regular services are on motorised dhows between Mtwara and Palma in Mozambique, and getting to either town involves significant overland travel in varying levels of discomfort. For the independent of mind and hard of buttock, this route is a treat, however.

Visas and red tape

Visas are not needed by citizens of most Commonwealth and Scandinavian countries or the Republic of Ireland. Everyone else, including US, UK and South African citizens, must get them in advance. On a recent visit I got my visa on arrival at Dar es Salaam and was charged US$35, but I recommend doing it before you go. Visa prices in neighbouring countries are often lower than in Europe or the US; for example, the Tanzanian High Commission in Pretoria, South Africa charges R135, tel: (+27) 12 3424393.

Currency

The Tanzanian shilling is a weak unit. In mid-1998 US$1 = Tsh658. US dollars are exchangeable everywhere. The country is slowly becoming familiar with South African rands as well.

Language

English and Swahili. Learning some Swahili will be very useful especially in the rural areas (most of the country) where little English is spoken.

Telephone

The country code is 255. Dialling from outside the country will cause ulcers. Internally, the system – if you can find a card phone – is not too bad. Important area codes are Dar es Salaam 051, Kigoma 0695, Mbeya 065, Tabora 062, Mwanza 068, Arusha 057, Moshi 055 and Zanzibar 054.

Tourist information

The Tanzanian Tourist Corporation is based in Dar es Salaam. If you need information, do not waste time trying to phone but go to the office on Maktaba Rd, near the New Africa Hotel.

Rail information

For Tazara bookings it is best to go to the Tazara station itself, approximately 5km from the city centre. To get there, take a bus from outside the post office on Maktaba Rd, or a taxi (US$3 from mid-town). Try and purchase your tickets at least a day or two before departure. There is a phone number but I have never been able to get through on it, although officials swear it is correct: 051 64191.

For bookings on the Central Railway to Kigoma or Mwanza, once again go direct to the station, this time the Tanzania Railways Corporation station on the corner of Railway St and Nkrumah St (opposite the Continental Hotel), tel: 051 26241.

Further reading
Philip Briggs' two books *Guide to Tanzania* (Bradt), and *East and Southern Africa: The Backpacker's Manual* (Bradt), are essential reading, the first for its comprehensive coverage of the whole country and the latter as an overview to the whole region.

Health
Take malaria precautions (see page 10).

Tazara Railway
The Tazara Railway is Africa's *Trans Siberian Express*. Traversing its full length between Kapiri Mposhi in Zambia and the Tanzanian capital of Dar es Salaam is supposed to take two days, but if things go wrong, as they frequently do, the journey can last a week. The railway was the result of landlocked Zambia's need for a safe rail link to export its copper, and Tanzania's desire to prove that, as a newly independent socialist country, it could shake off the shackles of colonialism. The philosophy behind the Great *Uhuru* ('Freedom') Railway, according to displays in the Zambia Railways Museum in Livingstone (see above), was to show up both 'the folly of imperialism with its kith and kin policy and perhaps the all-weatherness of socialist ideals'.

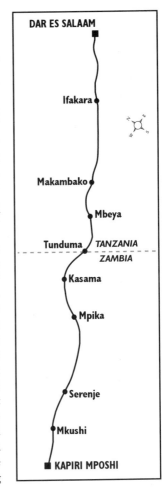

The railway was to be a triumph for the newly independent African states. In fact the idea had been first floated as far back as 1947 but, according to Zambian railway historians, surveys had found the line to be economically unjustifiable, 'because they realised its political implications particularly to their interests in the region'. Two surveys, one Canadian and one British, had been completed and both concluded the line would be unviable. However, the Chinese thought otherwise and an agreement between the People's Republic of China, Tanzania and Zambia was signed in 1967. China granted a 988 million yuan interest-free loan, payable over 30 years, to cover construction, training and locomotives. Zambia and Tanzania are still trying to service this massive debt.

Construction started from both ends in October 1970 and proceeded rapidly, driven by a huge work-force which, at its peak, consisted of 38,000 Tanzanian and Zambian labourers and 13,500 Chinese technical and engineering staff. It took 1,687 days to build the *Uhuru* – 320 bridges, 22 tunnels, 147 stations and 2,225 culverts. The first train traversed the full length of the line in October 1975, two years ahead of schedule.

The Tazara is the only way to travel by rail from Zambia to Dar es Salaam. It is popular among travellers heading for Malawi – in fact most backpackers going south tend to get off at Mbeya, just north of the Zambia–Tanzania border, and head into Malawi by bus.

The Tazara's Achilles heel is its single track. If anything happens to a train on that slender thread, traffic inevitably bunches up and stops. On one trip, a derailment near the one-horse siding of Mlimba, 500km (310 miles) from Dar es Salaam, delayed us for 36 hours. There was no water, and the food was starting to go off by the time we were moving again. Yet it was still a fascinating experience. The railway is a life-line for many, being the only consistently safe transport in the region, derailments notwithstanding, with an eclectic mix of travellers, traders and the usual con artists looking for more than a train ride.

There are two express trains per week, the Tanzanian-run *Kilimanjaro* and the Zambian-crewed *Mukuba*, between Dar and Kapiri, departing from each terminus on Tuesdays and Fridays. Local trains also leave Dar and Kapiri on Mondays, Wednesdays and Saturdays and terminate at Tunduma on the Tanzanian side of the border. The Tanzanian locals pass through the Selous Game Reserve during the day and you are sure to see quite a bit of game.

Times
Kilimanjaro/Mukuba Expresses

Eastbound

dep	Kapiri Mposhi	14.16 Tuesday, Friday
arr	Dar es Salaam	06.43 Thursday, Sunday

Westbound

dep	Dar es Salaam	17.34 Tuesday, Friday
arr	Kapiri Mposhi	07.14 Thursday, Sunday

Other scheduled stops (from the Tanzanian end) include Ifakara, Mlimba, Makambako, Mbeya, Tunduma (just inside Zambia), Kasama, Mpika, Chitambo and Serenje.

Fares

First class	Tsh42,000 (about US$60)
Second class	Tsh27,500
Third class	Tsh13,300

Accommodation

New trainsets built in India have replaced the ailing Chinese coaches. Compartments are large enough, with probably the widest bunks of any African trains. Four people share in first, six in second. Third class is the usual stuff-in of humanity, animals and baggage. First class coaches have communal showers (cold) and wash rooms. Tazara trains all have refrigerated baggage cars 'in which you may load up to 50kg of meat or your other perishables', according to the ever-helpful brochure.

Eating and drinking

Tazara expresses all have full dining cars whose chefs serve 'international dishes'. What this really means is that the Tanzanian chefs serve Zambian chicken and rice, while the Zambian chefs cook the same chickens Tanzanian style. Connoisseurs will no doubt be able to distinguish the subtle differences. As always *sadza* is served with just about everything. Meals start at Tsh2,000. You are supposed to get a free bottle of water per day in your compartment if you are travelling first; we got one at the beginning but it was not repeated.

Other lines in Tanzania

Tanzania's central railway runs from Dar es Salaam via Tabora to Mwanza on Lake Victoria and from Tabora to Kigoma on Lake Tanganyika. Trains leave Dar for Kigoma on Tuesday, Wednesday, Friday and Sunday and depart in the opposite direction on Tuesday, Thursday, Friday and Sunday. The trip takes around 40 hours and costs around US$39 in first and US$29 in second. A line branches off the central railway at Tabora and runs to Mwanza, the biggest and best-run port on Lake Victoria. Here you can catch a ferry to Bukoba and Musoma, both in Tanzania, or one of the weekly boats across the lake to Port Bell in Uganda and Kisumu in Kenya.

Ferries leave Mwanza for Bukoba at 21.00 or 22.00 every day except Wednesdays and Fridays, returning the following day at the same time. Fares are US$14 in first class, US$10 in second and US$5 in third. There are also local ferry services to some of the islands that dot this part of the lake.

Trains leave Tabora for Mwanza at 20.00 on Tuesdays, Wednesdays, Fridays and Sundays and in the other direction on Tuesdays, Thursdays, Fridays and Sundays, departing at 19.00. Fares are about half the full fare between Dar es Salaam and Mwanza. The connection to/from trains to Dar es Salaam or Kigoma is pretty efficient as these things go.

By steamer across Lake Tanganyika

The steamer trip down Lake Tanganyika, Africa's deepest and second-largest lake, can hardly be overrated. The lake is the cleanest of the three great lakes of the Rift Valley with crystal clear water lapping onto lush green shores.

The Tanzanian Railway Corporation also operates the steamer on Lake Tanganyika. The MV *Liemba*, assembled on the lake shore by the Germans before World War I when Tanzania was German East Africa, does a round trip every week between Kigoma, Bujumbura in Burundi and Mpulungu in

Zambia. It leaves Kigoma at 16.00 on Wednesday and arrives Mpulungu at 10.00 on Friday, turning back at 16.00 and arriving at Kigoma at 10.00 on Sunday. At 16.00 on Sunday, the boat heads north, reaching Bujumbura at 10.00 the next day, turning around at 16.00 to arrive in Kigoma at 10.00 on Tuesday. Tickets for the voyage from Kigoma to Mpulungu are US$25 in first class, US$21 in second.

Dar es Salaam

Some people just love this city, others loathe it. I am afraid I am one of the latter, finding it neither pleasant to spend time in nor cheap. Dar is the cultural and bustling heart of the country, despite having been recently replaced as the capital by the bland, central town of Dodoma.

Founded in 1866 when the Sultan Majid of Zanzibar built a palace there, it grew slowly into a trading centre but really only boomed when Germany set foot in Tanganyika in 1877. The city became the capital of German East Africa in 1881.

Most travellers pass through Dar on their way to or from Zanzibar, tending to give the city a miss. There are plenty of relics from its past, though. Architecture-buffs should not miss the German-influenced **buildings** which sit strangely among the other Arab influences. Examples include the Lutheran Church on the corner of Sokoine Drive and Maktaba Rd, and St Joseph's Cathedral, also on Sokoine Drive. **Museums** include the National Museum with its renowned hominid fossil displays and the Village Museum which is based on Tanzania's living and building traditions.

The diverse cultures which have developed the city give it its overriding atmosphere and despite the punishing humidity (I have never been so heat-exhausted in my whole life), its street life is vibrant and diverting, if only briefly.

If you want **beaches**, head for Oyster Bay which is close to the city (and busy on weekends) or go north to the Kunduchi beach resort.

Local **transport** consists of mini-buses or saloon taxis, both reasonably cheap. The best way to get a feel for the place is to amble around slowly. Keep tabs on where you are!

Steam in Tanzania

Tanzania has just one steam locomotive left, No. 2927, a Tribal Class 2-8-2. The locomotive was finally restored in 1997 after a protracted overhaul, part of which involved retrieving one of its number plates from a British enthusiast. The loco's overhaul provoked some press criticism that Tanzania Railways Corporation was wasting money while a shortage of serviceable diesel locomotives continued to hamper daily operations. The latest reports are that No. 2927 has subsequently been returned to work as Dar es Salaam station pilot which means it shuffles rakes of passenger coaches in and out of the station yard, taking away the empty trains after arrival and bringing in fresh coaches before departure.

Accommodation
Mid-price
Hotel Continental Nkrumah St, one block from Tanzania Railways' station. Doubles start at US$25 per night. There is a reasonable restaurant downstairs and the shaded verandah will shield you from the punishing heat of Dar's streets. Taxis to and from the Tazara station cost Tsh2,000, about US$3.

Rungwe Oceanic Hotel Situated on Kunduchi Beach, it has comfortable rooms with hot water, fans and net. US$25–US$30.

Budget
Luther House Sokoine Drive, tel: 051 46687. A single or double with communal bathroom costs US$6–US$8. It is popular and will probably need to be booked in advance.

MOZAMBIQUE
Mozambique is a long, thin country, lying between inland mountain ranges and a 2,500km-long palm-fringed coast. A victim of the Cold War and apartheid destabilisation (see History, below), Mozambique's genuinely smiling people are rebuilding their country, and tourism is one of the largest foreign exchange earners. The country is a former Portuguese colony and this influence remains in architecture, language and food, as well as a general unhurried approach to daily living.

The country has superb diving, deep-sea fishing and general beach lazing. Inland, rehabilitation of various game parks is in progress. However, much of the country was heavily mined during the war and, clearing forgotten mine fields is going to take some time.

The northern part of the country (above the Zambezi River) was less affected directly by the war but getting there overland can take some time because of poor road conditions and the fact that there are still only two bridges over the wide Zambezi. Astounding sights in the north are Ilha de Moçambique, the former capital with its centuries-old Portuguese fort which has survived hundreds of years of turmoil, and the ancient town of Ibo.

Getting there
By air
Just two airlines operate between Europe and Mozambique. Portuguese carrier TAP has flights from Lisbon via Madrid and LAM, the Mozambican national airline, flies to Lisbon and Paris. Being a sparsely trafficked route, flying from Europe direct to Mozambique is going to be expensive. The only flight to the Americas is by Brazilian airline VARIG which has a connection to Rio. You might do better to fly to South Africa or Zimbabwe where competition has resulted in significantly lower air fares.

Regionally, Mozambique is well-served by the national airlines of the surrounding countries with regular flights from South Africa, Zimbabwe, Malawi, Swaziland, Angola and Lesotho.

By rail

There are four rail links into the country, one each from Swaziland, South Africa, Zimbabwe and Malawi. Of these, only the train from Swaziland – actually a service from Durban, South Africa (see page 129) – is a through train. The train across the South African border from Komatipoort is actually a shuttle operated by Mozambique's railway authority while passengers heading to or from Zimbabwe down what is called the Beira Corridor, have to cross the border on foot to pick up their respective trains on the other side.

In northern Mozambique, a through train is supposed to run from Cuamba across the border to Liwonde in Malawi every week. Do not count on it – in this part of the world, trains often run when they want to.

By sea

South African shipping line Unicorn Lines sails freighters twice monthly between Durban and Maputo, Beira and Nacala, on a 12–14 day round trip. The ships have accommodation for six passengers in three cabins. Full fare one way is R3,000, although cheaper options are possible such as Durban–Maputo which costs R1,000. The schedule depends on cargo and weather so you may have to wait a few days. Using the ships opens up all sorts of possible itineraries especially for getting from South Africa into northern Mozambique and returning overland.

Currency

The metical (plural: meticais) is the local currency. At the time of writing the exchange rate was around US$1 = Mt11,000–12,500. SA rands and US dollars (nothing bigger than $20) are also accepted for cash payments throughout Mozambique. Travellers' cheques are useful only in major centres. You can change money at any bank but you will get a better deal at the *câmbio* (private bureaux de change) in Maputo, Beira, Nampula, Pemba and Tete. There is a vibrant currency black market but I recommend caution in using it – it is not legal and you will be dealing with some of the slickest operators on the planet.

The influx of highly paid aid workers has distorted the local economy and things like accommodation can be relatively expensive compared to other countries in the region.

Language

Portuguese is the official language and it is essential to learn a few phrases. English is sometimes understood close to the borders of Zimbabwe and Malawi and in Maputo. I have also met a few Mozambicans who speak fluent German (a legacy of the Cold War and East German 'interest' in the country) but cannot speak a word of English.

Visas and red tape

Visas are required by all foreigners and these should be arranged in advance from the nearest Mozambique consulate. I have heard of recent cases (mid-1998) of travellers crossing from South Africa being able to buy their visas at the border, but there has been no official announcement and it would be best not to risk it. When you get your visa, make sure that the number of days shown on it amply covers the time you intend spending in Mozambique.

In most countries, the single-entry visa costs US$35 and is good for a 30-day stay. If you are heading from South Africa or Zimbabwe, it may be cheaper (if not easier) to arrange your Mozambique visas there. The consulate in Johannesburg (corner of Jeppe St and Nugget St, tel: 011 336-1819) charges R135 and takes one week to issue the visa. If you don't like queues, use Johannes Travel Service on the second floor of the consulate building – they will do all the legwork.

Mozambican embassies are closed on Wednesdays.

Telephone
The international dialling code for Mozambique is 258 and important area codes are Maputo 01, Beira 03, Nampula 06, Chimoio 051 and Xai-Xai 022. The phone system is remarkably good considering there is not a single strand of telephone wire left between Maputo and Beira (it was stolen during the war) and the new cellular network will make life even easier.

Health
Malaria precautions are essential. Sun protection is also advised. Be very careful of cuts and grazes, particularly coral cuts from the beaches, as they go septic quickly.

Tourist information
Mozambique is still getting to grips with the information side of tourism. There are offices in Maputo and Beira but the best sources of information are other travellers or the staff at the larger hotels. Maputo used to have a brilliant twice-yearly information booklet called *Time Out*. I couldn't find it on my last trip although I was assured it still exists.

Rail information
Go to the station in person and make yourself clear. That travellers actually want to travel by train is still not a widely understood concept in Mozambique.

Further reading
Philip Briggs' *Guide To Mozambique* (Bradt), is excellent and one of few comprehensive guides to the country.

The rail system
Mozambique's railways are a real colonial exercise. There are five different systems, none of which actually connect, and there is no north–south link which can make travelling a real hassle, unless you really like buses, of course. Still, Caminhos de Ferro de Moçambique (CFM), the state-owned rail operator, has some useful train services for travellers going to and from Mozambique, as well as one classic African bush rail experience.

The services (covered in detail later in this chapter) are as follows:

- **Goba–Maputo** South Africa's *Trans-Lubombo* train runs twice weekly to and from Durban via Swaziland, crossing into Mozambique at Goba and terminating at Maputo.
- **Komatipoort–Maputo** Daily shuttle service connecting with South Africa's *Komati* train to and from Johannesburg.
- **Beira–Manica** Daily shuttle to Zimbabwe border.
- **Nampula–Cuamba** Daily, goes on to Malawi border at Liwonde once a week.
- **Xai Xai–Manjacaze** Weekly steam-hauled, narrow gauge train.

The train services are a lot more reliable than they were a few years ago and most of the war-weary coaches have been replaced with second-hand carriages from South Africa. Tickets are also amazingly cheap, making rail a vastly better alternative to catching minibus taxis. Even so, travel in Mozambique is a lot more difficult than in South Africa, for example; things simply do not work as well as they do over the border. But if you adopt an attitude of *não probleme* and let it wash over you, the rewards are immense.

History

The first Europeans to set foot in Mozambique were Portuguese seafarers in the 15th century. A fortress capital was built on Ilha de Moçambique, well up on the north coast of the country. From here, Portugal commanded an extensive trade in spices, slaves and ivory.

The settlement in Delagoa Bay, the site of present-day Maputo, was a backwater until the late 19th century. By then the power base in the region had shifted, gold had been discovered in the Transvaal and Delagoa Bay became an important port almost overnight. The bay provided a fine natural harbour, although it silts up rapidly and has to be dredged often. The opening of the railway between Delagoa Bay and Pretoria in 1895 boosted the local economy even further.

However, Portugal always ruled its colonies hard and did not follow the examples of France and Britain when they began granting independence to their possessions in Africa in the 1960s. Frelimo, Mozambique's first popular liberation movement, was formed in Dar es Salaam in 1963. The movement, whose policies were based on Marxist principles, began a military struggle in the late 1960s. Led by the charismatic Samora Machel, the guerrillas were supported by the Soviet Union which was pursuing a policy of expansion all over Africa. The war dragged on for many years but it was more of a 'police action' than a full scale conflict. The military coup in Portugal in 1974 changed everything. The new government wanted to be rid of its expensive and troublesome colonies in Mozambique, Angola and Guinea-Bissau and democratic elections were hastily organised.

Frelimo took Mozambique in a landslide victory. However, the thought of Russians pouring in to the eastern seaboard was too much for neighbouring white Rhodesia to bear. Rhodesia was itself then embroiled in a liberation struggle against Marxist-backed rebels and Mozambique offered these liberation movements safe training bases in the bush. Rhodesia responded by funding a group of disaffected Mozambicans who called themselves Renamo or the Mozambican National Resistance.

Renamo's tactics were brutal and the country ground to a halt as people abandoned their farms and fled to the relative safety of the cities. When white Rhodesia succumbed in 1980, the South African government, even more fearful of the Communist threat on its north-eastern borders, continued to supply and support Renamo. The senseless war dragged on for nearly two decades before a cease-fire was negotiated in 1992.

Elections were held in 1994, and once more Frelimo swept to power. The country is now a multi-party democracy. Rebuilding the country's infrastructure, which was almost entirely destroyed during the fighting, is being hampered by the estimated one million land mines left over from the civil war.

Maputo

Formerly called Lourenço Marques, Maputo was once a playground for South Africans who flocked here for cheap prawns and tropical weather. Independence in 1974 changed everything, and it was only in the 1990s that South Africans began returning in numbers. Unfortunately, too many of the returnees are the kind of people who give tourism a disgusting name – neo-colonialism is rampant.

Maputo feels like a lost southern European capital, which it is, really. The Portuguese influence is all-pervading, from the architecture to the smells of *peri-peri* chicken in the streets. The railway **station** is a classic colonial edifice, complete with a brass cupola designed by the great Gustave Eiffel of tower fame. The building has recently undergone a UN-sponsored renovation which has included a bizarre lime green-with-white-trim paint scheme.

Some of Maputo's nicest features are its *avenidas*, lined with jacarandas and flame trees, or palms in the case of the exquisite Marginal, a boulevard which runs along the seafront of the city. Many of the buildings are decaying colonial relics, adding to the kooky atmosphere of the place. Some of the newer, socialist-inspired edifices are only half-finished.

The city's more interesting buildings are the glittering white **cathedral** on Av Josina Machel, the geological museum (formerly a synagogue) on Av 24 de Julho and the **Mercado Central** (central market) on Av Karl Marx. There is a pre-fabricated metal building, also designed by Gustave Eiffel, in the quiet Jardim Tunduru (Botanical Gardens), just below the cathedral.

The city is not short on **museums** either – the better ones are the Natural History Museum, the Museu de Revolução on Av 24 de Julho and the Museu Nacional des Artes on Av Ho Chi Minh. Art exhibitions and shows are held at the Centro de Estudios Brasileiros, a cultural centre on Av 25 de Septembro.

Catembe, the dilapidated town across the bay, is just a short ferry ride away. Board at the ferry dock at Av 10 de Novembro; sailings start at 08.30 and run every half-hour.

Eating and drinking

There are sidewalk cafés on the main streets (Av 24 de Julho and Av 25 de Septembro), the **Continental** is one of the best, along with loads of restaurants and quite a few wild night spots, particularly in the **Feira Popular**, a tacky but vibrant fairground which contains a cluster of little bars, eateries and night-clubs scattered around the dodgem cars.

Peri-Peri, on the east end of Av 24 de Julho serves the best *peri-peri* chicken in Mozambique; it seems the farther north in the country one goes, the tougher the chicken gets; it may be that the chickens walk the whole way. Mozambique is also famous for its prawns, which have recovered from the pillaging Russian fishing fleet, and *lulas* (calamari) served in succulent, unbattered chunks. Best place for prawns is **Bar Rossio**, opposite the Hotel Central, near the railway station. The **Costa do Sol** is a popular restaurant at the north end of the Costa do Sol, with superb fish and curries, and one of the places with a guaranteed supply of Laurentina and Impala, superb Mozambican beers which provide a welcome relief from the South African Breweries products more generally available.

Night-life

Street- and night-life is very Latin in style. Maputo pounds at night. **Rua de Bagamoio**, near the station, is lined with bars while the Feira Popular is also, well, popular. **Clube Mini Golfe** on the Costa do Sol is a pumping night spot located in the grounds of a mini-golf course. The club is basically an open-ended hangar with jungle growing in and the Euro-trash and salsa-spinning DJ sitting under a giant clam shell. The night markets, located on open bits of land in the city, are the best places to drink cheaply – try **Mercado do Povo**. The bars here are tiny affairs, sometimes with room for just two or three people but you can get anything you want.

Safety

Like all big cities, Maputo has the same curse of street crime. The government has done a lot to disarm the people and there are not nearly as many guns around as there used to be. Some areas are particularly unsafe and, wherever you are, you should take a taxi at night. Be careful around the Central Market where pickpockets will fight over the rights to your wallet, and do not change money with the hustlers on the street – they win every time, and it is illegal anyway.

Accommodation

If you can afford it, try the **Polana Hotel** on Av Julius Nyerere. This colonial monolith has been restored. You can watch corpulent businessmen close deals, while malaria-stricken aid workers recover at the pool side. The coffee milk-shakes are outstanding and you do not have to be a resident to sit out on the terrace and drink one. Singles start at US$135 a night.

Hotel Central Rua da Bagamoio, near the railway station, has cheap but very clean rooms for about US$10 a night. Although the area around it is not the nicest, there is a reasonable night-life and the hotel itself is very safe.

Fatima's Backpackers Av Mao Tse Tung. Doubles US$15, dorm bed US$6, camping US$3. Fatima knows everything about Maputo so this is a reason for staying here. Clean rooms, reasonable part of town.

Hotel Cardosa Av Patrice Lumumba, and **Hotel Tivoli** on Av 25 de Septembro are also worth a try.

Getting around

There are some taxis (look for decrepit black and yellow Peugeots or Mercedes) and various local buses. Longer-distance buses north are run by Transportes Virginia, which leave from a depot on Av Karl Marx near the Hotel Universo, or Transportes D'Oliveiras, which go from their depot at Praça 16 de Junho on the western end of Av 24 de Julho. Both companies' buses for Beira leave around 05.00, those for Xai Xai and Inhambane go at midday.

Maputo to Komatipoort

This daily shuttle service connects with the Johannesburg–Komatipoort *Komati* train in South Africa (see page 85). In Portuguese colonial days this train was known as the *LM Mail*, (named for Lourenço Marques, as Maputo was then known).

Crossing the border from South Africa into Mozambique is like time travelling, so different are the two cultures. Immediately you will be surrounded by Portuguese-speaking people, architecture transported straight out of southern Europe and smells of *peri-peri* chicken and chips. The general attitude is a lot more laid back, too, despite the fact that the country still has terrific problems in the wake of its long civil war.

The train used to run through from Johannesburg to Maputo and back three days a week and became a favourite for cigarette smugglers. Hours were lost at the border crossing as the South African Army and police searched passengers, their luggage, and the train, and Spoornet decided to stop running through trains. Instead, CFM bought some second-hand coaches from South Africa and began running a daily shuttle from Maputo to Komatipoort on the South African side of the border. Most of the regular passengers are traders, migrant mine-workers, and the usual rash of thieves, conmen and smugglers, many of whom will immediately try and befriend you in the hope of deflecting some of the heat from customs and immigration.

Passengers using the shuttle clear South African customs at Lebombo, a police halt in the bush next to the electrified border fence which is supposed to keep illegal immigrants out of South Africa but does not. Mozambican customs are then cleared at Ressano Garcia in a crowded, sweaty office on the station platform. Then it is a clear run down to Maputo, over twisting track along the valley of the Komati River, over a hot dry plateau of scrubby bushes and then lush green, heavily populated, marsh land as the train runs into Maputo.

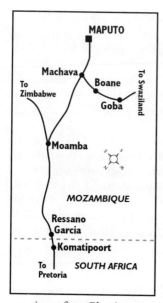

If you are heading for Maputo, sit on the left hand side of the coach all the way. Just out of Ressano Garcia, the train starts passing some of the silent echoes of the country's 17-year civil war – wrecks of entire trains lying in the bush, an utterly desolate, weed-choked brick factory with its slender chimneys still standing defiant, and burned-out tanks at abandoned stations. As the line approaches Maputo's satellite towns of Boane and Machava *shambas* crowd close to the tracks and children run alongside in their screaming hundreds, cheering the train into the city, some cadging a free ride on the coach running boards.

The shuttle runs daily from Maputo in the morning and returns in the late afternoon. Scheduled departure time is 05.30 from Maputo. In reality, it goes – and returns – at any time after. Clearing customs can mean an inordinate delay, especially on the South African side where documents and baggage are often examined at length. The train takes 2–3 hours to cover the 110km from between Komatipoort and Maputo. The timings depend heavily on what sort of work-over the train and its passengers get from customs officials on both sides of the border.

Main stops are: Komatipoort, Ressano Garcia (Mozambique), Chanculo, Movene, Moamba, Pessane, Tenga, Matola, Machava, and Maputo

Fares

Maputo–Ressano Garcia

| First | US$5.00 |
| Third | US$0.80 |

Goba to Maputo

This service from Durban in South Africa was launched in April 1998 in response to demand for a direct Durban-Maputo service. Before, train travellers would have to go via Johannesburg. The *Trans-Lubombo* has now cut the journey time from 50 hours to 22 hours. It is a fantastic way to get into Mozambique, not least because it is the only proper through train between the country and South Africa, as well as taking in some of Swaziland's beauty.

The route is one of Africa's prettiest. In Swaziland, the track follows the ancient route of several rivers including the wide Usuthu, while the Lebombo Mountains march along in the east. After crossing the border at Goba, the train then rolls along a river course, dropping steadily towards the coastal plain. After Goba, there is little human presence – the civil war drove most rural dwellers into the cities and the fear of land mines has largely kept them there – but there are plenty of crocodiles, pondering this new intrusion. There are plenty of wrecked trains too, blown off the track by rebels and still rusting in place years later.

By Boane, the vegetation has become lush and sub-tropical and *shambas* cram up against the lineside. The children shriek and wave and dance as the train passes, cheering the train all the way across the low-lying plain into Maputo.

Timings depend on how quickly customs are cleared and once in Mozambique, the train does not stop. Stations on the route after Goba are Boane, Matola, Machava and then Maputo. The South African and Swazi sections of the route are described in Chapter 7, pages 129–34.

Beira to Machipanda

Mozambique's central railway runs from Beira, the country's second city, to the Zimbabwe border at Machipanda. One passenger train runs daily over this line, leaving Beira at 06.30, returning at 12.00. It is a great way to get into

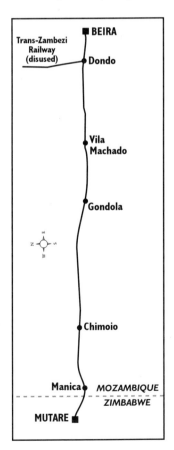

Mozambique from Zimbabwe, especially if you are planning to head south along the coast towards Maputo. The ride itself is not as scenic as the Maputo–Ressano Garcia–Komatipoort line, although the countryside around the border is quite mountainous and dramatic.

The 280km journey takes about 5-6 hours depending on all the factors in the world – is the locomotive in working order, was the train shunted on time, are there obstructions on the track. At least the scruffy thing runs and every day too. Fares recently were around US$10 for the full journey but these seem to fluctuate according to who is in charge on the day. There is no dining car so take your own food and plenty of water.

The best scenery is on the climb into the hills near Machipanda. Spare a thought for the driven workers who pushed Rhodes' 2ft gauge railway from the humid nastiness of the coast into these hills, battling malaria, heat and wild animals.

Stops after Beira include: Dondo (a junction for the war-stricken and long-abandoned Trans Zambezi Railway to Moatize and Malawi), Inchope (the main road to the south breaks away from the line), Gondola (an old watering point in steam days), Chimoio (a large-ish transit town), and Manica.

Beira

Beira is a great place to spend a few days, even though there is not a lot to do except soak up the atmosphere of a decaying colonial backwater. Sights worth seeing include the old Grand Hotel on the beach-front, a huge, rotting edifice which was abandoned in the 1950s and which has now become an informal squatter camp for the homeless. There are goats in the old ballroom and sizeable trees growing out of the roof.

The nearby ship graveyard is another bizarre, uniquely Mozambican, sight. The estuary is the last resting place of various rusting ships and fishing trawlers which have been rammed onto the beach and left there. There is a kind of informal ship repair industry, but most of the vessels here are way past any rejuvenation.

Take a walk around the town itself. The Portuguese flavour is imprinted in its streets and the few sidewalk cafés in its main business district. The smell of *peri-peri* chicken, woodsmoke and rotting garbage permeates everything – you will know where you are.

TEN WEEKS TO LICHINGA

The bush war brought Mozambique's trains to a halt. The rebels watched every line, ambushing any train they saw. In some parts of the country, whole trains still stand abandoned on the line, wheels rusted to the tracks. On the Trans-Zambezi Railway from Beira to Malawi and Moatize in western Mozambique, whole lengths of steel rail were lifted and bent around the trees in an attempt to ensure that no trains ever ran on that line again.

It was years before the government tried to run a train from the northern port of Nacala to Lichinga on the shores of Lake Malawi. By mid-1990, the people of Lichinga were desperate for fuel and a train was dispatched from the coast into the rebel-held province of Niassa. There were 800 tonnes of goods on board, a military escort and a number of passengers braving the journey.

It took ten weeks to cover the 800km. The average speed was 11km a day. One passenger died on the trip while a woman gave birth on the same day. Passengers took their own food and cooked it on open fires wherever the train stopped for the night. The line had to be rebuilt in places where rebels had removed and burned the sleepers and dumped the rails in the bush. On board was one Red Cross official with a tin of aspirins and various other pills, cotton wool and bandages. Fortunately for him, and the passengers, the train was not attacked and Lichinga was relieved.

Accommodation

There are quite a few hotels, but many of them are the dodgiest of fleapits. Best mid-range option is the **Hotel Miramar**, one block back from the beach-front road. A double room costs around US$20 a night with hot shower. Ask for a front room on the second floor – the view is terrific.

Eating

Just around the corner from the Hotel Miramar is a restaurant of the same name which serves a good variety of Portuguese dishes, including the ubiquitous *peri-peri* chicken and chips and very cheap fried chunks of *lulas*. You can sit on the outside terrace and watch the ocean and the few remaining expats get on with their lives.

Nampula to Cuamba

The passenger service on this almost forgotten railway in the north has been increased to five times a week, but though the line continues on as far as Nacala and Lumbo on the coast there are still no regular passenger trains on that section of the route.

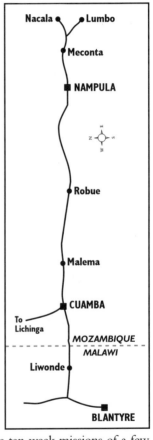

The daily Nampula–Cuamba journey is a real African train ride. The coaching stock has seen much better days, but no-one seems to mind. After all, it is the lack of a restricting baggage allowance that really appeals.

Amazingly, there is even a dining car although the menu options are limited to chicken and rice with tomatoes and onions, chicken giblets, and Coke to wash it down. Wherever the train stops, fruit and vegetable sellers will soon arrive to compete fiercely for your custom.

The usual wrecked trains, tanks and ruined stations proliferate along the way. The scenery is lovely though, especially around Cuamba where sugar-loaf granite outcrops dominate the landscape.

Timings for the approximately 450km journey fluctuate wildly but are down from the ten-week missions of a few years back, like the one described at left. Most of the railway between the ocean and Malawi has now been refurbished and trains move along at a relative lick. Expect to spend 5–10 hours on the train. At the time of writing, we had no clear idea of any proper fare structure. It's free if you slum it with the locals on a flatcar or in one of the boxcars!

Once a week, the train runs on from Cuamba as far as Liwonde in **Malawi**, which is great if you happen to be there on the right day. One traveller told me she had waited two weeks for the train to Malawi but was told to check at the station every day to see if it was 'ready'. She arrived one morning, apparently on time, only to be told it had left during the night. If you do make it, remember this is a hard ride and you will more than likely be riding on an open flatcar, along with hundreds of others, exposed to punishing heat or driving rain.

Take a poncho and plenty of food and water. And always keep a close eye on your kit.

Getting to Nampula/Cuamba
Nampula is not as isolated as it used to be. The roads to the south have been partially repaired and it is possible, if desperately uncomfortable, to ride by truck and bus from Beira (and Maputo). A better bet for getting to this region might be the regular Unicorn cargo boats which sail between Durban and the northern Mozambican port of Nacala (see page 258 for more details).

THE XAI XAI TRAIN
If you want to decide whether you would like riding this train, then here is what happened to me.

Night came fast. We had been blasting along for five hours or so and Manjacaze was a distant 20km (12 miles) behind. The railway meandered through thick, unpopulated bushveld. The train lurched and stumbled along the bent rails, falling into the gaps where one rail did not quite join the next. Sitting in the coal bunker, facing forward, it looked and felt as if the train was descending an endless flight of stairs.

Things were not going well for the crew. One of the cylinder covers had been blasted off during the long, savage climb out of Manjacaze, so in effect, the steamer was only working on one side. The driver was hanging on to the throttle with bony arms, forcing it open against the terrifying vibration of the loco. I was crouching on top of the coal, having what basically amounted to a soot bath, watching flaming embers arcing through the black African night.

Shortly after sunset, the train derailed for the first time. From my high perch on top of the engine, I saw the passenger coach stagger into the air and then lurch violently from side to side. The brakemen alighted at speed, screaming for the driver to stop. The argument over who was going to get sweaty re-railing the errant wagon started before the driver even shut the throttle, and it was a while before the two brakemen hauled out the massive re-railing jacks.

Bush mechanics is a wonderful skill and we were soon on the move. The headlight was broken and the crew were leaning out of the cab, keeping a strained lookout for animals or fallen trees. The stoker swung his shovel, and the fierce orange glow spilled out of the firebox,

Cuamba is served by a patchy bus service to the Malawi border. Rather try and get the weekly train to Liwonde and take a bus from there.

Trains in Malawi

Malawi has a very ragged passenger train service. Little investment and decades of poor maintenance mean that much of the railway and its rolling stock is in shoddy condition. Most travellers use the buses. In mid-1998, the air-brake hoses on a crowded passenger train ruptured at the start of a long descent and the train ran away out of control. Many people were killed and hundreds seriously hurt.

The government has since stepped up its efforts to generate private sector investment in the system. Until then, use your common sense.

Xai Xai to Manjacaze

This route is served by a weekly steam-hauled, narrow gauge train. This is a ride on the ultimate African bush railway. The narrow gauge (2ft 6in/76cm)

lighting the bush. The engine shook and roared and lurched. We sat in the coal, sharing smokes with the crew, sensing rather than seeing the overhanging trees. A fat yellow moon crept into the sky.

A while later as the train laboured up another endless hill, the tank-wagon drifted off the track. The familiar screech of tortured metal filled the night.

I was now exhausted and scared, slapping mosquitoes, spooking myself with fantasies of bandits and praying for dawn. Urged on by the now simmering passengers, the brakemen worked swiftly to rerail the errant wagon, but it was still an hour before the driver put his hand on the throttle and the real fun started. The locomotive erupted, spewing soot and embers into the night, shaking and jerking like a wounded buffalo. He quickly closed off the throttle and it settled. He tried again and again, but this was the little engine that couldn't. The train stood unmoved.

The driver called up his brakemen. It was decided the engine would carry on alone to Xai Xai for repairs and return the next day to fetch the train. The conductor was sent to tell the passengers; they sent a lynch mob back. The driver sagged visibly and dispatched his conductor to drop the freight wagons. He pulled the pin out of the coupler and the two wagons rolled, unlit and untended, back into the darkness. We were kicked off the loco and banished into the ugly atmosphere of the coach where the talk was seditious. 'This is a crap country. Nothing works here.' 'I wish we were still Marxist.'

It was 02.00. The engine blew fire into the sky and we inched slowly up the hill.

line no longer has any apparent reason for being. It transports almost no freight except for the bundles of house-building poles and firewood carried by the few passengers. Its survival is remarkable, defying both economics and the law of the jungle. There are just two trains a week, one in each direction, leaving Xai Xai at 07.00 on Fridays and returning on Sunday. The return journey takes three days and the return fare is about US$5.

Xai Xai

Xai Xai is 200km (125 miles) north of Maputo. To get there take a Transportes Virginia bus from the stop on Av Karl Marx near Fatima's backpackers or a Transportes d'Oliveiras coach from the bus station at the west end of Av 24 de Julho. The fare is around Mt20,000 (about US$2). It is a three-hour journey.

There is a hotel in Xai Xai but it is quite dingy and maybe not too safe. Rather catch a *chapa cem*, a pick-up truck with benches in the back, and head for the campsites at the **beach** (Praia do Xai Xai), 14km (9 miles) away. If you do not want to camp there is also the expensive **Complexo Touristico Halley** which has doubles starting at US$50 per night.

Future Possibilities

Many of Africa's railways are in disarray, the result of decades of upheaval, instability and war. A lot of those railway journeys are probably gone forever and yet analysts, sitting in countries far away, often do not register how resilient African railways are. If there are two strips of metal on the earth then there is a chance something will move along it. The ramshackle Xai Xai railway in Mozambique proves this.

THE BENGUELA RAILWAY, ANGOLA

The Benguela Railway is a privately-owned line, running from the Angolan port of Lobito and cutting straight across central Angola, into the Democratic Republic of Congo (formerly Zaire) and just not quite reaching the northern Copper Belt in Zambia. The 'Benguela' was legendary, a well-built copper carrier, using wood-burning Garratt steam locomotives.

Two decades of civil war in Angola have all but destroyed the railway. Bridges are blown or mined, track lifted, embankments and cuttings imploded. A small section from the coast as far inland as Benguela is said to be operational, but it has been at least 20 years since a train ran the full length of the railway.

Hope for its future has been raised as Italian company Tor di Valle begins work on rebuilding the link, in spite of negative comments from watchers. In payment, the company has secured the huge eucalyptus forests which the railway grew to provide fuel for its steam locomotives. Rebuilding is expected to take some time, a few years at least.

If they do pull it off, though, the way will be open for one of the world's greatest train trips – an east–west crossing of Africa, from Indian to Atlantic oceans, spanning cultures, religion, and turbulent history. It will be a big deal and depends on political developments as much as progress with the railway.

At the time of writing, peace talks between Angola's MPLA government and the rebel Unita movement had broken down once again – commentators have lost count of the times the talks have failed – and both sides were bristling. The United Nations mission to Angola admits its task is almost impossible. Most Angolans are war-weary in every sense and with any luck, the majority will prevail so they can get on rebuilding their lives. If they do, the potential to experience some of Africa's most dramatic train rides will hopefully follow.

THE SMUGGLERS' TRAIN TO THE JUNGLE

Before the old government was toppled in Zaire, trains would regularly cross the border between that country and Zambia. On the Zambian side, entrepreneurial Zairoise would stock up on cigarettes and other contraband and hide it loosely on the train, before heading back into Zaire. They would basically commandeer the whole train and no-one told them to do otherwise.

The railway into Zaire has not been operating for some time. Zaire's railways were bad enough on good days; the change of power and the subsequent violence have shut them down. When the situation stabilises, and it will because it always does, perhaps the trains will start running once more.

FROM SEA TO SEA

One can just about take a train all the way from the Indian Ocean at Durban on South Africa's east coast (or alternatively from Maputo in Mozambique) all the way across the continent and end up on the shores of the Atlantic Ocean at Swakopmund in Namibia. Almost, because there is a 260km gap between the railway town of De Aar (on the Cape Main Line between Johannesburg and Cape Town) and Upington near the border with Namibia.

Regular passenger services ended in 1991 and for years the Namibian trains were stopping at the border, from where the unfortunate passengers would have to make their own way as best they could. After two years of negotiations, TransNamib got permission to run its train to Upington and back twice a week. While the situation has been dramatically improved by terminating the service in a town rather than at a wind-swept, bleak desert border post, one still has to try and find alternative transport from or to Upington.

A lot of travellers have told me they would prefer to use trains to and from Namibia rather than the cramped overnight buses; there is certainly a growing train-using market out there, waiting to be tapped. TransNamib would like Mainline Passenger Services, the South African passenger train operators, to reinstate the former service between De Aar and Upington. There has been some resistance to this idea but, as tourism booms in South Africa, let us hope that the powers that be will sit up and listen to the growing cry.

MOZAMBIQUE – STEAM TRAINS AND ELEPHANTS

A few years ago, the Mozambican government granted US millionaire James Blanchard exclusive commercial rights to develop a stretch of southern Mozambique. The deal included the revitalisation of the Maputo Elephant Reserve (with its very war-weary animals) and the repair of the railway from Maputo to Salamanga which has been closed for decades because of war damage. The idea was that tourists arriving in Mozambique would board a steam train in Maputo and ride through the bush country to one of the new resorts on the coast.

Things are happening very slowly, however, and no trains have run as yet. CFM, the Mozambique railway authority, has apparently set aside a few steam locomotives for heavy overhaul to run on the line. It is a great idea, but could be some time in the making.

FURTHER READING
Railways
The Great Steam Trek, CP Lewis & AA Jorgensen (Struik 1978) is a beautiful photographic account of South Africa's steam locomotives with dollops of lovely evocative writing thrown in. Other railway histories are Sydney Moir's *24 Inches Apart* (Janus Publishing 1981) and his fine *Namib Narrow Gauge*, still one of the only definitive books on Namibia's early railway history. The latter two are out of print but specialist bookshops may be able to help. Also out of print but worth hunting for is Jose Burman's *Early Railways at the Cape* (Human & Rousseau 1984).

Travel literature
There is no shortage of books on African travel. Look out for Dervla Murphy's *South from the Limpopo* (John Murray 1997) and Nick Middleton's *Kalashnikovs and Zombie Cucumbers* (Phoenix 1995), still one of the only travel books ever written on Mozambique. *Letters to Daniel*, Fergal Keane (BBC/Penguin 1996), although not entirely about Africa, contains some of the most moving dispatches filed on this continent. If you can find them, South African travel writer Lawrence Green's three superb books – *A Decent Fellow Doesn't Work* (Howard Timmins 1963), *Tavern of the Seas* (Howard Timmins 1946) and *Where Men Still Dream* (Howard Timmins 1945) are evocative and rich travel histories of South Africa and the region generally before and after the two world wars.

History
One of the best general accounts of the history of the region is Richard Hall's *Empires of the Monsoon: A History of the Indian Ocean and its Invaders* (Harper Collins 1996) which successfully covers 1,000 tumultuous years of east and southern African history. Thomas Pakenham's *Scramble for Africa* is an excellent review of Europe's colonial ambitions on the Dark Continent. *The Boer War* (Weidenfeld and Nicolson 1979) by the same author is probably the best account ever written on this crucial era of South African history. A good work on general South African history is *History of South Africa* (L Thompson, Yale 1990). A specialised but outstanding work on the Anglo-Zulu War of 1879 is D Morris' *Washing of the Spears* (Abacus 1965, reprinted by Pimlico 1995). Worthy books on the South African struggle against apartheid include Nelson

Mandela's *Long Walk to Freedom* (Abacus 1994) and, post apartheid, *Tomorrow is Another Country* by journalist Alistair Sparks (Struik 1994) and Shaun Johnson's *Strange Days Indeed* (Bantam 1994).

Fiction

Southern Africa has produced some of the world's finest fiction. Notable works include: Andre Brink's *Dry White Season*, *Rumours of Rain* and *Chain of Voices*; Olive Schreiner's *The Story of an African Farm*; J.M. Coetzee's *Waiting for the Barbarians* and *Life and Times of Michael K*; Joseph Conrad's *Heart of Darkness*; Justin Cartwright's *Maasai Dreaming*; Tsitsi Dagarembga's *Nervous Conditions*; Bessie Head's *When Rain Clouds Gather* and *Maru*, Chenjerai Hove's, *Bones*; Doris Lessing's *The Grass is Singing* (and her autobiography *Under My Skin*); Dambudzo Marechera's *House of Hunger*; Charles Mungoshi's *Coming of the Dry Season*; V.S. Naipaul's *Bend in the River*; Alan Paton's *Cry the Beloved Country* and *Ah, But Your Land is Beautiful*; and Olive Schreiner's *The Story of an African Farm*.

Health

Wilson-Howarth, Dr Jane, *Bugs, Bites & Bowels, the Cadogan Guide to Healthy Travel*, Cadogan 1995.
Wilson-Howarth, Dr Jane, and Ellis, Dr Matthew, *Your Child's Health Abroad: A Manual for Travelling Parents*, Bradt 1998.

Travel guides

Southern Africa by Rail by definition cannot cover the whole region in detail. For fuller coverage of the individual countries, I would recommend the range of Bradt guides: *South Africa*, *Mozambique*, *Malawi* and *Tanzania*, all by Philip Briggs, and *Zambia* and *Namibia* by Chris McIntyre. In addition there is *East and Southern Africa: The Backpacker's Manual* by Philip Briggs. A good guide to Zimbabwe and Botswana is Barbara McCrea and Tony Pinchuck's *Zimbabwe & Botswana* (Rough Guides 1996).

COMPLETE LIST OF GUIDES FROM BRADT PUBLICATIONS

Africa by Road   Bob Swain/Paula Snyder   £12.95
Africa, East and Southern: The Backpacker's Manual
   Philip Briggs   £13.95
Albania: Guide and Illustrated Journal   Peter Dawson/Andrea Dawson/Linda
   White   £10.95
Amazon, Guide to   Roger Harris/Peter Hutchison   £12.95
Antarctica: A Guide to the Wildlife   Tony Soper/Dafila Scott   £12.95
Australia and New Zealand by Rail   Colin Taylor   £10.95
Belize, Guide to   Alex Bradbury   £10.95
Brazil, Guide to   Alex Bradbury   £11.95
Burma, Guide to   Nicholas Greenwood   £12.95
Cape Verde Islands   Aisling Irwin/Colum Wilson   £11.95
Central America, Backpacking in   Tim Burford   £10.95
Central and South America by Road   Pam Ascanio   £12.95
Chile and Argentina: Backpacking and Hiking   Tim Burford   £11.95
Cuba, Guide to   Stephen Fallon   £11.95
Eastern Europe by Rail   Rob Dodson   £9.95
Ecuador, Climbing and Hiking in   Rob Rachowiecki/Mark Thurber/Betsy
   Wagenhauser   £12.95
Eritrea, Guide to   Edward Paice   £10.95
Estonia   Neil Taylor   £11.95 (spring 1999)
Ethiopia, Guide to   Philip Briggs   £11.95
Galapagos Wildlife   David Horwell/Pete Oxford   £14.95   (summer 1999)
Ghana, Guide to   Philip Briggs   £11.95 (summer 1998)
Greece by Rail   Zane Katsikis   £11.95
Haiti and the Dominican Republic   Ross Velton   £11.95   (spring 1999)
India by Rail   Royston Ellis   £11.95
Laos and Cambodia, Guide to   John R Jones   £10.95
Latvia, Guide to   Inara Punga/William Hough   £10.95
Lebanon, Guide to   Lynda Keen   £10.95
Lithuania   Gordon McLachlan   £11.95 (spring 1999)
Madagascar, Guide to   Hilary Bradt   £12.95
Madagascar Wildlife   Hilary Bradt/Derek Schuurman/Nick Garbutt   £14.95
Malawi, Guide to   Philip Briggs   £10.95
Maldives, Guide to   Royston Ellis   £11.95
Mauritius, Guide to   Royston Ellis   £11.95
Mexico, Backpacking in   Tim Burford   £11.95
Mozambique, Guide to   Philip Briggs   £11.95
Namibia   Chris McIntyre   £12.95
North Cyprus, Guide to   Diana Darke   £9.95
Peru and Bolivia: Backpacking and Trekking   Hilary Bradt   £11.95
Philippines, Guide to   Stephen Mansfield   £12.95
Poland and Ukraine, Hiking Guide to   Tim Burford   £11.95

Romania, Hiking Guide to   Tim Burford   £10.95
Russia and Central Asia by Road   Hazel Barker   £12.95
Russia by Rail, with Belarus and Ukraine   Athol Yates   £13.95
South Africa, Guide to   Philip Briggs   £11.95
Southern Africa by Rail   Paul Ash   £11.95
Spain and Portugal by Rail   Norman Renouf   £11.95
Spitsbergen, Guide to   Andreas Umbreit   £12.95
Sri Lanka by Rail   Royston Ellis   £10.95
Switzerland by Rail   Anthony Lambert   £10.95
Tanzania, Guide to   Philip Briggs   £11.95
Uganda   Philip Briggs   £11.95
USA by Rail   John Pitt   £10.95
Venezuela, Guide to   Hilary Dunsterville Branch   £12.95
Vietnam, Guide to   John R Jones   £11.95
Your Child's Health Abroad   Dr Jane Wilson-Howarth/Dr Matthew Ellis
   £8.95
Zambia, Guide to   Chris McIntyre   £11.95
Zanzibar, Guide to   David Else   £11.95

Bradt Guides are available from bookshops or by mail order from:

Bradt Publications
41 Nortoft Road
Chalfont St Peter
Bucks SL9 0LA
England
Tel/fax: 01494 873478
Email: bradtpublications@compuserve.com

Please include your name, address and daytime telephone number with your order and enclose a cheque or postal order, or quote your Visa/Mastercard card number and expiry date. Postage will be charged as follows:

UK: £1.50 for one book; £2.50 for two or more books
Europe (inc Eire): £2 for one book; £4 for two or more books (airmail printed paper)
Rest of world: £4 for one book; £7 for two or more books (airmail printed paper)

Index